MEN OF COURAGE

EDITED BY WILLIAM PARKER

True stories of present-day adventures
in danger & death

PLAYBOY PRESS

Terror in the Air, p. 15, from "Ten Hours of Terror," by Joseph P. Blank, *True* magazine, February 1962. Copyright © 1962 by Joseph P. Blank.

The Race Driver Who Wouldn't Die, p. 37, from "Go, Hercules! Go! Go! Go!" by Charles N. Barnard, *True* magazine, June 1967. Copyright © 1967 by Charles N. Barnard.

They Couldn't Break Billy Dean, p. 57, from "The Undefeated Dignity of Gen. Bill Dean," by John Dos Passos, *True* magazine, February 1961. Copyright © 1961 by Estate of John Dos Passos.

Run to Glory, p. 69, from *Four-Minute Mile*, by Roger Bannister. Copyright © 1955 by Roger Bannister. Reprinted by permission of Dodd, Mead & Co.

Death on the Slopes, p. 79, originally appeared as "Death on the Slopes," by Curtis W. Casewit, *Man's Magazine*, April 1965. Copyright © 1965 by

Pyramid Publications.

Escape from Devil's Island, p. 93, from *Papillon*, by Henri Charrière. Copyright © 1970 by William Morrow & Co., Inc., and reprinted with their permission.

Shot Down over Russia, p. 101, from *Operation Overflight: The Story of U-2 Spy Pilot, Francis Gary Powers*, by Francis Gary Powers with Curt Gentry. Copyright © 1970 by Francis Gary Powers and Curt Gentry. Reprinted by permission of Holt, Rinehart & Winston, Inc.

Manolete's Last Dance with Death, p. 117, from *Glorious Triumphs: Athletes Who Conquered Adversity*, by Vernon E. Pizer. Copyright © 1966, 1968 by Vernon E. Pizer. Reprinted by permission of Dodd, Mead & Co.

Bloody Road to Usumbura, p. 129, from *Congo Kitabu*, by Jean-Pierre Hallet. Copyright © 1965 by Jean-Pierre Hallet.

MEN OF COURAGE

Published simultaneously in the United States and Canada by Playboy Press, Chicago, Illinois. Printed in the United States of America.

PLAYBOY and Rabbit Head design are trademarks of Playboy, 919 North Michigan Avenue, Chicago, Illinois 60611 (U.S.A.), Reg. U.S. Pat. Off., marca registrada, marque déposée.

Playboy Press hardcover edition published 1972. Playboy Press softcover edition published 1972.

The cover photo is by Marcel Ichac from the book *Annapurna*, by Maurice Herzog. Copyright © 1952 by E. P. Dutton & Co., Inc., publishers, and used with their permission and that of Jonathan Cape Limited, London, England.

To Don and Claudette,
whose patience and understanding
made this project possible.

TABLE OF CONTENTS

Out of the night that covers me,
Black as the pit from pole to pole,
I thank whatever gods there be
For my unconquerable soul.

WILLIAM ERNEST HENLEY

PREFACE

"If you think of death, you might as well give up racing." These words were spoken by Bud Werner, whose losing ski race with death, in the form of an avalanche, is one of the chronicles of dangers narrated in this volume. Werner's life and death are graphically narrated in Curtis W. Casewit's story of *Death on the Slopes*. Some defy death and win. Others lose. The men with John Kennedy on PT 109 made it back to life. Young Kennedy, almost single-handed, made the rescue of the crew possible. His story adds another dimension to the courage of self-preservation—that of self-lessness, of courage for the sake of others. Manolete, the greatest of bullfighters, was gored to death at a time when his skill and daring were being doubted; in this final encounter between bull and matador, the two antagonists died together. While he was in the hospital, Manolete asked, "Did I kill the Miura?" Yes, the black, dangerous animal had died from the matador's sword.

Danger, adventure, death—these are the themes that run through the narratives in this book. There is sustained suffering, as in the case of Jean-Pierre Hallet, whose hand was blown off by dynamite but who drove the *Bloody Road to Usumbura* with one hand to find a hospital 70 miles away. Jim Hurtubise, *The Race Driver Who Wouldn't Die*, was told that the skin grafts on his horribly burned body would freeze his hands into one position. But he thought only of getting behind the wheel and told the doctors that he made his living "grabbing hold of something round." They fixed his hands cupped just enough so they could hold the steering wheel of a racing car. The crash left him so horribly burned that he should have died in transit to the hospital. How Jim sustained himself through weary, incredibly painful months of skin grafts, and exercise of new skin that split and healed, is one of the true classics of the genre, for Jim not only found the will to survive but made it back to the track to race again.

Back to danger! Back, once again, to the uneven match with death. Just what is it that prompts men to provoke fate over and over again? As you read these true and accurate accounts, you may wonder. And you may also look within, examining your feelings of participation, of identification with

9

these men in their moments of high danger. When Francis Gary Powers flew his last U-2 spy mission over Russia, he considered himself just a skilled aviator on a routine mission, but within minutes he had to decide whether to destroy his plane, whether to release the ejection mechanism or use his parachute, whether to kill himself with the poison he carried or give himself up to his Russian captors. And when Captain Byron D. Rickards and his crew on Continental Airlines flight 54 suddenly faced the pistols of a father-and-son team of skyjackers, they had to face hours of crucial decisions unprepared.

Here are the reactions and fates of men under pressure, men like you and me who, by choice or chance, came face-to-face with death. They acted out, each in his own way, a drama that symbolizes dangers that are rarer and rarer in our civilization but that hold an undiminished fascination for all of us. There is, within every one of these stories, the moment in which men test themselves. Those who have chosen such tests of their own free will are perhaps better prepared than those who encounter them accidentally. When Henri Charrière planned his *Escape from Devil's Island,* he was provoking fate as he had done all his life. The Frenchman's frantic attempt to save the life of his comrade shines through what would otherwise be just another escape story. His whole existence had been the outlaw's challenge of organized society—with all the mixed elements of Robin Hood and Al Capone. Our civilization encourages the defiance of routine existence to be channeled into sports, adventure and exploration; yet in cases such as Charrière's even the criminal wins a measure of admiration through the very daring of his undertaking and earns his passage home into organized society.

Men still act nobly under pressure. This book is a document of such manhood. The ability to react courageously when the chips are down is part of that larger entity we call human character. It is the spirit a man develops within himself that enables him to be what we call "brave" on demand. The common bond that links the men in this book is their ability to handle a "moment of truth" in a heroic way. When that moment came, they were not found wanting. They stood tall, graceful in their strength. They were men.

And yet how diverse are their stories! How many faces

courage wears! Some men seek danger; others have danger thrust upon them. For some, danger is a calculated means of reaching a goal; others must smell danger in every breath to feel alive. The faces of courage are equally diverse. It can be quick as a reflex, or it can be sustained for hours, days or longer. It is everything from the athlete's willingness to push his body beyond the limits of its endurance to the fight for life itself. Sometimes courage is a toughness of spirit that has nothing to do with anything physical——such qualities as dogged determination, standing up to mental torture for long periods of time or just doing supremely well the job for which one has been trained.

Those who seek danger most often do so because they have some great goal in mind that will set them apart from their fellowmen. It is the compulsion to prove themselves, their bodies, their spirits, their very souls. Of this breed, nothing is quite so terrifying as the challenge that Peter Gimbel set himself——to film the great white shark in its natural habitat, baiting it to violence with reeking horseflesh. He filmed it from a cage, but that cage could have ended up as his coffin, so vulnerable was it to the power of this savage 4000-pound vulture of the deep. To catch such a monster takes physical strength, but to go back into the dark waters time after time for one more close-up when it would have been much easier to say, "Cut, print it, and let's get the hell out of here," takes a rare breed of man.

Equally rare and equally pure in spirit is such a man as Maurice Herzog, who led the French climbing team that conquered the heights of Mount Annapurna in the Himalayas. Such a goal is incomprehensible to anyone except another mountaineer. To stand beside Maurice as he and his colleague hastily take a couple of snapshots of each other on the 26,493-foot summit is to share an emotional purity that is growing rare in an increasingly adulterated, polluted world. It is man conquering nature and yet embracing nature with all his soul.

One man in this same heroic mold is the diminutive Red Grant, last of the batmen in the barnstorming world, whirling down to earth in their birdlike costumes in death-defying stunts. The near disasters he himself encounters in his chosen profession would chill the blood of the bravest. The deaths of his air-circus colleagues leave the big question, Why does a man expose himself to danger like this? Perhaps it is for the thrill of flight on the most primitive level, the type of inspiration that drove the Wright brothers to take to the air in their fragile machine.

The instinct toward self-preservation is basic in man. For men of courage there is always a choice in that split second between life and death. Do you accept death as an easy way out of the struggle for life, whatever the cost? One hero in whom Americans can feel enormous pride is General Billy Dean. Captured by the Communists in the Korean War, Dean withstood brainwashing, torture and interrogation for months without cracking.

The supreme example of courage in the line of duty is that of the heroic crew of *Apollo 13*, who had to turn back to earth while rationing their evaporating fuel reserves. Captain James Lovell's low-key description of the epic flight makes the quick thinking and resourceful action seem almost routine. But courage can never be just routine. In spite of his incredible cool, the nervous stress of those fateful hours comes through.

The courage of the athlete whose drive to excel above and beyond the efforts of ordinary men sets him apart in a unique way. Roger Bannister looked failure in the face when the wind kicked up before his projected assault on the four-minute mile. It would have been all too easy for him to postpone his attempted record run to another day, *any* other day. But the time was now, and he went ahead anyway. Jerry Kramer tells the inside story of the famous "frozen" game at Green Bay, between the Packers and the Cowboys, that climaxed the 1967 National Football League season. His playing winning football in 13-degree weather is as pure a type of courage as that shown by those who climb mountains. Nowhere does Jerry mention or apparently consider the risk of permanent injury on the frozen ground under 500 pounds of opposing linemen. Winning the game is what matters. There is the quieter brand of courage displayed by two policemen doing their duty, out of the limelight, despite pressure and constant danger. One was a young man, Colin Barker, who took care of some toughs in the Haight-Ashbury district of San Francisco in a way that did credit to the force. The other was a quiet, methodical country cop, Sergeant Edgar Croswell, responsible for the Apalachin roundup, who went on with his investigation despite pressure from politicians to drop the case. His work dealt a serious blow to the Mafia's organization.

One supreme lesson can be learned from the stories in this book: Men face tremendous problems today—no matter what their roles in life. These tales of drama and adventure show that, when it comes down to ultimate survival, man is capable of overcoming Herculean obstacles. This indomitable ability to survive has to suggest that—our predictions to the contrary—the human race has a future.

Our daily computerized lives make it less and less possible to test our own courage under pressure. Spectator sports threaten to crowd out the average man's participation, and the neighborhood sandlot seems to be going the way of the old swimming hole. Yet many a man is tempted to seek danger now and then, if only to show that he has what it takes. Rather than doing it with daredevil driving tactics on a superhighway, he is better off seeking such challenges in sports, camping, hunting or simply in the 101 challenges that he meets in daily life.

In this book an attempt has been made to keep the selections contemporary. For this reason dramatic adventures from the Twenties and Thirties, such as Charles Lindbergh's ordeal in flying the Atlantic or the saga of doryman Howard Blackburn, who allowed his hands to freeze around the oars so he could attempt to row himself and his frozen mate 100 miles to safety, do not appear. Readers will undoubtedly have favorite stories of their own that didn't make this particular lineup.

The material that follows, though, produced by such well-known writers as the late John Dos Passos, Ernest K. Gann, John Hersey and Martin Caidin, to name a few, should prove more than just exciting reading. Such stories tend to reaffirm man's belief in his own resources and, in the words of William Ernest Henley, his "unconquerable soul."

WILLIAM PARKER
Groton, Conn.

TERROR IN THE AIR

By Joseph P. Blank

*Airline hijacking was not so common in 1961, the time set-
ting for this tale of heroism in the air. The wild rash of hi-
jackings to Cuba had not begun, and that made the shock
of this particular incident even harder to take for the people
involved—and the nation. The plane was a Boeing 707 four-
engine jet liner bound from Los Angeles to Houston with 67
passengers and a crew of six. Two of those passengers, Leon
Beardon, 38, and his 16-year-old son, Cody, were to become
the pivotal characters in a real-life drama that involved hundreds of airline personnel, airport police, local police, the
FBI and even President John F. Kennedy and directly threatened the lives of 71 people on the aircraft. The exemplary
courage of the pilot, Captain Byron D. Rickards, his crew
and Border Patrol commissioner Leonard Gilman, who happened to be a passenger aboard that Continental Airlines
flight, kept a major tragedy from happening.*

At 2:00 A.M., August 3, 1961, the stewardess's call buzzer
sounded and a small light winked on over the head of a
passenger in the coach section of Continental Airlines flight
54. Until this moment the flight of the big, sleek $5,400,000
Boeing 707 jet liner had been completely routine.

It had left Los Angeles International Airport at 11:30
P.M., August 2, bound for Houston with intermediate stops
at Phoenix, El Paso and San Antonio. At 1:06 A.M. it roared
off the Phoenix runway with 67 passengers and a crew of six
and, with its four jet engines howling, climbed steeply into
the black sky for the one-hour run to El Paso. Fifty minutes
later, when the plane was flashing through the night at 27,000
feet, graying, rugged-faced Captain Byron D. Rickards, 52, a
flier since 1927, turned the controls over to First Officer

15

Ralph L. Wagner and made radio contact with Air Defense Command for the relay of instructions from the Air Route Traffic Control Center at El Paso.

The sound of the buzzer interrupted 21-year-old stewardess Lois Carnagey's chat with a group of air-force recruits on their way to San Antonio for basic training. She walked up the darkened aisle, noting that only a few passengers were awake, stopped at Leon Beardon's seat, turned off the call button over his head and leaned down to hear his request.

Beardon, a spare, blond man of 38, looked up at her pleasantly, shoved the barrel of a .38-caliber pistol into her middle and softly said, "To the cockpit." He arose, followed by his 16-year-old son, Cody, who had been sitting next to him. The younger Beardon clutched a .45-caliber automatic, which he kept mostly hidden under his sport shirt.

They walked through the coach section and into the first-class section, where the other stewardess, 22-year-old Toni Besset, an ebullient, vivacious blonde, stood. Toni smiled as the three approached, and Lois said, "He's got a gun."

Toni said, "Oh," and the smile froze on her face.

"You come along, too," the elder Beardon told Toni.

In the forward lounge they walked past director of passenger services Louis Finch, who was busy checking his ticket records. Lois opened the cockpit door, and they filed into the small compartment. Second Officer Norman L. Simmons, the plane's engineer, looked up irritably. Lois announced, "The man has a gun!"

Simmons moved his eyes from Lois's frightened face to Beardon's grim expression to the gun. Wagner, 38, a veteran of 21 years in the air and the father of four children, screwed his head around to ask why visitors were in the cockpit. Captain Rickards, concentrating on the radio, saw Wagner's mouth open in surprise, and he glanced back.

Leon Beardon pointed his gun at Rickards and said, "Turn the plane forty-five degrees to the right and maintain radio silence. We're going to Cuba." He was poised and calm and spoke in a conversational tone. Rickards stared at him. A week earlier, after headlines reported the hijacking of a Miami-to-Tampa Electra, Rickards's wife had asked him what he would do if a hijacker ever pointed a gun at him, and he had said, "I don't know." He considered the question academic; such things could happen, of course, but it couldn't happen to him.

No one in the cockpit moved. The plane streaked through the night. The voice from Air Defense Command, code-named Sad Pal, squawked over the radio: "ATC [Air Traffic Control] clears Continental Fifty-four from present position to the El Paso VOR [a radio station that guides the plane in]. Descend and maintain one one thousand [11,000 feet altitude]. Over." Sad Pal waited for the plane to follow regulations by repeating the instructions.

Leon Beardon moved his gun a little and said, "Captain, did you change the course?"

"No."

"You'd better do it."

Sad Pal came over the radio: "Continental Fifty-four, Sad Pal. Did you copy the clearance?"

Rickards told Beardon, "We can't fly to Cuba. We only have an hour's fuel."

"Captain. . . ."

Rickards then felt scared. The plane did carry only one hour's fuel. But if Beardon was crazy and didn't believe him, he might start shooting. It could mean the lives of every person in the plane. Casually and matter-of-factly Rickards said, "Mr. Simmons will show you the fuel gauges. You can see for yourself."

Simmons, 46, with more than 20 years' and six million miles' experience in the air, showed Beardon the gauges for the center tank and the two outboard auxiliary tanks and explained the calibration.

Sad Pal came in again: "Continental Fifty-four, Sad Pal. Did you copy the clearance?"

Beardon said, "All right, go to Monterrey, Mexico."

"We can't," Rickards replied. "I don't have charts for the route, and we'd probably crash in the mountains. Besides, the Monterrey runway is too short for a jet. We've got to land in El Paso."

"That's right," Simmons agreed. "We'd all get killed, and what's the point of that?"

Sad Pal patiently said, "Continental Fifty-four, Sad Pal. Did you copy your clearance?"

"We'd better answer that call," Rickards said. "If we don't, they'll send something up here to find out what the trouble is."

Beardon nodded. "But no extra conversation."

Rickards looked at Wagner. "I'll take the controls. You

handle the radio. Tell them OK." Leon Beardon held a gun on Lois Carnagey, whom he had ordered to sit in the jump seat behind the pilot.

As Rickards sloped the big ship down to 11,000 feet, he knew that the situation could explode at any moment. Beardon and his son acted calm, and Rickards wanted to keep them that way. He didn't want the guns in the Beardons' hands to fire, and he tried to think ahead to avert a situation that might trigger the guns. "We'd better inform the passengers about what's happening," he told Beardon, "and we'd better tell the people on the ground, so they know your intentions."

"That sounds reasonable," Beardon said. "Tell the people on the ground there are four of us here. Tell them we're coming in to fuel up only. No passengers get off or get on. No one comes around the plane except the fueling crew. I don't want any trouble. So if everybody goes along with what I say, nobody'll get hurt."

Wagner tuned in to the Continental flight-operations office, relayed Beardon's message and asked for immediate clearance to land. He knew Rickards wanted to get the plane out of the air as fast as possible. In a few seconds the control center came in: "Continental Fifty-four, the active runway is twenty-two, wind southeast at four."

Rickards began his approach to the El Paso airport. Lois could feel Leon Beardon's gun against her back. She acted calm but was all jelly inside. "Could you point that gun away from me?" she asked. "I'm afraid of guns." Beardon complied, then told Toni to take care of the passengers and tell them to sit still after the plane landed. Toni stepped past Cody Beardon crouched in the cockpit doorway facing the passenger compartments and holding the .45 concealed behind the crook of his arm.

In the forward lounge Toni tapped big Lou Finch, a 38-year-old father of five children, and said, "Lou, they've got guns and want to take the plane to Cuba."

Lou grinned up at her. He and Toni often kidded each other during flights.

"I mean it, Lou. They mean business. They don't want any passengers to leave the plane."

Lou glanced back and saw Cody Beardon's gun. As Toni walked down the aisle, he got on the public-address system and said, "Please keep your seat belts fastened after landing. Until further instructions there will be no deboarding or boarding in El Paso." Several passengers groaned and asked each other, "What now?"

In the cockpit Leon Beardon leaned toward Rickards and said, "Captain, I wouldn't want anything to happen on this landing."

"Don't worry. Nothing will." Rickards had no intention of trying to play tricks with a 100-ton airplane that was going to contact the concrete runway at 115 miles an hour. He just wanted to get his passengers and airplane down safely. He smoothly touched down, put the four engines in reverse thrust to slow down the onrushing craft, then taxied off the runway and switched off the engines. He peered through the cockpit windows. He couldn't see a single human being or the slightest indication of activity. The airport looked deserted. It was 2:16 A.M. Leon Beardon told Lois to stay with the passengers.

Lou Finch walked down the aisle, stopping at each row of seats and quietly telling the passengers, "This plane is being hijacked by gunmen. They want to take it to Cuba. Try to be calm." His report was met by a variety of expressions. Some passengers stared uncomprehendingly at him. A few said, "You're kidding!" Women involuntarily clutched their children, while others covered their faces with their hands. A middle-aged man told Finch, "Let's fight 'em right here in the plane. Let's make a stand in our own country!" Finch told him to stay put. In the forward compartment a woman sobbed audibly, and her husband put his arms around her and tried to comfort her. He beckoned to Lois. "My wife is pregnant," he pleaded. "Can't she get off, please?" The woman added, "I'm six months' pregnant. I'm afraid for the baby." She again began crying.

Lois walked to the cockpit and explained the problem to Leon Beardon. He thought for a moment, then said, "We don't want any babies born aboard, do we? Bring her up here." Satisfied by the obviousness of the woman's condition, he said, "All right, we'll let 'em off." To Rickards he said, "Tell them to wheel the stairs up to the plane, and we'll let this couple off. Tell them to be careful. No funny business."

Lou Finch interrupted. "Why don't you let all the El Paso passengers off? In fact, why not all the passengers? You don't need them for what you want to do. And it'll lighten our load."

Beardon considered the suggestion for a full minute and said, "All right. But I want four hostages. I don't want any soldiers or recruits, because the Cubans may shoot them when we land in Havana. If we can get four volunteers, the rest can leave."

Finch made the request for volunteers over the PA system as Lois and Toni moved down the aisle. The first volunteer was 24-year-old Jack Casey, a Continental office employee. A few weeks earlier Casey had been transferred from the airline's Denver office to the Houston office.

The second volunteer was Leonard Gilman, 43, a deputy regional commissioner for the Border Patrol in southern California. Lean, athletic, capable, Gilman had been on his way to Brownsville, Texas, on business. He didn't identify himself; he merely said, "I'll stay."

As Lois passed down the aisle, 19-year-old Truman Cleveland, a private first class in the army returning from Pacific duty to Fort Bliss at El Paso, caught her arm. He said, "I'll stick with you."

Finch got on the PA system again. "We need one more volunteer," he said urgently. Luis Erives, a 26-year-old U.S. Army veteran of Mexican parentage who was on his way from Los Angeles to visit his dying mother in northern Mexico, looked around. He heard men explaining to each other that they had families or important business engagements. He saw frightened women and children. He motioned to Lois and said, "I'll stay."

Lois and Toni shepherded the four hostages into the forward lounge, and the other passengers filed out. Some looked admiringly at the crew and hostages and said, "Good luck." Others kept poker-faced or wore weak grins of relief. Toni, ever the airline stewardess, took her post at the door and bade the passengers a cheery "Good night." One recruit grinned at her and said, "Have a good time in Cuba," and she smiled. "You have fun, too." In leaving the plane, a man asked Leon Beardon, "If I stay, will you let one of the stewardesses go?" and got a hard, curt "No!" Gilman touched one woman at the end of the line and quickly whispered, "Listen to what I say, please. Here is my card. When you get into the terminal, go to a telephone, call the Border Patrol, and tell them I'm on the plane."

After the cabin doors were locked and the stairs pulled away, Leon Beardon ordered Lois into the cockpit, where he held the gun on her and told Captain Rickards to direct the airport to start fueling the plane. Cody Beardon stood at the cockpit door, his gun pointed toward the hostages. Thus far, he hadn't uttered a word.

Captain Rickards radioed the instructions and stared into the night. He couldn't see any activity. He wondered what was happening, what was going to happen.

Within two minutes of Captain Rickards's report of the hijacking from the air, the news was flashing out of the El Paso airport by radio, telephone and teletype to every part of the country. Within five minutes cars were racing toward the airport—the FBI, the Border Patrol, local Continental Airlines men and women, El Paso police, state troopers, sheriff's deputies, the El Paso mayor and councilmen, newspaper reporters and photographers. The Air Defense Command alerted jet fighters to take off on seconds' notice to track the captured jet liner when it took to the air. In Denver, the home base of Continental Airlines, president Robert F. Six and other airline executives were hurriedly dressing, while a crew at Stapleton Airfield was servicing a jet-prop Viscount to fly them to El Paso. At Fort Bliss a major general ordered out his car to take him to the airfield and alerted a company of troops, in case it was needed.

In Washington the Federal Aviation Agency, the FBI and the Justice Department were conferring to determine facts and coordinate their activities.

In the offices of every daily newspaper in the country and in many other parts of the world, teletype machines were chattering out the news of the hijacking and copy-desk men were composing headlines.

Outside the plane the chief problem faced by the local and federal agencies was a scarcity of facts. Were there four hijackers as reported by Captain Rickards (a deception by Beardon to inflate his power) or two men as described by the freed passengers? "At the outset there were many unknowns, and these unknowns just continued," said Edward Parker, a deputy chief at El Paso Border Patrol headquarters. "To what extent were the hijackers armed—just pistols or perhaps sawed-off shotguns and submachine guns as well? What was happening to the two young stewardesses, and how were they taking it? What were conditions in general in the airplane?

"And who were the hijackers? At the beginning we thought they were Cubans. Fanatical Castro patriots? Maniacs? If we pressed them, would they destroy the ten captives in the plane? We didn't know; so we had to sweat out each minute."

The Beardons came from Coolidge, Arizona. The father had a criminal record dating back to 1941 and had been convicted of grand theft, forgery and first-degree robbery. In 1955 he had been a mental patient at the Arizona State Hospital, to which he had voluntarily committed himself because he was "depressed." In Coolidge, where he had left his wife and three younger children, he had worked off and on as a used-car salesman. At the time of the hijacking he was on parole from a five-year-to-life sentence.

The involved agencies and the law officers, who were keeping out of sight in the airport administration building, agreed on one need: time. They had to have time to find out what was happening in the airplane and time to work out a plan. They decided to agree to whatever the hijackers wanted but to stall, delay, do anything to buy time without jeopardizing the safety of the ten hostages.

Inside the big plane, nearly half as long as a football field, the tension had eased off. The Beardons appeared calm in their command of the situation. The hostages, as if by silent agreement, tried to be equally cool. They wanted to avoid any kind of crisis that might push the Beardons into action with the guns.

Suddenly Leon Beardon turned away from the window through which he had been staring, called to Finch and said, "I want to see the identifications of the four men who stayed." With Cody Beardon watching, Gilman had no chance to stuff his credentials down behind a seat. In the cockpit the elder Beardon noted Gilman's credentials and called in, "Inspector, are you armed?" Gilman said he wasn't. Beardon came out, covered Gilman with his gun and told his son to frisk the official.

Then he turned to Rickards. "Radio them to get this plane fueled."

Rickards obeyed. In a few minutes a tank truck slowly circled toward the plane. The refueling crew hooked the hoses into the plane, then puttered around trying to look busy. They pumped no aviation kerosene into the plane. The three flying officers looked at the fuel gauges, understood what was happening and exchanged quizzical looks of wonder.

In the lounge Toni and Lois made and served coffee and handed out the little packs of five cigarettes that normally are given to passengers on air trips. Leon Beardon said he didn't mind the hostages moving around, one at a time, and stretching their legs or using the washroom.

Toni tried to draw young Beardon into conversation, and they soon were chatting about surfing and water-skiing. Toni laughingly mentioned that she had been studying Spanish and maybe she'd have a chance to test her fluency. Leon Beardon said, "You'll be well treated in Havana. Don't worry about a thing." His son asked Toni if there was any champagne aboard the plane. "No," she lied, "we only carry it on first-class flights."

Beardon returned to the cockpit and examined the gauges. His face hardened, and he told Rickards, "Look, I said we'd get along if I wasn't crossed. Tell them to get the plane fueled."

Rickards contacted Wayne Curto, manager of the Continental office. "The man, here, with a gun says to get the plane fueled," he said. "He is listening to both ends. We're just relaying messages."

"All right," Curto replied. "We just had a little trouble getting the fueling machinery started. The company suggests a change of planes, because you may have trouble landing the jet in Havana. We have a DC-7 flying in from Houston, and it should be here by nine-thirty. We can make the transfer in the open and assure that nothing will happen."

Beardon said, "Tell him nothing doing."

"I don't know if Havana can take a jet; we'll need eight thousand feet of runway," Rickards exaggerated. He knew that a jet had landed and taken off from the Havana airport without difficulty.

Curto was following Continental president Six's instructions. From the air Six had told the El Paso office to try to make an exchange of aircraft. The transfer might enable the law officers to act, and it would also permit the company to keep in service an expensive airplane that was capable of bringing in $25,000 a day in revenue. "But don't do anything to jeopardize the safety of the hostages," Six directed. "If that becomes an issue, let the airplane go."

Beardon rejected Rickards's avowed fear. "You'll make it," he said.

Outside, the trucks started their refueling motors. The ground crew set the motors on idle speed, and the fuel just dribbled into the tanks. In the cockpit the flight crew watched the needles on the gauges barely move, and they knew that the fueling was going to take a long time. It took a half hour to pump a few hundred gallons, and then Curto radioed that the two trucks had exhausted their load and would have to go to the bulk plane for more kerosene. This took another half hour. Then the battery on one of the refueling trucks went dead, and the truck had to be towed away. Beardon was becoming visibly irritated. He saw an American Airlines refueling truck on the field, and he told Rickards, "Tell them to use the American Airlines truck." The message went to Harold Spores, Continental's El Paso manager of flight operations, who took time "to find out about it," then reported, "American won't allow it. We have no reciprocal agreement with them."

Beardon accepted this excuse but angrily said, "Tell them to keep on fueling." The hostages could see that Beardon's temper was growing edgy. Simmons looked at Rickards, lowered his eyes to a two-foot-long flashlight at his feet and whispered, "I could clobber him."

"You'd better hold it, Norm," Rickards said. He wanted no shooting, especially around the two stewardesses.

At the cockpit door young Beardon told his father he had to use the washroom, and the elder Beardon said, "OK. Give me your gun." As the fully cocked .45 changed hands, Leon Beardon slipped his finger in front of the trigger and the gun fired, sending a bullet between Simmons's feet. Everyone in the cockpit jumped, and the concussion partially deafened Simmons. Lois, who had kept iron-bound control, dropped to her knees and began sobbing. Toni slumped into Simmons's lap and began crying softly, "Do you think we'll get out of it? Do you think we'll be killed?" Simmons patted her shoulder and said, "It's all right. Everything'll be all right." At the same time he wondered whether he'd ever see his wife and 12-year-old daughter again. In the lounge Private First Class Cleveland turned to Finch and said, "Boy, oh, boy, those guys in the army told me never to volunteer for anything."

Nobody knew whether or not the shot was deliberate. It probably was accidental, because it occurred without provocation. To save face, Leon Beardon said, "That'll show you I mean business." He handed the empty shell to Toni, saying, "Here's a souvenir for you." Still shaky, she put the shell in her mouth. It occurred to her that her mouth was a silly place to keep the shell; so she dropped it into her brassiere.

The tension and suspense now were drawing taut everybody's nerves. Border Patrol official Gilman could feel his insides tightening. His only plan at the time was to do what he could to keep everybody calm. He knew he couldn't make a pass at either Beardon while they held guns at full cock. In the confined cabin any shot carried the chance of hitting someone. Gilman was particularly concerned about the two girls. He rose from his seat and stepped toward Leon Beardon, who brought his gun up and said, "That's far enough, Inspector."

"Be reasonable about this," Gilman urged. "If you attempt this flight to Cuba in a jet, we'll probably have to belly-land. Why not let the girls go? You don't need them. The rest of us will take our chances."

Beardon considered this for a moment, then shook his head. "They get paid to take their chances," he decided. "They stay." He turned back into the cockpit. "Let's get this plane off the ground, Captain."

"They're not finished fueling, and I'll need charts for the flight to Havana."

"Well, you get on the horn and tell 'em, by God, to get them, and let's go. I'm fed up with this stalling."

Rickards requested the charts. In ten minutes a maintenance man brought the charts up the steps to the front cabin door. Rickards checked them, found they were inadequate and requested more. Another blue-coveralled man came out of the administration building with a batch of charts. The flight crew, watching the man approach, knew he was not a bona fide employee. He wore highly polished brown dress shoes. Beardon suspected the man and told Rickards, "Tell him to stop. Tell him to open the top of his coveralls. I want to see that he's not wearing a bulletproof vest." The man, an FBI agent who was hoping to get a glimpse of conditions in the cabin, obeyed Rickards's shouts. Beardon refused to permit the agent near the door and ordered him to pass the charts to the cockpit window with a pole. He then scrutinized each chart for written messages.

After a glance at the fuel gauges Beardon said, "OK, Captain, let's go."

Rickards, like all the hostages except Gilman, had reached the end of his patience. He had swallowed too much coffee, smoked too many cigarettes, waited too long for something to happen. He contacted Spores on the radio and said, "The man, here, wants to go."

Spores: "We're not through fueling." The ship now contained enough fuel for the trip to Havana.

Beardon: "This is it, Captain. We're getting the show on the road. No more stalling."

Rickards to Spores: "Things are getting pretty tight here. We'd better move."

Spores: "This matter is now out of our hands. The government has taken over."

Rickards: "I can appreciate that, but there's a man here pointing a gun, and he says we're going."

Spores: "All right, but. . . ."

Rickards contacted the tower and requested clearance to fly at 35,000 feet to Houston, where he would request further clearance. The tower obtained clearance from the Air Route Traffic Control Center and returned to Rickards: "Thirty-five thousand. Runway four. Runway wind is northeast at six."

Rickards: "Thank you."

Trucks came in to start the jet engines. The stairs were pulled away. The refueling trucks drove off. Messages were streaming out from the airport. At nearby Biggs Field, two jet fighters roared into the sky. In the jet liner the hostages had strapped themselves into seats, and, as the engines howled, Finch nodded to Casey and said, "It's about time we stopped jacking around and got going." The Beardons crouched in the cockpit, their guns poised. Simmons and Wagner had their eyes glued to the instruments.

Captain Rickards released the brakes and began moving the big plane down the ramp, past the administration building. Harold Spores, Continental's flight-operations manager in El Paso, came over the radio: "You'll never make it." Rickards thought, *They must be planning something. What?*

The voice of a man in the El Paso airport control center was heard in the radio room of the Federal Aviation Agency: "The airplane is now taxiing past the tower!" Perspiration began to show through the shirts of several agency executives. They knew that the airplane would never leave the ground.

The decision had been made in Washington by President Kennedy in consultation with his aviation advisor, Najeeb Halaby, administrator of the Federal Aviation Agency. In telephone conversations with the president, Mr. Halaby had laid out the known facts of the hijacking, and the president had weighed the risks in both permitting the jet liner to depart and forcing it to remain on the ground. If the plane took to the air, there was no way to tell what the gunmen— they still were unidentified—would do to the hostages. Furthermore, it was intolerable to allow the gunmen to break the laws, kidnap citizens and defy all federal and local law-enforcement agencies. The blow to United States prestige would be lamentable. Lastly, two commercial liners already had been hijacked to Cuba, and this business had to stop.

The manner of stopping the jet liner was left to law officers at the scene. The FBI, with Agent Francis Crosby in charge, was directing the police action. Crosby and Edward Parker, a deputy chief of the Border Patrol in the El Paso area, agreed that it wouldn't be effective to halt the plane peacefully. The jet liner could have been easily immobilized by deflating the tires or fouling the engines or jamming a couple of big fire trucks against the landing gear. None of these measures, however, would have prevented the gunmen from threatening to kill a hostage unless corrective action permitted the plane to take off.

From the air, now within an hour of El Paso, Robert Six suggested, "Wait until the last minute; then shoot out the tires when the airplane starts taxiing." Crosby agreed that this kind of violence was best; the results would convince the gunmen that the plane was physically incapable of taking to the air and no threats or reprisals could alter that fact.

As the big jet started to move, a maintenance man on the ramp telephoned the Continental office: "They're rolling!" It was now 6:50 A.M., and four and a half hours had passed since the plane touched down. Curto dropped the phone and shouted to Crosby, "Now's the time to stop the plane!" Crosby sprinted out.

The plane taxied ponderously but smoothly about 300 yards and was making a right-hand turn into the runway, when a squad of four green Border Patrol cars came screeching out from behind the maintenance shops. Drawing alongside the plane, Border Patrol and FBI men fired at the ten big tires with rifles and submachine guns.

Rickards didn't hear the shots, but he saw tracer bullets skipping down the concrete taxi strip, and he cried, "My God! They're shooting at us!" He knew that the law officers must be firing at the tires. It was real, yet unreal. *This is just like the movies,* he thought.

"Keep going!" Leon Beardon yelled.

Rickards wondered why the tires didn't go flat. Bullets were piercing the tires, but, with their tremendous air pressure, they were deflating slowly. The plane lurched a little, and Simmons shouted, "You can't take off! The tires are going!"

"Keep going!" Leon Beardon yelled.

Several bullets hit the cabin. Lois and Toni flung themselves on the floor of the lounge. A bullet crashed through the window near Erives's head, and a piece of flying glass cut Finch's cheek. As Finch dropped to the floor to protect himself, he shouted at Casey, "What the hell are they shooting at *us* for?"

Gilman shouted, "Stay in your seats! The bullets will ricochet up through the floor!" No one heard him.

In the cockpit a light on the fire-control panel suddenly glared red, and Wagner shouted, "They've shot out number-two engine!" He pulled the lever that released fire-extinguishing fluid into the engine, and Rickards cut the power. The jet liner halted. All ten tires were down, and kerosene was streaming out of the disabled engine.

For a few minutes no one in the airplane spoke. Rickards stared down through his window. A crowd of nearly 200 law officers, officials and airline people milled around the plane. A fire crew was spraying a broad circle of foam to prevent ignition of the leaking kerosene. A few hundred yards from the plane, hundreds of spectator cars lined the road.

In Washington congressmen stormed over the crime. It was generally assumed the hijackers were Cubans. A California senator said, "It is an act of war and should be dealt with accordingly." A New York representative was ready "to quarantine Cuba and throw a naval and air blockade around her until Castro purges himself and gives proof that he will not permit a recurrence of such excesses."

A wave of hypercaution swept the air agencies, airlines and airports of the nation. By teletype, the FAA urged flight crews to lock cockpit doors and authorized them to carry sidearms. At all major airports security police carefully scrutinized passengers. In Boston two airlines gave all Miami-bound passengers "close checks." At the San Francisco and St. Petersburg airports, passengers awaiting embarkation were questioned because nearby persons had overheard the word *hijacking* in their conversations.

In the airplane the Beardons and the hostages had no conception of the ruckus provoked by their escapade. With a sigh, Rickards turned to First Officer Wagner and Simmons and said, "Let's finish the logbook. We're not going anyplace." To Leon Beardon he said, "This airplane has had it. It can't move."

"Let's take the DC-7 deal," Beardon said.

"We don't have a rating to fly that airplane. It'll have to be another crew."

"Ask them about it."

Rickards contacted Harold Spores, who said, "Yes, we can go through with it. A DC-7 with a volunteer crew is flying in from Houston. Should be here at nine-thirty."

Beardon spoke to his boy. "With all that high-powered stuff out there," he said, nodding toward the guns, "they'll never let us transfer. We'll never make it alive."

"Where you go, I go," the boy said. Throughout the ordeal he had never wavered in his coolness. He betrayed tension only by periodically wiping his sweaty gun palm on his dungarees. He kept his gun on full cock at all times.

Leon Beardon held his gun near Lois's head and told Rickards, "You get on the radio and tell them I mean business, and I want to know what kind of security I can have in transferring to the DC-7."

FBI agent Crosby answered. "You have a guarantee of safe-conduct to the DC-7 and assurance that the airplane will take off and leave the El Paso area. That is all I can guarantee."

At the same time, Border Patrol official Ed Parker was talking by telephone to his Washington headquarters. Parker was a pilot, and he suggested that he and another Border Patrol man make up the DC-7 crew. Although not rated to fly a DC-7, Parker figured that during the time the hijackers entered the plane, the engines warmed up and the plane taxied to the runway, he and the crew would be able to work out a move to overpower the hijackers. The plan was approved.

A half hour later, however, administrator Halaby discussed the projected transfer with the president, and the president disapproved. The government would make no humiliating deals with criminals, he decided. FBI headquarters passed the decision to Agent Crosby.

In the plane a light flashed on the door-indicator panel, showing that the door to lower 41, the electronics-equipment compartment in the belly of the plane, had been opened. A person in 41 could enter the cockpit through a grate in the floor. The three flying officers ignored the light. Wagner casually crossed his legs and tried to cut off the view of the light with his foot, but Leon Beardon noticed it. "Why is that door open?" he asked. Simmons answered matter-of-factly, "Oh, that's just a two-inch vent that lets hot air out of the radio compartment." The light soon winked out as an FBI man completed some exploration and left the plane.

There was nothing to do but wait. Everybody was sick of coffee. The cigarettes were gone, and the dedicated smokers were driven to lighting up butts. Casey passed out some of his cigars. The temperature in the plane was around 100 degrees Fahrenheit. Nerves were getting raw, and few words were exchanged. With the constant view of all the guns outside, Leon Beardon was growing more tense. He must have realized that the ring was tightening around him.

Gilman now began to worry more about what might happen inside the plane. He didn't know how Beardon would respond to growing pressure. He didn't like the way the boy behaved. He was too cool. If the father told him to shoot a hostage, he might immediately respond without thinking. Gilman felt he had to distract the father and prevent any kind of irrational, impulsive idea from snowballing in his mind.

He left his seat in the forward compartment and strolled easily toward Leon Beardon in the lounge. Beardon watched him and said, "I don't want any funny business. I don't want to hurt anybody unless I have to."

"I'm not up to any tricks," Gilman assured him. "Maybe I can help you. You're worried about the transfer to the DC-7. All right, we can get the plane to taxi up here. We can order all those people away. Then you and the boy and I will leave. I'll walk between you. Nobody'll take a chance on shooting and hitting me."

Beardon weighed this idea. He kept looking out the window at the armed guard.

Gilman felt he might be wavering and said, "Why don't you give me your gun and give up and walk off the plane? That way there's no chance of anybody getting hurt. I can guarantee you a fair trial."

"I can understand your attitude, Inspector," Beardon answered, "but you don't understand mine."

"No, I don't. It's hard for me to understand a father bringing his son into a thing like this. You must be escaping from a crime."

"I'm not escaping from a crime."

"Why *are* you doing it?"

"I have my reasons. This has been thought out a long time, and you're not going to talk me out of it. Anyway, it's a good way for me to get to Cuba. I think the Cuban form of government is better than ours. I prefer it. I intend getting there and bringing the rest of my family down legally. They'll pay their way. I didn't have the money for the trip."

"Well, you picked a pretty expensive way to get there. You say you like Castro, but you're not doing him any favor by bringing down a hijacked United States plane. It's just going to put pressure on him."

"Don't you worry about that."

Gilman and Beardon talked easily, almost amiably, and the conversation obviously distracted Beardon. Toni and Lois felt grateful to Gilman, who appeared sure and confident. Lois reached into her flight bag, pulled out her knitting and industriously occupied herself with the needles.

At about 9:15 A.M. Beardon said, "Where's the DC-7?"

Rickards checked by radio, and Spores reported that its arrival was delayed. Actually, the airplane had landed out of sight of the jet liner.

Then Parker, of the Border Patrol, got on the radio and told Rickards that the law agencies wanted absolute assurance that the hostages were safe. He asked that each hostage give his name and address. He also was very curious about Gilman, whom he knew well as a man of prompt decision and action.

Beardon warned Gilman not to try any code on the radio. When Gilman gave his name and address, Parker said, "How's the produce business?"

"All right."

"Business is slow around here," Parker said, "and we can ship a load of red onions right now, if you like." Parker was improvising a code; "Red Onions" was the name of a spirited horse once owned by Gilman, and Parker wanted to know if Gilman thought that law officers (red onions) should rush into the plane.

"Negative," Gilman replied, "negative." He felt that the situation in the plane was in adequate control, that time was working against the gunmen and that it would be foolhardy to make a move that could precipitate shooting.

"That was an interesting code, Inspector," Beardon allowed. "What was it all about? What did you tell him?"

"Negative. You heard me say it. It means everything is all right."

"Look, we're all getting along well," Gilman said. "Why don't you uncock those guns? If one of them goes off and somebody is hurt, the people out there will never allow you or a plane to leave."

Beardon uncocked his gun and told his son to do the same. Gilman continued his chatting with the elder Beardon. His manner so disarmed the gunman that Beardon said, "Inspector, I'll put my gun away if you give me your word you won't do anything." Gilman solemnly agreed, and Beardon shoved the gun into his belt, then later shifted it to his hip pocket. Cody Beardon still held his gun. After more talk Gilman suggested that the father take his son's gun. Beardon reached for his son's gun and put it in his other hip pocket. Toni said, "Oh, thank God."

Gilman felt better with only one man armed. He decided to try to keep matters running as they were as long as possible. If Beardon reached for a gun, however, he would jump him. Gilman caught Simmons's eye and looked at Cody Beardon. Simmons slightly nodded his head in understanding: If Gilman made a pass at the father, Simmons was to take the son.

The forward lounge of the plane contained a television set, and somebody flicked it on. A local news program was on the air, and TV cameras at the airport showed the plane with the crowd around it. The news broadcaster was enthusiastically describing the shooting and the number of armed law officers impatiently waiting to get at the gunmen. Simmons, afraid that the Beardons would become excited, said, "That thing'll have to be turned off. It's interfering with radio reception." Toni switched off the set.

Leon Beardon again was growing impatient, and he asked Rickards to find out about the DC-7. It now was 10:45 A.M. Agent Crosby replied, "We have our instructions from the highest authority. There will be no trades or deals. I demand that you surrender peaceably. If anybody on that plane is hurt, you'll hang for it."

Leon Beardon gave Gilman a look of mixed consternation and anger. "But they agreed," he said.

Gilman said, "Take it easy. Let me talk to him." He explained Beardon's attitude to Crosby, who replied, "I'm willing to come aboard and discuss it." Crosby felt the closer he got to Beardon, the faster the episode might be closed.

"Just a minute," Gilman said. To Beardon he asked, "How about giving up? Give me your guns and we'll get off the plane, and it'll all be over."

"No. Tell the FBI man to come aboard. But unarmed. And alone."

A crew rolled the stairs to the forward door of the cabin. The Beardons sat in the forward lounge, which cut off their view of the rear of the plane. Gilman nodded to the three hostages, Finch and the two girls and said, "Why don't you people go to the rear of the plane while we talk here?" Lois put away her knitting. Casey shook Cleveland, who was sleeping, and said, "Let's go." Simmons left the cockpit, letting the door close on Rickards and Wagner, and pushed open the cabin door for Crosby. At that moment he easily could have stepped out of the plane and dashed down the steps to freedom, but escape didn't occur to him. He closed the door after Crosby entered.

As the two law officers, with Simmons standing by, began talking with the elder Beardon, Gilman noticed a red light blink on at the rear of the plane. He knew that the rear cabin door was open. Told to go to the rear of the plane, the group had kept on moving to the door, opened it and dropped into the arms of the police on the ground. The four men were immediately handcuffed and held until identified. The two girls were hustled off to a car.

With the cockpit door closed, Rickards and Wagner were isolated. As they waited for the next development, they heard noises below them, and then the electronics-compartment grate opened. An FBI agent and a Border Patrol man, .45s in hand, crawled into the cockpit. They nodded to the pilots and crouched by the doorway.

Wagner whispered to Rickards, "If they open that door and start poppin' off with those guns, we'll get it. We're right in the line of fire."

Rickards leaned toward the two lawmen and said, "Do you mind if we leave?" They nodded consent.

Wagner tossed an escape rope out, squeezed through the cockpit window and lowered himself to the ground. Rickards crawled through the electronics compartment in the belly.

In the lounge Crosby told the Beardons that the transfer to the DC-7 was out, period. He was forbidden to make any deals. Beardon accused the FBI of reneging on a deal, and Crosby said, "Orders are orders. Now, why don't you just come along?"

Beardon's voice rose. "Before I'd step through that door and let American officers arrest me, I'd kill myself."

Gilman gave Simmons a darting look and swung his right fist at Beardon's jaw. The blow stunned Beardon and broke a bone in Gilman's hand. Simmons grabbed at the elder Beardon's arms, while Crosby lunged at Cody Beardon and put a hammerlock on him. The two law officers stepped from the cockpit and pulled the guns out of Beardon's hip pockets. Then Gilman and Crosby walked the Beardons out and down the steps.

It was 11:50 A.M. in El Paso, and nearly ten hours had passed since Lois Carnagey felt Leon Beardon's .38 poke into her stomach.

At the federal court trial in El Paso, Leon Beardon was

charged with kidnapping, obstruction of interstate commerce and violation of the Federal Motor Vehicle Theft Act. His attorney asked for a verdict of not guilty by reason of insanity. A jury took 22 minutes to return a verdict of guilty. On October 31 a federal judge sentenced him to life in prison.

Cody Beardon pleaded guilty under the Juvenile Corrections Act to transporting a stolen vehicle across state lines and was sentenced to a correction institution until the age of 21.

In the aftermath Congress passed a law making the crime of hijacking an airliner a capital offense.

THE RACE DRIVER WHO WOULDN'T DIE

By Charles N. Barnard

In a sport where the dangers are so obvious they go unspoken, Jim Hurtubise drove like a man who didn't know they existed. He was a leadfoot, a crowd pleaser. And then, one day at Milwaukee, it happened. Crash! Oh, he'd been in plenty of smashups during his 15 years of car racing, but this time a new element was added: fire! Just a week before, he had seen two drivers incinerated in a towering column of black smoke at Indianapolis. But he hadn't dwelt on it; he never did. Now, suddenly, he was in the midst of a roaring alcohol fire that mushroomed to nearly 1000 degrees of blistering heat in 30 seconds—three times enough heat to fry an egg! The track crew extinguished the blaze quickly, but the damage had been done. In addition to other burns, Jim Hurtubise's hands had been broiled like meat on a barbecue! That should have finished Jim's racing career right there— but it didn't. He fought back through months of painful hospital care and rehabilitation, determined to drive again.

It was in Milwaukee, Wisconsin, on June 7, 1964—a long time ago now. A particular automobile race is not usually so well remembered, not even by a driver. But third-degree burns heal slowly and in pain, and the scars will always make Jim Hurtubise remember the day.

There were 36,285 people at Fairgrounds Park that afternoon. The weather was bright and hot, and the gathering crowd—burdened with coolers full of beer on ice or standing in long lines to buy hamburgers and cigars—shimmered with excitement. Every staccato revving of an engine before the race stirred these people like nervous bees. They had come to see the big names—the Mantles and Namaths and Clays of racing—men and cars who had, only eight days before, contested for the rich 500-mile prize at Indianapolis. It's the same each year in this sport: The races at Phoenix and Trenton come first, in March and April. Next, the big one at Indy on Memorial Day. Then Milwaukee, first week in June. By then the men and the automobiles are as fast as they will be all year.

The Milwaukee track is an asphalt-paved one-mile oval, almost flat in the turns. A concrete wall about three feet high surrounds its outer perimeter to keep spectators safe from the cars. Drivers don't like walls wherever they are, but otherwise they don't complain about Milwaukee. They can average over 100 mph there with today's machinery, and they can win $10,000 in the hour it takes to finish 100 miles.

This day there were 22 cars lined for the start, some of them the new lightweight rear-engine designs, some the heavier front-engine roadsters that had dominated American track racing for a decade. The bodies were brilliant in candy-apple reds, frosty whites, tangerine, opalescent green, all of them slung low between big, wide black tires.

Hurtubise would drive a front-engine roadster he had built himself. He had been building cars as well as driving them from the time he was a teen-ager helping out around his father's gasoline station near Buffalo, New York. Now he was 31, and although he had yet to win at Indianapolis, he had won at a lot of other places, and he was as fast as any man. He was also a great favorite with the crowd—a happy sort of competitor, with eyes that often sparked with mischief. Another driver, A. J. Foyt, then the national champion and winner in the week past of the Indianapolis race, was also at the wheel of a front-engine car. Veteran Roger Ward, a former champion and Indy winner, would drive one of the new rear-engine cars.

From the start of the race it was clear that this day belonged to these three. The 19 other drivers would play no particular part in the drama of the next half hour. This was to be a swirling battle between Foyt, Ward and Hurtubise, and the thunder of their three engines made a single hole in the air each time the cars lapped the track. As the Milwaukee *Journal* described it the next day, "First Foyt and Ward battled, then Hurtubise joined them and for nearly twenty laps they raced around the track, down the straights and through the turns, looking more often like one car than three.

Until Hurtubise crashed, the racing was some of the finest ever seen here."

The crash was a beauty, too. Not, some in the crowd thought, the *best* one in Milwaukee's memory, but if you were lucky enough to have a seat near the fourth turn. . . .

It came on the 52nd lap, arriving like an uninvited guest, dirty, unwelcome, ugly. And, when it happened, the speed of time seemed suddenly to change. Action that had been swift, smooth and deceptively safe was now slowed in agony. The picture flickered, and events that brought binoculars up to the eyes (and soon forced them down again) unfolded like a slow-motion film. Watch this now, it said; study what you see happening there on the fourth turn; notice this, remember that, because later somebody is going to ask questions.

As in most accidents, what happened was a hundred things or a thousand all crowded into long, long seconds—micro-movements of metal and muscle suspended in time. The first of these occurred, unseen, in the oily darkness of a gear case in the rear of Ward's leading car. Something broke under the killing twist of 600 horsepower. Gears that were cut and polished to mesh with only thousandths of an inch to spare suddenly ground onto each other. The Ward car, traveling at about 110 mph, bucked and switched its tail as the rubber of its rear tires burned on the asphalt. Foyt, barely a yard behind and moving 16 feet every tenth of a second, some-how had time to receive the alarm through his eyes, to feed the data through his brain, to move his arms and hands on the steering wheel and to change course just enough to miss the stricken Ward.

A yard behind Foyt, crowding, straining and occupying the same second of time, Hurtubise. He processed the data, too: Trouble ahead. Pull on the wheel; turn right toward the out-side of the track. Get around Foyt from the right rear. . . .

At over 100 mph, when two exposed racing wheels touch, tread to tread, the laws of dynamics say that the one coming from the rear climbs the one in front. Hurtubise's left front wheel touched Foyt's right rear and went over it. The Hurtu-bise car leaped for the sky like a thrill driver mounting a ramp. Lifted by the left side first, it twisted in its flight, bank-ing more sharply right, moving almost lazily through the air, still intact but doomed.

In this same segment of time, Ward, his wheels seizing, was slowed to perhaps 75 mph and headed for the infield grass. Foyt, passing Ward, was unaware that a fellow driver was now airborne behind him.

And Jim Hurtubise was on his way down.

His left foot was pressing with desperation on a brake pedal. The brakes, working, stopped the spinning wheels in midair. But the car still flew. It nosed down in a diving turn to the right, and it hit the outside wall of the track with the right front wheel first.

Some of the spectators have seen nothing so far, their attention scattered elsewhere. Now, however, Hurtubise announces his arrival for all to see and hear. The right front wheel, machined from magnesium, explodes in a blinding flash as it hits concrete with the power of an artillery shell. The driver, with broad harnesses of webbing over each shoulder and another belt across his middle, receives the shock of impact through his entire body. A hundred times the force of gravity tears at the belts but cannot rip them loose. A form-fitting extension of the cockpit seat, designed to hug Hurtubise's right side, now exerts a crushing force on his rib cage. Three ribs, the fifth, sixth and seventh, crack. One of them punctures Hurtubise's right lung, collapsing it. The internal wound begins to flood his chest cavity with blood. He is still conscious. His bare hands still grip the useless steering wheel. The action, tormentingly slow, continues.

The right front wheel, torn free, bounces from the wall, then crashes back through the cockpit of the car, leaving a rubber bruise on Hurtubise's white coveralls. A piece of disk-brake-lining pad, scorching hot, is popped from the front wheel, takes a high, arching trajectory to the rear and lands between Hurtubise's back and the upholstery of the seat. There it will smolder, leaving two circular burn marks.

So far the crash is survivable. But it isn't over yet. In the next seconds the dreaded thing happens. Unseen in the mashed wreckage, the rigid front axle has been driven backward through the chassis. In its path is a 15-gallon auxiliary tank full of alcohol-blend racing fuel. The axle strikes the tank a blow, crushing it like an accordion. The fuel, compressed, builds an irresistible pressure, blowing open the hinged filler cap and bucketing down into the aluminum bathtub of the car body.

Now, its engine silenced, the car reacts to the unyielding

strength of the wall. It recoils and, slowly, tail first, on three wheels, it rolls back toward the center of the track, clanking and scraping its ruptured parts on the asphalt like a broken crab. The driver sits motionless in the cockpit, his helmeted head slumped forward, goggles still in place, his hands still instinctively braced in place on the wheel.

Somewhere, inevitably, there is a spark. And then an inferno.

In the track infield men run with fire extinguishers in their hands. The crowd, on its feet now, makes pitiful sounds. Sirens growl as red trucks move. Yellow caution flags flap at drivers who still circle the track. They steer low around the inside, reducing their speed. As each goes around, he can see the wrecked car in the middle of the fourth turn, and he knows Jim Hurtubise is burning.

In 15 years of racing it was his first taste of fire—the hated risk that makes most drivers shake their heads help-lessly in wordless fear and disgust. A week before, he had seen drivers Sachs and MacDonald incinerated in a towering column of black smoke at Indianapolis. Others he knew had gone the same way: Roberts, O'Connor, Vukovich—all of them dead or dying in the flames. But Hurtubise never had time to concentrate on fear of fire or anything else. In a sport where the dangers are so obvious they go unspoken, he drove like a man who didn't know they existed. In the slang of racing, he was a charger, a leadfoot. As a consequence, he was also a crowd pleaser. No matter what he drove, he stuck his foot hard on the gas rod, and the fans knew it and in their way acknowledged that here was a man who would keep his end of the bargain with the people who bought the tickets. Charge!

They discovered it first at Indianapolis in 1960, when, as a 27-year-old rookie, he set new one-lap and four-lap qualifying records over 149 mph. After that they called him Hercules. In 1961 he came back to lead the 500 for 35 laps before he burned the pistons out of his engine. In 1962 he went the distance to finish 13th at 135 mph. And in 1963 he found himself at the wheel of the biggest, most powerful machine of them all—a supercharged 800-horsepower called the Novi. It was, for race fans, a dream combination of man and machine. It was Burton making love to Liz; it was Patton in a tank; it was Cooper at high noon. The Novi was a bellowing V8 that could run over everything in sight as long as it stayed in one piece. But it had killed drivers, torn the treads off tires, blown the expensive guts out of its engines and broken the hearts and bank accounts of everyone who had ever tried to make it a winner. Now, in 1963, it was Hurtubise's turn to ride the bad stallion and show the crowd he really was Hercules.

In qualification runs he quickly gave them back the price of admission, howling around the two-and-a-half-mile oval at over 150 mph. He started the race in the center of the front row, was slowed by a fouled spark plug on the parade lap, dropped back into seventh position entering the first turn, then wound the engine high and tight to blow the plug clean and plunged down the back stretch like a man aiming a bazooka. In five-eighths of a mile at 175 mph, with the Novi's blower crying like a high wind, he passed the six cars in front of him and thundered into the third turn in the lead.

Hurtubise couldn't hear the Indianapolis crowd that day over the sound of his engine, but if he could, it would have sounded like a love song. Hundreds of thousands stood screaming his name as the red car, obscene with power, the bright chrome of its exhaust pipe already blued with fire, swept out of the fourth turn and onto the main straight in first place. It was the fastest first lap in the history of the race. Hurtubise! Hercules! Go! Go! Go!

He went. For 102 laps he went, until an oil leak stopped the Novi. In those 255 miles he had given his fans thrills they would relive for years. He had planted himself as firmly as a monument among the drivers who—win, lose or hit the wall—would always get a sort of Roman thumbs-up from the crowd. Hurtubise knew this, and it made him love racing the more. Now he had tasted both the fame and the money. He had led 32 other men around the arena. And some day soon, he promised himself, he would win it all.

There is something about this 500-mile automobile race in Indiana that does things like that to the men who have tried to win it. Like a run for the presidency, it stirs ambitions that will not again be quiet. For a young American race-car driver like Jim Hurtubise from North Tonawanda, New York, by way of a hundred dirt tracks and county fairs, it is a reach for a kind of immortality—the chance to make a mark in a book that will never be erased—and to make the kind of money that puts kids through college. For over half a century this strange seduction has lured men to the two-and-a-half-mile track each Memorial Day—and has beckoned them back again after they have lost, after they have won—and even after they have been maimed in their quest.

For Jim Hurtubise it was not the great race that nearly took his life away, but almost surely it was the narcosis of Indianapolis that made him fight back from horrible disablement to try again.

When the Milwaukee rescue workers reached the car, 15 gallons of fire were boiling inside the body and on the track beneath—alcohol fire, burning watery clear, with patches of blue and puffs of smoke rising from whatever it touched. In ten seconds it was everywhere, blistering paint, buckling aluminum, eating black and brown spots into the white fabric of the driver's coveralls, turning exposed flesh a strange, bad color. In 30 seconds it reached nearly 1000 degrees of heat, frying deep into every crevice and pore where the fuel had spread. Then, in another 30 seconds, geysers of white powder whumping from the extinguishers had strangled it. But a minute's fierce cooking had been done—three times enough heat to fry an egg—and now a life hung in the balance.

Jim Hurtubise remembers hitting the wall. He remembers seeing men running with the red extinguishers in their hands. Then the gray, uncertain fog of semiconsciousness puts his memory out of focus.

In North Tonawanda, New York, Jane Hurtubise has taken her three children, Karen, Patricia and Andy, to a local amusement park for an afternoon of fun while their father is away at work. Soon the public-address system will call her to the telephone to take a call from Milwaukee.

They flipped open the quick-release buckle of his harness and lifted him, gently but quickly, from the car. It wasn't easy, with other cars flying by, everything covered with white extinguisher powder, the track still wet with fuel and parts of the car still hot—not easy to pull 165 pounds of man out of a tight seat, not wanting to grab him hard, not knowing where the pain was or what might be broken or ready to peel off.

The rear door of the ambulance swung wide; the stretcher,

white-sheeted, rolled out and back, and when the door closed on Hurtubise and the young man in a white uniform who pressed a stethoscope to his neck, the fog cleared and the clouds of pain rolled in.

"I remember the ambulance ride. I remember the siren. It was only about a half mile to the hospital. I was beginning to feel the burns then."

At the hospital they gave him something for the pain, and then, even before they started to cut the clothes off his body, they could see this was going to be bad. The fire had burned up between his legs, scorching flesh from just above the ankles to mid-thigh. Like a torch, it had reached up then to his arms and to those parts of his face that were not covered by the goggles, helmet or kerchief. The end of his nose and his nostrils were seared. But the parts that looked the worst were the hands. They were broiled like meat on a barbecue.

It was 2:30 in the afternoon now. In North Tonawanda, Jane Hurtubise, numb with fear, was putting her children into their grandmother's house and getting herself ready to fly to Milwaukee. At Fairgrounds Park, driver A. J. Foyt went on to finish 100 turns around the track and win $9830. When his car rolled to a stop after the checkered flag, mechanics found a small dent in the tail where Jim Hurtubise had passed in his flight. This would take only a few minutes to fix—but at the same time, at West Allis Memorial Hospital, doctors were beginning a much bigger repair job. They could see that their patient needed the maximum care that medicine could give a burn victim and fast. They also knew the place that could help him best—the U.S. Army's Brooke Medical Center at San Antonio, Texas. Hurtubise, a veteran of Coast Guard service, was eligible to go there. So, from Milwaukee, at about 7:00 P.M., the call for help went out.

"Brooke General," as army people call it, is an old military hospital, solid-looking, dignified, brick-walled, with red tile roofs. It sits in the hot Texas sun and looks down the broad, green parade ground of Fort Sam Houston. It has ministered to the hurt and maimed of several wars. Since the coming of atomic weapons, Brooke has looked ahead to a new kind of warfare in which most soldiers would not be shot through with steel and lead but burned by the fires of fusion. As a consequence, the doctors of Brooke have made themselves specialists in what heat can do to human flesh—and what medicine can do about it.

The only outward sign of urgency about Brooke is a large, flat square of bare concrete near the main entrance. This is where the helicopters bring work for the doctors in the third-floor burn ward: from fiery battles in Vietnam, from airplane crashes in Germany, from a kitchen in Japan where a soldier's wife has been torched by a cookstove—or from a racetrack in Milwaukee where a veteran has been hurt earning his living.

When Brooke got the call from Milwaukee, a team of air-evacuation specialists went into action. By 9:00 P.M. a C-131 Samaritan hospital plane was ready to leave San Antonio. In addition to its flying crew, a "burn team" consisting of a doctor, Captain William Mills, Jr., and a medical orderly, Sergeant Billy Mask, were the only other passengers. They flew through the night for six hours, and by 3:00 A.M. they were standing by Jim Hurtubise's bedside.

His wife had arrived before them. She was allowed to see her husband briefly. She remembers now that he never moved in the bed, that he showed no signs of recognition. She worried about his face—what it would ever be like again. Then the horror swept over her in waves and she fainted, and nurses carried her out to a chair in the hall.

When the Brooke team got to him, Hurtubise was awake. It was now 12 hours after the accident, and he had had all the emergency care this place could give him. His burns had been washed and dressed. Later a report would say that his mental state was normal. When he saw Dr. Mills, he asked for something to drink; the terrible thirst of the burn victim had begun. Through every square inch of seared flesh he was now losing fluids—plasma, salts, damaged red blood cells, body water. But they couldn't give him anything to drink. There was a five-hour flight back to San Antonio, and liquids cause air sickness.

By 5:00 A.M. the three men—patient, doctor and orderly —were in an ambulance on their way to the airport. By 6:00 the C-131 was airborne again. Army regulations didn't permit Jane Hurtubise to go with her husband on the military plane. Wearily, still stunned, she made her way to the airport to make connections with a commercial flight for San Antonio.

Aboard the C-131 Hurtubise lay in a litter, dozing and

waking. Mills and Mask watched him constantly. They removed some of the dressings from his wounds. They inserted a tube at his right ankle for the replacement of body fluids. Occasionally Hurtubise would try to rise. Once, in his fiery delirium, he asked if they would let him get up and walk around the plane. They told him no. He doesn't remember any of this flight now, but the men who were with him do.

At 11:00 A.M. the C-131 arrived at Kelly Field, and from there a helicopter lifted Hurtubise and the doctor and the sergeant to the pad in front of Brooke. By then the reporters and photographers were gathered. They saw the stretcher lifted out and saw it transferred inside. Hurtubise remembers the cameras and the crowd, nothing more.

And so, by noon on June 8, Jim Hurtubise had arrived at the place he would spend the next nine months. They wheeled him in through swinging doors at the end of the ward, down a short hall and into the 85-degree heat of an intensive-care room, where they put those who may not live.

It was now less than 24 hours since he had pulled on the "flameproof" coveralls and the helmet and the rubber-soled shoes and the face kerchief and slid himself down into the tight seat behind the wheel in Milwaukee. He should have been on his way back to North Tonawanda, New York, today. Instead he was in Texas, being weighed on a scale that would measure every ounce of him that was draining away. Then they put him in a hospital bed with his arms and hands elevated on pillows at each side, and they started pumping stuff back into his veins. In the first 24 hours he would get 5000 cc. of electrolyte solution, 850 cc. of plasma, 2000 cc. of 50-percent dextrose and water, 500 cc. of whole blood, plus some tetanus toxoid and penicillin. They inserted a chest tube to evacuate air from his chest and reexpand his right lung. They washed the burns again and covered them with a cold-cream-like substance called sulfamylon to fight infection.

At this point there was no question that Hurtubise was in mortal danger. There was one chance in three that he would die—in a few days or a few weeks. He says now that he never thought about this and didn't even know that the other shapes lying in beds in the sterile, windowless cell of the intensive-care room were people also fighting such bad odds. He remembers that everyone he saw—doctors, nurses, technicians, therapists—wore face masks and looked alike. He played a game with himself: identifying these people by means of voice alone.

When members of his family came in the first days, they also wore face masks: his wife, Jane; his brother, Pete, who had been his mechanic at Milwaukee and who had sat on the pit wall and wept while the smoke rose; his father, Ernest, who got the news of his son from a man who paddled three miles in a canoe to find him at an island cabin in Georgian Bay on Lake Huron.

Before they entered the burn ward, a doctor gave them a briefing on what to expect. "Even so," says a nurse at Brooke, "when they first see a patient here, visitors always just look and say nothing. Sometimes what they see is hard to believe. And sometimes they can't take it. We had so-and-so here, the movie star. He came to cheer up the patients, but he got sick himself."

Hurtubise's father is a big, genial man. He spent nine days at the hospital, "the roughest nine days of my life. But Jim, he must be part Indian or something. He never showed any feelings. He just talked about getting well. To me it looked like he had only a fifty-fifty chance."

By now the exact extent of his burns had been calculated: 42½ percent of his total body area. Of this, almost 25 percent was second degree and the remaining 18 percent, third degree. The second-degree burns looked yellow-red and were supremely painful in the first 24 to 36 hours. Some day this skin would recover. The third-degree burns were deeper: brown, gray and black. Because the flesh had been destroyed forever, including the nerve endings, third-degree burns are not unbearably painful. Most patients at Brooke are given drugs for only a few days. Hurtubise remembers the pain, but he remembers the fear for his hands more.

"I was with him when he first got a good look at them," says his father. "He just shook his head and grunted."

A doctor explains: Hurtubise could see his hands because they were not bandaged, but he probably didn't interpret what he saw. He could still move them slightly.

On the third day the work of removing dead tissue began in the operating room, and two days later the first attempt to cover the third-degree burn areas with skin grafts was made. With this, the process of putting Hurtubise back together again began.

In a small room across the hall from the intensive-care room there is an ordinary kitchen-style refrigerator, and stored on its shelves are plastic containers of skin. Some of this skin is taken from pigs, some from dogs and some from human cadavers, both Negro and white. None of it can ever be successfully grafted onto a living person, but it is used as an interim, or preparatory, step before some of the patient's own undamaged skin can be transplanted to burned areas. This is what they used as a lifesaving covering for Hurtubise.

When he came out of the operating room, Hurtubise had new hands—not good ones or useful ones, but hands that looked like they had been sewn into a clumsy pair of Frankenstein gloves, each gray-white finger stitched in place with black thread and with wider strips of hairless, dead-looking dog skin stuck on the backs up to a point above the wrists. Now at least the system of tendons that moved his fingers was covered. Whether the fingers would ever actually move again remained for time to tell. If the grafts could be kept on for five to six days, the hands would be ready for permanent covering with his own skin.

Within three days came the first bitter blow. The grafts had failed and had to come off. Hurtubise took the disappointment well. Within a week a new pair of skin gloves were sewn in place, and this time they took.

By now, ten days after arrival, Hurtubise was up and down out of bed three or four times a day, and he was well enough to be moved out of the intensive-care cell and into the open ward. The chest tube had been removed, and his lung had reinflated normally. This made possible a daily half-hour bath in a giant stainless-steel tub called a Hubbard tank. The tank is cruciform in shape so a man can be immersed with his arms outstretched while nurses hose off skin debris and the sulfamylon salve with a high-pressure spray. It is the worst pain of all, and the cries heard in this room are the most pitiful in the hospital. As a substitute for screams, Hurtubise decided to sing—anything, any song with words that could be bellowed out by tortured lungs. He asked the doctors and nurses to sing with him—to sing loud so the men outside the room would just hear, "You are my sunshine, my only sunshine."

Hurtubise remembers that getting out of the warm water was the worst part. "When my leg burns were still all bare and they lifted me out of that tank, I'd shiver and shake and feel colder than I'd ever felt in my whole life. My skin— everywhere where there *wasn't* any skin—it felt like it was being pushed with needles all over."

As he emerged from the critical life-or-death stage, his days began to take on a routine: the Hubbard tank in the morning, whirlpool treatments in arm tanks in the afternoon. Every week or so they took him back to the operating room and put him to sleep and planed strips of skin from his body for transplanting onto his arms and legs. The strips are called split-thickness grafts. If the skin on his abdomen was 20/1000ths of an inch thick, a whirring tool called a dermatome took 18/1000ths of it, leaving a wound that itself would take two weeks to heal.

Once, when they needed a lot of skin to cover the big burn areas on his legs, the dermatome stripped his entire back from shoulders to buttocks. Then Hurtubise spent the next 52 hours on his stomach.

Finally the day came when they had Jim Hurtubise all covered with his own skin. The next job was to make him move his arms and legs—and, if possible, his hands—in as normal a way as possible. Skin grafts shrink as they heal, and the new skin on Hurtubise's arms became so tough and tight that he could not bend them to bring a spoon to his mouth. To solve this problem and to make silverware easier for his excruciatingly sensitive hands to grasp, spoons and forks were taped onto pieces of wood four to six inches long. These "blocks" formed extensions so he could reach his mouth and feed himself.

By the end of June, Hurtubise was beginning to show the people at Brooke that he was a tough one. Doctors and nurses draw no comparisons, of course. To them every patient in the burn ward is making a heroic fight. But Hurtubise is remembered for a certain stoic strength. A nurse says, "He never said, 'I'll try,' when we asked him to do something. He just did it. And he never said, 'I can't.' The first time a doctor asked him to make a fist with his hand, he just closed his eyes and then tightened up those fingers as far as they would go without a word. Sometimes it takes a patient a full five minutes before he can make a move, and we stand there and say, 'More, more, more.' But Jim just *did* it."

"My arms and legs were bad, too," says Hurtubise. "I couldn't bend them much at all. I'd try, but every time when I really tried, the skin would crack and bleed and I'd have to stop. I couldn't squat, either. The scar tissue on my legs wouldn't let me. But I'd squat anyway, and something would give a little more every time."

By July Jim Hurtubise was beginning to think of his future. He knew there was no longer any doubt that he would live. The question was, *how* would he live? What would he—what *could* he—do? By now his hands, although covered and healed, did not look capable of much useful function. The grafts had formed webs of skin between the fingers like the feet of a duck. These had to be cut apart. Even then, burn damage to the extensor tendons on the back of the hands had drawn the fingers up into a fixed clawlike position such as kids make when they try to scare other kids. If the hands would ever be useful again, they had to be formed into some more functional position. The doctors told Hurtubise they could fix the fingers permanently into a number of positions, but once done, there would be no changing them—ever.

Hurtubise didn't waste time deciding.

"I told them I was a guy who made his living grabbing hold of something round," he says, turning an imaginary steering wheel with both hands. "I told them to fix the hands so I could do that."

Whether anybody realized it or not, Hurtubise had made up his mind that he was going to drive again—not just the family car, either, but something like that Novi, something with all those wild horses under his foot, something that would bring that Indianapolis crowd up out of the seats and squeeze the wind from their lungs in one more long cry of Hurtubise! Hercules! Go! Go! Go!

So once more they took Hercules back to the operating room, and this time they pushed stainless-steel wires into the tips of his fingers and down through the marrow cavity of the bones. They "cross-pinned" each joint in the opposite direction. Then, gently but firmly, they bent the fingers for the last time. In three weeks they would be fused finally and the wires could be removed, and each hand would be cupped enough to hold the steering wheel of an automobile.

After that a few people at Brooke suspected what it was that Hurtubise was going to try to do.

"Oh, he talked about the Five Hundred all the time, of course," says one nurse. "All the time, the Five Hundred." But no one believed him. He could build a doghouse in the physical-therapy shop, yes. And when they let him out for a little fun on weekends, he could grasp a glass of beer—if it was one of those tall, thin pilsner glasses. He was even learning to write again; the first time he signed his name was on a birthday card for his wife. The nurse who helped him says it took several minutes, but you could read it. But drive a race car again? Well, hardly—but you don't tell that to a man who has just had himself wired for the job.

Hurtubise received a lot of mail from his fans during his days in San Antonio. Ten thousand letters. Jane Hurtubise remembers that when the first 100 arrived on the first day, she went out and bought 100 printed thank-you cards and began to address them. But at the end of the first week, the letters were being delivered to Brooke in mail sacks—and Jane gave up. Many of the letters contained money. One little girl said she would send Jim her allowance, but it was too small; so she was sending her lucky two-dollar bill instead. Most of the mail also brought messages of encouragement: "Get well fast, Jim. . . . We miss you, Hercules. . . ." And in a neat, careful hand: "Dear Jim: I know I will see you drive at the great Indianapolis 500 again someday."

Sure you will, kid—but first I've got to drive a car again—any car, any old Detroit sedan, anything with four wheels and a gas pedal and a steering wheel. Some weekend when they let me out of here for a beer, I'll do it.

The automobile-racing establishment had been good to Jim Hurtubise during his trial. He had been a member of the lodge in good standing, and now that he was hurt, help had come from all directions: from race promoters, tire companies, other drivers, manufacturers. They provided his family with many favors, including a rent-free house—and a car.

It was a 1963 Oldsmobile 98 sedan, and one weekend in August when Jane drove up the Brooke driveway to take her husband out, Hurtubise decided he would try. With stiff arms and legs, he swung toward the driver's door. With his left hand, the steel wires still protruding from the fingertips, he reached for the door handle. But his thumb could not punch in the door button. He tried, while his wife watched, until the pain of trying was too much, and then he stopped and let her drive him home.

A week later he tried again. This time he had given the problem some thought, and he was ready. Carefully keeping his balance, he lifted one foot and pushed the door button with the toe of his shoe, pulling the door toward him with one hand at the same time. The door swung open.

"My hands were still so tender that I couldn't turn the key in the ignition. I tried, but the pressure of the metal on my fingers was too much. So I wrapped the key in Kleenex— made a big, soft ball of it—and then I could turn it and start the engine.

"It was the same with the steering wheel. I could hook my hands on to it, but it felt so hard I had to wrap more Kleenex around it to be able to hold on at all. And if I bumped one of those wires sticking out of my fingers, it hurt like hell. I didn't drive far that first day. Just far enough to know I could."

Later he pulled some of the wires from his hands himself. One nurse at Brooke still remembers Jim handing her one of the wires. She thought it was a Hurtubise practical joke; she still does. But the doctors know better. They know that the guy nicknamed Hercules had indeed pulled his own wires.

"We knew about the wires, but we didn't know he was driving a car," says Colonel Walter S. Switzer, the clinical director of the burn ward. "But when a man is recovering, he can do whatever he wants to try as far as we are concerned. It was up to Jim if he had this ambition to drive again. It wasn't up to us to tell him not to. Even if he got into an accident and burned again, we'd be ready to treat him again."

After two months the doctors decided that the little finger on Hurtubise's left hand was actually dead. The fire had charred bone-deep, and there were no signs that the finger could even be wired. On August 7 it was amputated. In another month Jim Hurtubise was ready to leave the burn ward. On September 17 he was discharged.

For the next five months Hurtubise was an in-and-out patient in another part of Brooke. Here they continued, with plastic surgery, to work on his hands. Some of the webs of grafted skin between his fingers were released, and other scar tissue was loosened.

In mid-October, four months after the accident, he went back to Milwaukee as a spectator at a stock-car race. He didn't tell anybody yet what was on his mind—and people who saw him would not have guessed. One friend reported, "He looked worse than when they shoved him into the ambulance." Another said, "His hands just sort of swung around at the ends of his arms."

In February he showed up at the Daytona, Florida, races. He looked better now. One hand was still bandaged from the last operation. Then, later in the month, he was ready to leave the hospital for the last time. When he said good-bye, he knew how lucky he was. In the nine months he had been at Brooke, he had seen three fellow patients die, including another race driver, Bobby Marshman.

He went back to North Tonawanda, to his house and his family and his friends—to his father's garage and to the shop behind his house, where he had built his race cars. Behind the shop, dumped with some other old discarded junk, were the smashed and scorched remains of the Milwaukee race car.

"When I looked at it, I could see what had happened, all right." The thoughts of a man making plans; the wrecked car was exhibit A of what to avoid the next time. That fuel tank shouldn't have been up front. I won't do that again. . . .

It was early spring now in upstate New York. It had been spring, a year ago, when he left. Now racing was about to begin for 1965. Hurtubise counted the time ahead: only three weeks until the Phoenix race. Six weeks until Trenton. Less than three months until Indy. . . .

He bought a bulldozer and a pickup truck and started to work to toughen himself. "I still couldn't handle small tools, but I could drive some, and there were days when I'd just get in the truck and drive all around all day looking for a place to go and something to do. I got a rowboat, too, and I'd row for hours to toughen the hands and get a good grip." By March he thought he was ready to crawl into a race car again.

"I knew if I was going to get into the Five Hundred in May, I'd have to show the U.S. Auto Club [official sponsor of the Indianapolis race] that I could handle a fast car. The Phoenix hundred-and-fifty-miler was my first chance."

First, however, the USAC wanted a statement from a doctor that Hurtubise was fit to drive. They wrote to Dr. Mills.

"The day he got the letter," says Jane, "Dr. Mills called me and asked what I thought. He said if it was up to him, he wouldn't sign it, but he said he knew how strongly Jim felt, and he wanted to know how I felt. I told him I couldn't live with Jim if they didn't let him drive."

Mills gave his OK. He wrote, "I don't know what it takes to drive a race car, but I think Jim Hurtubise can drive anything with four wheels."

Although he lost his brakes early in the race, Hurtubise drove a steady, conservative race at Phoenix and finished fourth. His hands were sore and swollen with pain for days afterward, but the race meant something important. Now he was no longer just a burn victim trying to toughen his hands enough to open a door or pull up the zipper on his pants— now he was a race driver again. The Phoenix crowd had cheered every mention of his name, and the sound reached his ears like an echo of the past—like that great sea surf of voices that had worshiped him at Indianapolis.

A month later, in April, he drove only ten laps of the Trenton race before his car failed, but on May 1 he finished third in a Plymouth stock car at the Yankee 300. This was three and a half hours of hard driving and gear shifting— enough to prove to USAC that he could probably manage the 500 miles at Indy.

The month of May has an almost mystic significance to the drivers, car owners, mechanics and thousands of other spear carriers who comprise the Indianapolis crowd. To be there in May is to be making The Scene—the biggest scene. To a driver, being part of it is like an Academy Award nomination to an actor, like a seat on the floor of a national convention to a politician. Never mind that he may not qualify fast enough for the race itself; never mind that the car may be a dog. If he's there, he belongs. In May 1965 Jim Hurtubise belonged again. USAC had OK'd him to drive, and he had a car he thought would go.

His story should really end here. He should have won the great race in 1965 and acknowledged the wild cheers of the crowd with a wave of his gnarled hands—and then, perhaps, retired. But sport is not Hollywood, and the hero doesn't always end up with the laurel wreath. Hurtubise, eager, his foot as strong as ever on the accelerator, crashed hard into the wall in practice. For a moment there was the explosion of magnesium wheels against concrete again. Then he walked away from the wreck, unhurt, even unshaken. An old friend who still had faith in Hercules offered him a chance to drive the old Novi again, and he took it, but in the race the hard-luck car and hard-luck driver completed only one lap together.

But Jim Hurtubise had come back—and the world of racing knew it.

THEY COULDN'T BREAK BILLY DEAN

By John Dos Passos

General William Dean was one of our first big heroes in Korea. Cut off from his retreating troops early in the war, he wandered through the countryside for 35 days, begging for handouts of rice from friendly villagers and eluding enemy patrols. Then, just when he thought he would make it back to the American lines, he was led into an ambush and captured. For the next three years the Korean Reds alternately froze him, tortured him and tried to brainwash him. But the general took all they had—and spit in their eyes!

When Major General William Frishe Dean turned up alive at Panmunjom after three years as a Communist prisoner, he did his best to keep people from making a fuss over him. No man could honestly claim to be ashamed of the Congressional Medal, that he admitted, but he explained that he came close to shame when he thought of the men who had done better jobs than he had without such recognition and died doing them. He kept reminding the reporters that he was a general captured because he took a wrong road.

"I lost ground I should have not lost. I lost trained officers and fine men. I'm not proud of that record," he said. "And I'm under no delusions that my weeks of command constituted any masterly campaign."

It puzzled General Dean that the American people insisted on making a hero of him all the same.

He described himself, with characteristic candor, as an "in-between curious kind of a general officer" who had never been to West Point, who hadn't seen action in World War One and who hadn't come up from the ranks.

As far back as he could remember, he had wanted to be a soldier. He was the son of a rural dentist, born and raised in Carlyle, the small county seat of Clinton County, in southern Illinois. Maybe it was on account of his mother's German blood that he was so carried away by the sight of soldiers drilling when his folks took him to the St. Louis World's Fair. He had a corn-belt childhood in the public schools, sold magazines to buy himself mail-order courses in physical culture.

As a kid he was a crank about physical fitness, weight lifting, dumbbells, push-ups, chinning himself. He was an inveterate hiker.

No student, he flunked the West Point exams after graduating from high school. The war was on in Europe, but he was too young to enlist without his mother's permission.

When the family moved to California, he enrolled in a prelaw course at the university. For spending money he worked as a stevedore on the San Francisco docks, as trolley conductor, washed dishes and even pounded the beat for a while as a student cop during the period when a Berkeley police chief was trying to interest college boys in the policeman's career. What he liked best about college was the Students' Army Training Corps.

He never did get a degree, but the army had a crying need for officers: Mighty few boys wanted an army career after the War to End War ended in the disillusioned peace. When Dean was 24, he managed to pass the required examination for a commission as second lieutenant in the regular army.

The man was a natural-born infantryman. Still a crank on physical fitness, he coached athletic teams, rode, played polo. A young lady whose horse ran away when he took her out for a canter while he was stationed at Fort Douglas, Utah, ended by becoming his wife. The Canal Zone was their honeymoon. They were happy in the army life. He served as a lieutenant for 12 years, was promoted to captain at 37, to major at 41.

He landed in France on Omaha Beach with the 44 men captured. As a general officer, he didn't believe in soldiers getting captured.

In 1947 he was military governor of South Korea, trying, through interpreters, to teach the Koreans how to run their sawed-off nation American style. Later he regretted he hadn't tried to learn more about the Koreans before he tried to do that job. At that he was known as "the walking general" because, instead of zooming about in a star-spangled staff car, he walked to his office in the morning. He was occasionally seen poking through the slums of Seoul or hiking far up into the hills to shoot pheasant. After elections, duly approved, he turned the problems of Korean self-government over to Syngman Rhee and left for a new tour of duty, in Japan.

One Saturday night in June 1950, General Dean and his wife attended a fancy-dress party at headquarters of the 24th Division at Kokura. They wore the Korean costumes they had brought away as souvenirs from Seoul. The costumes were admired, but the general, who was six feet two, remembered that the robes were much too short for him. He was uncomfortable in the hard stovepipe hat of a *yang ban*.

Next morning the North Korean army, trained by Russian instructors and armed with Russian heavy tanks, crossed the 38th parallel. World War Three, here it comes, they told each other at headquarters in Kokura. General Dean's troops were scattered all over the southern islands of Japan. Regiments were under strength. A bare 15 percent had seen combat. Men were soft from occupation living, PX beer and the delicate attentions of the Japanese girls they shacked up with. They didn't know where the hell Korea was and couldn't care less. While they were busy tending the refugees, military and civilian, who came out in planeloads, orders came to hold South Korea.

General Dean found himself, after a number of false starts, fumbling around in the fog on a C-45 looking for the Taejon airstrip. That highway and railroad junction in the middle of the peninsula had been picked for the hub of defense. Looked like a good place for headquarters on the map.

The fog down in Taejon was thicker than in the air above it. Everybody was on the run. No communications. No intelligence a man could rely on. Fifth-column work. At ROK headquarters slit-eyed officers were yelling "Communist" in each other's faces. For an American who didn't know the language, it was hard to tell friend from foe.

Before General Dean had time to set up his headquarters organization, the Communists had broken through down all the arterial roads. Their heavy tanks outclassed the American light tanks that had already been nearly obsolete when the fighting stopped in Europe five years before. Ammunition was short. Nobody knew the terrain. Some outfits were putting up a scrap, a few brave men selling their lives high, but nothing was holding anywhere.

It was decided to move headquarters southeast down the railroad to Yongdong. Communications were so bad General Dean decided he'd be better able to judge what was going on if he stayed awhile in Taejon.

One hot July morning the general woke to the sound of gunfire. The problem that day was how to pull out of Taejon while there was still time. He spoke afterward of the "somber poetry" of combat. "The phrase *fight and fall back* has a brave sound," he once remarked in recalling the scene, and he remembered vividly then the smells of the Korean summer morning, the rice-paddy muck and human excrement and the punky reek of smoldering thatch, laced now and then with the sharp sear of cordite. "Bone-wearying" was how he described the fighting that day and the days before it.

Communist tanks were already in town.

A general's business is to give orders. Although he still had one telephone line open to the rear, General Dean and his aide and a Korean interpreter were so thoroughly cut off there were no orders left to give. He decided that if he couldn't give orders, he could at least give an example.

Taejon was full of infiltrators wearing the white clothes of the country people, turncoats sniping out of windows. Dean got the clerks and cooks and messengers of the regimental command together into a party to stalk tanks. Fight and fall back. In covering the retreat, they accounted for a number of snipers, made unsuccessful attacks on a couple of Communist tanks they found waddling about without infantry support. The last many of the retreating troops saw of General Dean, he was blazing away with his .45 at a tank that rumbled unconcernedly by. "Dean losing his temper" was how he explained it.

At last he got hold of a man with a bazooka who still had ammo, for a wonder, and crawled with him up into a plastered room overlooking a narrow shopping street. They found themselves looking down the muzzle of the cannon of a Communist tank. The general indicated a spot at the base of the cannon. The bazooka fired point-blank. A horrible screaming came from inside. Two more rounds. The tank was out of commission, and the street was quiet.

The general was keeping a list that day of men he intended to decorate for bravery. (He'd been feeling a little guilty, so he said, about skimping on decorations in the European theater.) He even had a dozen or more medals in his jeep all ready to pin on.

Dean's brave men never did get their decorations. Things moved too fast. Already it was dusk and time to evacuate what was left of the regimental post. Some light tanks sent up to relieve them were having a hard time holding their own in a fire fight with the Communist armor. His troops were clumsy about taking cover, Dean thought sadly—hadn't played enough cops and robbers when they were kids.

The main road out was jammed with jackknifed trucks and burning half-tracks. The road was under fire as far as you could see. In a squall of bullets the general's jeep roared through an intersection into a wrong road. No way to turn back.

They came on a bunch of men talking surrender under a wrecked truck. Some were wounded. Dean filled his two jeeps with the wounded and as many others as could climb aboard. They drove careening into a Communist roadblock. Nothing to it but to take to the ditches.

Dean's aide was wounded. Afterward Dean told of how proud he was of this Lieutenant Clarke for the way he kept the 17 men together as they crawled through the muck of a bean field. One of their Koreans, a well-dressed one, fell into a "honey pit." Later Dean remembered waiting for dark on a riverbank and delivering a lecture about putting halizone tablets into your canteen before you drank the water.

Carrying one man too badly hurt to walk, they crossed the river at dark and climbed a steep mountain spur, hoping to cut back to the road beyond the Communist roadblock. The wounded man was delirious. He drank up all the water they had and kept calling for more. At a point on the mountain, while Lieutenant Clarke was giving his little outfit a rest, Dean thought he heard water in a gully. He slipped away from the group and started to climb down. He never knew how he came to trip and plunge headfirst down the hill. He blacked out.

He must have rolled a hundred yards at least, because

when he came to, he was lying alone on the hillside in the black night. His shoulder seemed to be broken. He was bleeding from a gash in the head. No sign of the other men.

About daybreak a Communist patrol almost stumbled over his carcass. Dean was conscious enough to hear the goatlike scamper of their feet up the stony slope. When they had gone, he dragged himself into a clump of bushes, where he lay all day groggy with pain.

By night he had himself in hand. His legs were all right. His head was clear. By favoring his shoulder, he found that in spite of the pain he could crawl. By the time he reached the top of the ridge, he was walking. All the boyish physical culture was standing by him now. He'd walk to the American lines.

He found himself, as in a nightmare, climbing handhold to handhold down a perpendicular cliff in a downpour of rain. He joined company with a young lieutenant, lost him again in a haze of weariness escaping from some Korean riflemen across a paddy field. Day followed day. He lost track of time.

For 35 days, hiding out by day in the rocky ridges and traveling at night, blarneying the country people out of a little rice now and then in the villages, he managed to escape capture. Gradually he made his way south toward the shrinking perimeter of the Pusan beachhead. He could already hear the distant rumble of American guns, when his luck failed.

A pair of Koreans named Han and Choi, whom he thought he'd secured as guides through to the American lines, led him into an ambush.

His shoulder was still agony. He was too weak from undernourishment and scurvy and dysentery to put up much resistance when 15 home guards jumped him on a moonlit road and trussed him up like a calf and dragged him off to the Communist police in the nearest town. Still he tried to fight so hard they would shoot him; he wanted his children to know he had put up a fight to the end.

On account of the language difficulty, he never really knew whether his guides had intended to betray him all along or whether they couldn't help themselves. They are said to have been paid five dollars for his hide.

Anyway, there he was, an American major general locked in an L-shaped cage, in which he could neither stand up nor lie down, in a small-town police station, a prisoner of war of the Communist Koreans.

Defeat. Captivity. This was like no other war in the nation's history. No more could any American general boast about how few men he'd had captured. All over Korea Americans were surrendering.

These were the kids who'd been soaked in wartime prosperity while their elder brothers manned the amphibious landings and the desperate beachheads and the floating bases and the great air strikes of World War Two, raised on the gibble-gabble of the radio between the family car and the corner drugstore and the five-and-ten.

Nobody had ever told them anything except to get more and do less.

Nobody had ever told them that to be an American meant anything more than to look at the comics and to drive around the roads in a new automobile, obtained on easy monthly payments, and to reach for packaged foods out of the Frigidaire; and, particularly, the army hadn't explained to them what they were doing in this lousy country that was all steep hills and muddy fields that smelled of human dung, helping one bunch of gooks fight another bunch of gooks that had a hell of a lot better tanks and seemed to know what they were doing. (United Nations—what the hell was the United Nations? Wasn't that a building in New York?)

General Dean had been proud of how few of his men surrendered in the European theater. He felt ashamed enough squatting in that little cage, a prisoner; he'd have felt worse if he'd known that four days after the fighting started, a captured officer of his own 24th Infantry Division was broadcasting enemy propaganda over the Communist radio.

After the stalemate and the exchange of prisoners across the 38th parallel, army authorities went to considerable trouble—statistics were collected, reports compiled, books written—to discover why, out of 7190 army men captured, 13 percent became out-and-out creatures of the Communists and roughly one-third collaborated in some way or other with the enemy. They were the "progressives."

There were so many informers that not one single man made good his escape from a prisoner-of-war camp (and you ask why the prestige of our nation has sunk so low in the world).

They'd all had some schooling, but no one had taught those poor kids that spirit, the little spark of God in every man, is what keeps man alive in adversity. The Communist indoctrinators were able to appeal to a sort of ignorant idealism that is the dead shell of the protestant ethics our fathers lived by. Idealism without ethics is no compass.

"One of the most difficult problems for a prisoner is maintaining his judgment," General Dean wrote later.

For judgment, read sense of right and wrong.

No one had told those kids that right and wrong was the inner compass that points true north. When army discipline broke down, they fell to pieces, each poor devil by himself. They didn't help each other the way the Turks did or the Marines. They didn't take care of themselves. If you can't help yourself, you can't help the next man. They wouldn't eat the gook chow—2730 let themselves die in captivity. Of the survivors, two-thirds confessed to the army investigators they had "played it cool."

Thirteen percent told the enemy nothing, wrote no confessions, joined no study classes, memorized no Marxist litanies. They were the "reactionaries." They had tough sledding, but they came out best in the end.

And with honor.

Fifty-year-old General Dean, with a broken shoulder and an infected foot, suffering from dysentery and every disease that fatigue and underfeeding brought in their train, would definitely have been described as a "reactionary." Dean had spirit enough and to spare.

For 30 years communism had been building a technique, using everything from the thumbscrew and the rack to the latest psychological methods of the scientific laboratories and dark and cold and solitude and starvation to kill God's spirit in man. They tried threats and misery on Dean, they tried rational argument, they tried luxury, but still Dean talked back.

Torture? No, they didn't torture him, not a bit.

He was taken first to a modern sort of penitentiary (he'd inspected it himself as military governor). The commandant suggested kindly that he must go on the air to explain to his family and friends that he was safe, that they were treating him with the deference his rank deserved and, incidentally, that the Communists were being welcomed as brothers by the Koreans of the south.

No, Dean wouldn't go on any radio.

The commandant asked him whether, if they turned him loose, he would continue to fight.

Dean said that if his country gave him a chance after the mess he'd made of his command, he'd try to do better next time and kill a lot more Communists.

Torture? No, they didn't torture him, not a bit.

He was taken north and put in the hands of a certain Colonel Kim, who was learned in the techniques.

It was Kim's business to try to make Dean sign a propaganda petition. At first Kim tried good food and pleasantries. He even sent a doctor to attend to Dean's dysentery. He offered him a pleasant country house and all the whiskey he wanted to drink and the assurance that he wouldn't be tortured.

Dean said he didn't drink whiskey.

Colonel Kim's geniality faded. He took to waking Dean up in the middle of the night.

About the time of the Inchon landing there was a break. Dean was hurried into Pyongyang, the Communist capital, and interrogated by the chief of security about the American plan of maneuver. He insisted on a written answer. Dean wrote it out with stiff fingers:

Fortunately, I do not have the information you seek. But even if I did, I wouldn't give it to you, because by so doing I would be a traitor to my country. So help me God, William F. Dean.

He was sent back to Colonel Kim. The real interrogation began. It was winter by that time. Day after day and night after night they made Dean sit on a hard chair in the light summer suit they'd given him when they took away his uniform. His infected left foot had swelled so he couldn't bear a shoe. He had lost so much weight that sitting on the hard, straight chair was agony. He had to sit on his hands. Sitting on his hands made them swell up almost as much as his foot. The interrogations seemed to be heading toward his trial as a war criminal. Colonel Kim and another Kim and a Ph.D. worked in shifts.

The room was cold, the temperature about 33 degrees. Colonel Kim complained because Dean's teeth chattered. Colonel Kim, who wore a heavy overcoat, said it wasn't cold at all. To prove it, he made Dean strip down to his shorts. Day after day they went on keeping him awake, starving him, freezing him, using old-fashioned third-degree methods. The only breaks were when Dean had to go running to the latrine.

No, they didn't torture him, not a bit. Colonel Kim interspersed his interrogation with references to the torture to come. At last Dean could stand it no more. Afraid he might tell something under torture in his worn-out state, he managed to steal the revolver off a sleeping guard. When the Koreans jumped on him from all sides, he couldn't get the revolver to fire. Dean was sorry for the poor guard, a simple fellow who had been nice to him. He was led away and probably shot for falling asleep on duty.

Somehow the desperation of Dean's act impressed his captors. Colonel Kim was seen no more. There was no more talk of torture. Doctors visited him. He was kept warm. His food became fairly decent. By that time MacArthur's army was sweeping north. Ill as he was, Dean was hurried in trucks and jeeps up to the Yalu and across into Manchuria for safekeeping as the Korean Communist army broke in pieces.

On that trip Dean could relax a little. Everybody was too busy to interrogate him. He wasn't treated too badly now that the Americans seemed to be winning.

Dean began to make observations. Already he had observed with some interest that sitting motionless, stripped to the skin, in extreme cold, his body, even in its weakened condition, somehow managed to retain a little warmth.

His guards were enemies, but they were sometimes friends. He became interested in what he was to describe as "the many-sided, kind and cruel, inventive, clever, stupid, resilient, unpredictable Korean character." Maybe getting to know these people was worth what he was going through. It would never have happened to an uncaptured general.

After the Chinese victories rolled back MacArthur's advance, he was spirited from place to place. He had an idea the Korean Communists were trying to keep him out of the hands of the Chinese. He wasn't mistreated, but he was never allowed out of doors. Months passed cooped in tiny rooms. He had no reading matter. They wouldn't let him play the local form of chess his guards played. To keep from losing his mind, he squared numbers and did square roots and kept track of the flies he killed. His biggest day he killed 522.

He began to be cozy with the Communist Koreans. A number of his guards were training to be officers. He became interested in their careers and helped them with their homework. He learned all he could about their Communist theory and practice.

"The most important discovery to me," he reported later, "was that the ordinary Communists who guarded me and lived with me really believed that they were following a route that would lead to a better life for themselves and their children. . . . It was easy for us to say they were mistaken but not so easy to explain to these men of limited experience just why their ideology must fail. . . . We can't convince them with fine words. We've got to show them something better. We must have an answer simple enough for the dullest to understand."

At last, after three years, Dean was exchanged with the rest at Panmunjom. The first Americans he saw were gaunt prisoners in a column of trucks. "Hi, General Dean!" they yelled. "Hi, General! We didn't know we were waiting for you." The Yankee voices sounded wonderful to him.

Soon afterward, with unaffected dignity, with perfect candor, he was telling his story to the world's press assembled at Freedom Village. Somehow, in everything Dean said, in everything he did while he was a prisoner, there had appeared that answer simple enough for the dullest to understand.

The American people were right to make a hero of him.

RUN TO GLORY

By Roger Bannister

Now bid me run,
And I will strive with things impossible.
JULIUS CAESAR

The loneliness of the long-distance runner is a very real thing.
It was particularly evident to Roger Bannister in 1954 as he
prepped for an attempt at becoming the first runner to break
the four-minute-mile barrier. First, the decision to even un-
dertake such a feat was a formidable challenge. What if he
failed? How could he face himself and his friends? Then
there were the long, often boring and sometimes painful
hours of training to be endured. And finally, when the day
came, the decision of whether or not to cancel because of
nearly gale-force winds. Then, in the race itself, how to keep
the mind from wandering from the task at hand, shutting out
the pain as tortured muscles drove his body faster and faster
down that last 300 yards! Willpower alone was hurrying him
toward the tape. . . .

I expected that the summer of 1954 would be my last competitive season. It was certain to be a big year in athletics.
There would be the Empire Games in Vancouver, the European Games in Berne, and hopes were running high of a
four-minute mile.

The great change that now came over my running was that
I no longer trained and raced alone. Perhaps I had mellowed
a little and was becoming more sociable. Every day between
12:30 and 1:30 I trained on a track in Paddington and had
a quick lunch before returning to the hospital. We called
ourselves the Paddington lunchtime club. We came from all
parts of London, and our common bond was a love of
running.

I felt extremely happy in the friendships I made there, as we shared the hard work of repetitive quarter miles and sprints. These training sessions came to mean almost as much to me as had those at the Oxford track. I could now identify myself more intimately with the failure and success of other runners.

In my hardest training Chris Brasher was with me, and he made the task very much lighter. On Friday evenings he took me along to Chelsea Barracks, where his coach, Franz Stampfl, held a training session. At weekends Chris Chataway would join us, and in this friendly atmosphere the very severe training we did became most enjoyable.

In December 1953 we started a new, intensive course of training and ran several times a week a series of ten consecutive quarter miles, each in 66 seconds. Through January and February we gradually speeded them up, keeping to an interval of two minutes between each. By April we could manage them in 61 seconds, but however hard we tried, it did not seem possible to reach our target of 60 seconds. We were stuck, or, as Chris Brasher expressed it, "bogged down." The training had ceased to do us any good, and we needed a change.

Chris Brasher and I drove up to Scotland overnight for a few days' climbing. We turned into the Pass of Glencoe as the sun crept above the horizon at dawn. A misty curtain drew back from the mountains, and the "sun's sleepless eye" cast a fresh, cold light on the world. The air was calm and fragrant, and the colors of sunrise were mirrored in peaty pools on the moor. Soon the sun was up, and we were off climbing. The weekend was a complete mental and physical change. It probably did us more harm than good physically. We climbed hard for the four days we were there, using the wrong muscles in slow and jerking movements.

There was an element of danger, too. I remember Chris falling a short way when leading a climb up a rock face depressingly named Jericho's Wall. Luckily, he did not hurt himself. We were both worried lest a sprained ankle might set our training back by several weeks.

After three days our minds turned to running again. We suddenly became alarmed at the thought of taking any more risks and decided to return. We had slept little; our meals had been irregular. But when we tried to run those quarter miles again, the time came down to 59 seconds!

It was now less than three weeks to the Oxford University versus AAA race, the first opportunity of the year for us to attack the four-minute mile. Chris Chataway had decided to join Chris Brasher and myself in the AAA team. He doubted his ability to run a three-quarter mile in three minutes, but he generously offered to attempt it.

I had now abandoned the severe training of the previous months and was concentrating entirely on gaining speed and freshness. I had to learn to release in four short minutes the energy I usually spent in half an hour's training. Each training session took on a special significance as the day of the Oxford race drew near. It felt a privilege and joy each time I ran a trial on the track.

There was no longer any need for my mind to force my limbs to run faster—my body became a unity in motion much greater than the sum of its component parts. I never thought of length of stride or style or even my judgment of pace. All this had become automatically ingrained. In this way a singleness of drive could be achieved, leaving my mind free from the task of directing operations so that it could fix itself on the great objective ahead. There was more enjoyment in my running than ever before, a new health and vigor. It was as if all my muscles were a part of a perfectly tuned machine. I felt fresh now at the end of each training session.

On April 24 I ran a three-quarter-mile trial in three minutes at Motspur Park with Chataway. I led for the first two laps, and we both returned exactly the same time. Four days later I ran a last solo three-quarter-mile trial at Paddington. Norris McWhirter, who had been my patient timekeeper through most of 1953, came over to hold the watch.

The energy of the twins, Norris and Ross McWhirter, was boundless. For them nothing was too much trouble, and they accepted any challenge joyfully. After running together in Oxford as sprinters, they carried their partnership into journalism, keeping me posted of the performances of my overseas rivals. They often drove me to athletics meetings, so that I arrived with no fuss, never a minute too soon or too late. Sometimes I was not sure whether it was Norris or Ross who held the watch or drove the car, but I knew that either could be relied upon.

For the trial at Paddington there was, as usual, a high wind blowing. I would have given almost anything to be able to shirk the test that would tell me with ruthless accuracy what my chances were of achieving a four-minute mile at Oxford. I felt that 2 minutes, 59.9 seconds for the three-quarter mile in a solo training run meant 3 minutes, 59.9 seconds in a mile race. A time of 3 minutes, 0.1 second would mean 4 minutes, 0.1 second for the mile—just the difference between success and failure. The watch recorded a time of 2 minutes, 59.9 seconds! I felt a little sick afterward and had the taste of nervousness in my mouth. My speedy recovery within five minutes suggested that I had been holding something back. Two days later at Paddington I ran a 1-minute-54-second half mile quite easily, after a late night, and then took five days complete rest before the race.

I had been training daily since the previous November, and now that the crisis was approaching, I barely knew what to do with myself. I spent most of the time imagining I was developing a cold and wondering if the winds would ever drop. The day before the race I slipped on a highly polished hospital floor and spent the rest of the day limping. Each night in the week before the race there came a moment when I saw myself at the starting line. My whole body would grow nervous and tremble. I ran the race over in my mind. Then I would calm myself and sometimes get off to sleep.

Next day was Thursday, May 6, 1954. I went into the hospital as usual, and at 11 o'clock I was sharpening my spikes on a grindstone in the laboratory. Someone passing said, "You don't really think that's going to make any difference, do you?"

I knew the weather conditions made the chances of success practically nil. Yet all day I was taking the usual precautions for the race, feeling at the same time that they would prove useless.

I decided to travel up to Oxford alone, because I wanted to think quietly. I took an early train deliberately, opened a carriage door, and, quite by chance, there was Franz Stampfl inside. I was delighted to see him, as a friend with the sort of attractive, cheerful personality I badly needed at that moment. Through Chris Basher, Franz had been in touch with my training program, but my own connection with him was slight.

I would have liked his advice and help at this moment but

could not bring myself to ask him. It was as if now, at the end of my running career, I was being forced to admit that coaches were necessary after all and that I had been wrong to think that the athlete could be sufficient unto himself.

In my mind there lurked the memory of an earlier occasion when I had visited a coach. He had expounded his views on my running and suggested a whole series of changes. The following week I read a newspaper article he wrote about my plans, claiming to be my advisor for the 1952 Olympics. This experience made me inclined to move slowly.

But Franz is not like this. He has no wish to turn the athlete into a machine working at his dictation. We shared a common view of athletics as a means of "re-creation" of each individual as a result of the liberation and expression of the latent power within him. Franz is an artist who can see beauty in human struggle and achievement.

We talked, almost impersonally, about the problem I faced. In my mind I had settled this as the day when, with every ounce of strength I possessed, I would attempt to run the four-minute mile. A strong wind was blowing that would slow me up by a second a lap. In order to succeed I must run not merely a four-minute mile, but the equivalent of a 3-minute-56-second mile in calm weather.

I had reached my peak physically and psychologically. There would never be another day like it. I had to drive myself to the limit of my power without the stimulus of competitive opposition. This was my first race for eight months, and all this time I had been storing nervous energy. If I tried and failed, I should be dejected, and my chances would be less on any later attempt. Yet it seemed that the high wind was going to make it impossible.

I had almost decided when I entered the carriage at Paddington that unless the wind dropped soon, I would postpone the attempt. I would just run an easy mile in Oxford and make the attempt on the next possible occasion—ten days later at the White City in London.

Franz understood my apprehension. He thought I was capable of running a mile in 3 minutes, 56 seconds, or 3.57; so he could argue convincingly that it was worthwhile making the attempt. "With the proper motivation, that is, a good reason for wanting to do it," he said, "your mind can overcome any sort of adversity. In any case, the wind might drop.

I remember J. J. Barry in Ireland. He ran a four-minute-eight-second mile without any training or even proper food—simply because he had the will to run. Later, in America, where he was given every facility and encouragement, he never ran a fast race. In any case, what if this were your only chance?"

He had won his point. Racing has always been more of a mental than a physical problem to me. He went on talking about athletes and performances, but I heard no more. The dilemma was not banished from my mind, and the idea left uppermost was that this might be my only chance. "How would you ever forgive yourself if you rejected it?" I thought as the train arrived in Oxford. As it happened, ten days later it was just as windy!

I was met at the station by Charles Wenden, a great friend from my early days in Oxford, who drove me straight down to Iffley Road. The wind was almost gale force. Together we walked round the deserted track. The St. George's flag on a nearby church stood out from the flagpole. The attempt seemed hopeless; yet for some unknown reason I tried out both pairs of spikes. I had a new pair that were specially made for me on the instructions of a climber and fell walker, Eustace Thomas, of Manchester. Some weeks before, he had come up to London, and together we worked out modifications that would reduce the weight of each running shoe from six to four ounces. This saving in weight might well mean the difference between success and failure.

Still undecided, I drove back to Charles Wenden's home for lunch. On this day, as on many others, I was glad of the peace that I found there. Although both he and his wife, Eileen, knew the importance of the decision that had to be made, and cared about it as much as I did myself, it was treated by common consent as a question to be settled later.

The immediate problem was to prepare a suitable lunch and to see that the children, Felicity and Sally, ate theirs. Absorbed in watching the endless small routine of running a home and family, I could forget some of my apprehensions. Charles Wenden had been one of the ex-service students in Oxford after the war, and some of my earliest running had been in his company. Later his house had become a second home for me during my research studies in Oxford, and the calm efficiency of Eileen had often helped to still my own restless worries. Never was this factor so important as on this day.

In the afternoon I called on Chris Chataway. At the moment the sun was shining, and he lay stretched on the window seat. He smiled and said, just as I knew he would, "The day could be a lot worse, couldn't it? Just now it's fine. The forecast says the wind may drop toward evening. Let's not decide until five o'clock."

I spent the afternoon watching from the window the swaying of the leaves. "The wind's hopeless," said Joe Binks on the way down to the track. At 5:15 there was a shower of rain. The wind blew strongly but now came in gusts, as if uncertain. As Brasher, Chataway and I warmed up, we knew the eyes of the spectators were on us. They were hoping that the wind would drop just a little—if not enough to run a four-minute mile, enough to make the attempt.

Failure is as exciting to watch as success, provided the effort is absolutely genuine and complete. But the spectators fail to understand—and how can they know—the mental agony through which an athlete must pass before he can give his maximum effort. And how rarely, if he is built as I am, he can give it.

No one tried to persuade me. The decision was mine alone, and the moment was getting closer. As we lined up for the start, I glanced at the flag again. It fluttered more gently now, and the scene from Shaw's *Saint Joan* flashed through my mind: how she, at her desperate moment, waited for the wind to change. Yes, the wind was dropping slightly. This was the moment when I made my decision. The attempt was on.

There was complete silence on the ground . . . a false start. . . . I felt angry that precious moments during the lull in the wind might be slipping by. The gun fired a second time. . . . Brasher went into the lead, and I slipped in effortlessly behind him, feeling tremendously full of running. My legs seemed to meet no resistance at all, as if propelled by some unknown force.

We seemed to be going so slowly! Impatiently I shouted, "Faster!" But Brasher kept his head and did not change the pace. I went on worrying until I heard the first lap time— 57.5 seconds. In the excitement my knowledge of pace had deserted me. Brasher could have run the first quarter in 55 seconds without my realizing it, because I felt so full of running, but I should have had to pay for it later. Instead he had made success possible.

At one and a half laps I was still worrying about the pace. A voice shouting, "Relax," penetrated to me above the noise of the crowd. I learned afterward it was Stampfl's. Unconsciously I obeyed. If the speed was wrong, it was too late to do anything about it; so why worry? I was relaxing so much that my mind seemed almost detached from my body. There was no strain.

I barely noticed the half mile, passed in 1 minute, 58 seconds, nor when, round the next bend, Chataway went into the lead. At three-quarters of a mile the effort was still barely perceptible; the time was 3 minutes, 0.7 second, and by now the crowd was roaring. Somehow I had to run that last lap in 59 seconds. Chataway led round the next bend, and then I pounced past him at the beginning of the back straight, 300 yards from the finish.

I had a moment of mixed joy and anguish, when my mind took over. It raced well ahead of my body and drew my body compellingly forward. I felt that the moment of a lifetime had come. There was no pain, only a great unity of movement and aim. The world seemed to stand still or did not exist. The only reality was the next 200 yards of track under my feet. The tape meant finality—extinction, perhaps.

I felt at that moment that it was my chance to do one thing supremely well. I drove on, impelled by a combination of fear and pride. The air I breathed filled me with the spirit of the track where I had run my first race. The noise in my ears was that of the faithful Oxford crowd. Their hope and encouragement gave me greater strength. I had now turned the last bend, and there were only 50 yards more.

My body had long since exhausted all its energy, but it went on running just the same. The physical overdraft came only from greater willpower. This was the crucial moment when my legs were strong enough to carry me over the last few yards as they could never have done in previous years. With five yards to go, the tape seemed almost to recede. Would I ever reach it?

Those last few seconds seemed never-ending. The faint line of the finishing tape stood ahead as a haven of peace after the struggle. The arms of the world were waiting to receive me if only I reached the tape without slackening my speed. If I faltered, there would be no arms to hold me, and the world would be a cold, forbidding place, because I had been so close. I leaped at the tape like a man taking his last spring to save himself from the chasm that threatens to engulf him.

My effort was over, and I collapsed almost unconscious, with an arm on either side of me. It was only then that real pain overtook me. I felt like an exploded flashlight with no will to live; I just went on existing in the most passive physical state without being quite unconscious. Blood surged from my muscles and seemed to fell me. It was as if all my limbs were caught in an ever-tightening vise. I knew that I had done it before I even heard the time. I was too close to have failed, unless my legs had played strange tricks at the finish by slowing me down and not telling my tiring brain that they had done so.

The stopwatches held the answer. The announcement came —"Result of one mile . . . time, three minutes . . ."—the rest lost in the roar of excitement. I grabbed Brasher and Chataway, and together we scampered round the track in a burst of spontaneous joy. We had done it—the three of us!

We shared a place where no man had yet ventured—secure for all time, however fast men might run miles in future. We had done it where we wanted, when we wanted, how we wanted, in our first attempt of the year. In the wonderful joy my pain was forgotten, and I wanted to prolong those precious moments of realization.

I felt suddenly and gloriously free of the burden of athletic ambition that I had been carrying for years. No words could be invented for such supreme happiness, eclipsing all other feelings. I thought at that moment I could never again reach such a climax of single-mindedness. I felt bewildered and overpowered. I knew it would be some time before I caught up with myself.

DEATH ON THE SLOPES

By Curtis W. Casewit

In the late 1950s and early '60s Buddy Werner was America's hottest skiing talent ever. Year after year his fearless and hell-bent style brought him to victory after victory in races around the world. But hard luck and untimely injuries dogged him, and the Olympic medal—the only one he really coveted —somehow seemed to always slip from his grasp. Finally, at age 28, discouraged and tired, he decided to quit and find a way to earn his livelihood. Things were beginning to straighten out. Then, one day, a man called him to make a ski movie in Switzerland. It would be a lark. He went and soon found himself skiing for his very life as a 600,000-ton avalanche of churning snow came spewing down the mountainside chasing after Werner and 15 other skiers with a vengeance. . . .

Buddy Werner skied as if his life depended on how fast he sped down the slope. It did! Behind him loomed an avalanche—a churning 600,000-ton, 400-yard-wide monster that snarled at first, then cracked the mountain open with a prodigious clap of thunder and finally roared after Werner and 15 other skiers with a vengeance.

For several days during April, 1964 they had been making a movie on the slide-prone slopes near St. Moritz, Switzerland. Out of the corner of his eyes Werner could see the film's producer, Willy Bogner, Jr., veering sharply to the right and out of the avalanche's path. Some women, part of the film crew, were shrieking with fear over the roar of the unleashed snow masses, and behind Werner a few of the slower racers already had been buried.

Werner went into a racing crouch, deep down for maximum speed. He intended to outski the encroaching "White Death." His life depended on it.

Buddy had always taken chances. All his life he'd needed

danger. Speed had become his mistress—even if it had shredded his ankles after a crack-up and torn out his tendons and yanked off his kneecaps. Once he had skied so fast that the inevitable crash necessitated his spending four hours on the operating table while doctors drilled steel screws into his shinbones.

Now Werner made a split-second decision. Under him the hill dipped for a steep mile. The lower part lay in the shade, which meant the snow would be extra fast down there. He could spy snow slabs at the bottom, thick, corrugated crusts iced by the winds. He steered toward the glacierlike mass with the force of a rocket. But the avalanche was accelerating, too. It licked at his heels. On his neck the air pressure was so strong that he could hardly breathe. Shivers ran down his spine. He crouched still lower, then planted his ski poles and came soaring through the air, leaving the avalanche and the crusty ground behind him.

He'd been faster than the killer slide.

Suddenly the whole valley turned mad. Another avalanche broke away from the opposite side of the mountain. Werner had already cleared most of the rough field and was heading toward the next precipice when the air blast made him crash. He struggled up again, *but it was too late*. He'd taken one risk too many. The enormous white tiger was clawing at him, mauling him.

He wasn't alone. A girl in tight stretch pants, Barbi Henneberger, had popped out of nowhere, then disappeared, swallowed up by the boiling white dusk. A crack racer, she, too, had managed to outski the first monster, but now mound upon mound of wet snow heaped over their young bodies.

They were still breathing—or so the doctors thought later —when others began their search with trembling fingers and the shovels of their skis. This was Switzerland, and ten minutes after the disaster patrolman Reto Raehs was ready for action. Before long he directed 150 rescuers and five specially trained avalanche dogs. Two helicopters and five doctors stood by.

But it's no picnic to find anyone blanketed by an avalanche. You think you know the buried skiers' last location. But you can't really be sure, because you were moving hysterically fast yourself. Besides, the snow is blinding white; you're as lost as if you are stranded in a desert. You can't tell if the victim has been swept down hundreds of yards farther—entangled in smashed skis, mouth filled with snow—or buried in his tracks.

The rescue chief distributed seven-yard-long wooden avalanche probe poles. Then he had the searchers form two long lines, and the poles were pushed slowly into the deep snow. Once in a while patrolman Raehs would glance balefully toward the movie team. He wondered at their naïveté in exposing themselves to a slope whose slides had killed other skiers before. In fact, the whole area had been closed for days, and the group had gone blithely past avalanche warning signals. . . .

"Can Werner still be alive?" someone asked a St. Moritz physician while the rescue team's efforts continued.

The doctor looked at his watch. *"Koennte sein,"* he said. "Maybe. You can last two hours under the snow. Sometimes longer. It depends on the depth and the amount of air."

The rescuers continued to dig furiously throughout the afternoon, the famous Swiss sun blazing down on them. Under the ink-blue sky the sweat ran down their tanned faces. Film maker Willy Bogner, Jr., wiped his wet brow. Ironically, the avalanche had buried his girl. He'd known Barbi for years. Bogner and Barbi had both been German Olympic-team members.

They found 23-year-old Barbi Henneberger after two hours. She was dead.

Then they found Werner. He, too, had suffocated. At 28 it was a terrible but logical end to a hard-luck career. . . .

Not unlike most children raised in the Rockies, Wallace "Buddy" Werner started to ski early. His parents put him on skis in Steamboat Springs, Colorado, at the age of two. At six he raced behind wild horses, dived on skis through hollow barrels, jumped from small hills. Shortly after, Olympic ace Gordy Wren taught Werner to jump from the big ones.

Even as a boy he was a daredevil. Seventy miles per hour at jump takeoff wouldn't faze him. Buddy had guts when it came to downhill running, too. He'd spurt through the steepest of forests on the barest of snow, hurling himself around tree stumps, diving over tree roots. One spring day he mistakenly hit a sandpile. He fell forward so hard that he broke both skis, sprained an ankle and tore his face. The ankle didn't matter, he said. It was the end of ski season, anyway.

Soon he beat the town's best skiers. By then Wren had taught him slalom (swerving through a series of flags on a steep course). At 15 Werner became national U.S. champion. He was off to the races.

Unfortunately, there was never too much money in the family. Buddy's mother clerked in a store, and his father worked for a trucking company to support Buddy and his brother and sister. Consequently, Buddy had to earn his own travel expenses. He made great sacrifices. For years he performed on the same pair of skis, often sharing them with his brother. He wore the same beat-up ski pants and a threadbare sweater. He didn't even go to the movies. Other youths already had cars; he needed the cash for train fare. Nor did he date girls. His only date was with the ski slopes.

In 1954, standing by as a reserve member of the American Olympic team, he got his chance when another racer broke his leg in Austria. Werner made his first trip to Europe and, at the age of 18, beat some of the world's best racers.

One morning his coach pulled him aside. "We're going to send you to the world championships at Are, Sweden."

"I'll train," Werner said.

"You always have. It's just a matter of technique now," the coach said. "You've got courage. That's what downhill takes. You also have strong legs. But I want you to ski lower. You're still too high, and that takes too much wind."

During the next week Werner flew down the icy snow walls in a deep crouch, gaining speed. Gravity would pluck hard at him, and the sudden bumps would propel him into the air. But he had fast reflexes, and he learned to right himself, to recover, skis landing with a smack, and to roar on. By the end of a week he was so fast that he stood a good chance at the world championships. His bags already were packed for Sweden when he took one more run. A bump tossed him. As he came down, he tried to ride it out, but he somersaulted, cartwheeled and hit the valley floor with a fierce impact. He tried to stand up but couldn't. He'd injured his kneecap and ruined his Olympic hopes. Bad luck—first installment.

By next winter he was ready again. He skied slopes when nobody else dared. He jumped at suicidal points—all to gain a few split seconds. Downhill racing to Werner was a sequence of calculated risks, a series of recoveries. Cal Queal, of the Denver *Post,* put it this way: "Buddy was a spring, a bubble, a hip-swiveling, steel-legged ballet dancer. He was a bomb, but beautiful."

Werner, to hone his craving for danger, took endless chances. Shy among people, reticent with words, he had a compulsion to express himself in daring action on the slopes. One day he was working out at Alta, Utah, with Willy Schaeffler, the rugged German coach who has trained some of the world's best racers. "I want you to rest this afternoon," Schaeffler told him. "Get some sleep."

It was spring, when the sun is strongest in the Rockies, and Werner's lips were badly blistered. He always tanned badly. The skin hung from his nose, which had layers of six different colors and a profusion of freckles.

"You look tired," Schaeffler insisted. "You've had enough for the day."

Werner didn't answer. His head turned toward the craggy teeth of the Rockies, toward the point that rose steepest behind the lodge. Schaeffler followed the glance. A small slide detached itself from the cornice. Like a large slab of white marble, it plumped heavily down, rolled over, dissolved into particles.

"*Gefaehrlich!* Dangerous!" Schaeffler said. "Worst slope here. Guess the rangers will blast it."

Werner grinned.

"Take off your skis and go to your bunk! No monkey business!"

Werner did as he was told, but when Schaeffler went to Buddy's bunk that afternoon, it was empty. The coach's leonine face looked out the window, where the mountain rose like an elongated Tower of Pisa. There was Werner, flying off the cornice. Schaeffler still recalls the thick, white snow board breaking off behind the racer, rumbling after him. Werner swung right and left, keeping ahead of it—a solo performance for his own benefit. Midway, the slide pulverized.

Just then a group of forest rangers that included the famous Monty Atwater drew up in a car, and Werner got chewed out. Undaunted, he tempted fate again and again.

By 1956 Europeans were becoming aware of him. He was the hottest skiing talent America ever produced. That winter he won the Grand Prix of Chamonix, defeating the best French racers in their own backyards. He won the Lauberhorn in Switzerland, and while the old Matterhorn looked on in disbelief, he won the Gornergrat Derby at Zermatt. The other skiers on the U.S. team paled beside Werner. "Buddy Werner and the Seven Dwarfs!" one paper commented.

This was an Olympics year, too. A reporter asked Werner about his chances. Buddy thought for a full minute. "There's only one place in a race," he said. "First and last." But mostly he wouldn't say anything. Outside he was calm—almost dull—but inside he burned with ambition. He'd dropped out after one semester at Denver University for the sake of the Olympics. He wanted an Olympic medal above all else.

Yet, even before the start, bad luck hounded him again. Tearing down at a terrific clip in training, he fell on the steep Olympic slope. Aghast, spectators watched the crumpled, snow-covered figure get up again and walk away. Only a broken ski.

Came the games. Eyes drawn together in narrow slits, lips a hard line, he had the race all won with his go-for-broke style, when he fell at the 54th gate. Ditto for the giant slalom, where he put all his hopes, skill, cunning and experience into the downhill, which was held the last day.

More than 50,000 people lined the treacherous course to watch the *Amerikaner*. Would he win his first gold medal? There were 86 competitors from 25 nations. That year Toni Sailer—already seven times world champion—was the overwhelming favorite. If Buddy could beat him. . . .

Sailer went first. He made the 11,480-foot course in a record 2:28.5 seconds.

"Bud Werner, U.S.A.!"

Werner looked relaxed. Like all top racers, he had developed nerves of steel. He tightened his crash helmet, slid into the starting slot. He had new skis. He had the perfect wax. Othmar Schneider, one of his coaches, slapped him on the back. "Good luck!"

"Ten seconds to go!"

Werner adjusted his goggles. Whipping rhythmically with the countdown, he was ready to burst out of the ring.

"Five . . . four . . . three . . . two . . . one. GO!"

He had an explosive start. *"Wunderbar!"* they shouted after him. His poles whipped furiously. Now he shot downward as if he were a cannonball. He was a blur as people timed him on their stopwatches. After 50 seconds he was gaining on Sailer's time. He banked in the curves at 65 mph, but you could hardly hear his skis. A whisper only. No friction. He knew each control marker like an old friend and chose the fastest, shortest line through each.

He blasted through a forest torpedo style. A final bump before the final schuss. Second-shaving strategy: He'd clear the hurdle by jumping before he came to it, roar through the air in a ball, then alight 100 yards farther down, just before the finish gate. But he was going so fast that something went haywire. House-high above the ground, he lost his balance. An edge of his ski dug into the snow at an angle. He rolled over a dozen times, his right ski flew off. He did not give up, went down the last stretch on one ski! The crowd gasped and roared at his acrobatics. Seldom had there been such applause.

But he'd lost again. He was 14 seconds behind Sailer. In 37th place.

His face was wet with snow and tears. He limped away—a few friends shielding him, consoling him. The only medal that really counted in his eyes—an Olympic medal—had slipped out of reach.

"He tried too hard," his coach said later.

He tried again in the Arlberg-Kandahar at Garmisch, Germany. That day the course was murder. In fact, a Canadian was thrown into a rocky ravine to his death. Half the racers didn't finish or mashed their legs to a pulp, broke their ribs on the ice, lacerated collarbones and shoulder blades. And one man, who hit a tree, had his nose torn off.

Werner was cool enough not to fight the inevitable. As he crashed, he relaxed and remained in one piece. Only his skis were shattered. Later, after they'd walked behind the Canadian's coffin through the narrow German street, a reporter asked Werner what he considered his chances to be for continued survival.

Werner thought a long time. The reporter turned to go, when Werner finally broke the silence. "If you think of death, you might as well give up racing."

"You have no fear, ever?"

Werner shook his head. "If you're afraid, you don't belong in the downhill."

In summer he'd scale Colorado's 14,000-foot peaks or walk for ten-hour stretches. He still had a hard time studying and still had no profession, but he needed money. He purposely chose a backbreaking summer job: telephone lineman in the Rockies.

On another occasion a rich insurance man paid for Buddy's training trip to Chile. Here Werner would submit to "leg-burning" (skiing 60 miles a day) sessions. For the hell of it he also took part in South American speed tests. Although the course was straight, the slightest mistake would be the last. Werner was clocked at 105 mph, but he didn't fall. His coaches were horrified by the risks he took. "Play it safe!" they kept telling him. "Stop being a hero!" He saw it in a different light and promptly pulled a lateral tendon.

Recovered, he entered the Inferno race in Mürren, Switzerland. Bar none, this is the world's roughest competition. Only the best ski racers have tried it. Only the sturdiest. After a single kilometer even a good skier goes to pieces; the Inferno sweeps down for ten kilometers, twice as long as other downhills. In all it drops 7000 feet—at some points as straight as an arrow. To complicate matters, there are almost no warning signals. The racer picks the route dictated by his own guts. For a few it means jumping over icy waterfalls and across glaciers.

It was Werner's turn. A few racers already had been clobbered. One had spilled in the first descent down Schilthorn Mountain, which resembles the top of the Empire State Building. A skier with a skull painted on his helmet gouged out an eye on a rock. The man ahead ended midway in screeching disaster.

As always, Werner looked calm. Only his eyes, glittering with fire, betrayed his inner emotions. He barreled down absolutely straight, seeking the most dangerous line. At the bottom he took off in flight, landed, blazed onward. Now the famous Plattwang schuss, which had fractured countless legs, caused two brain concussions. Directly beneath was a glacier. Most racers bypassed it altogether, traversing the long way round, at the cost of seconds.

Thousands of people waited for Werner. No one knew

how fast he went. Seventy? Eighty? Not even the experts realized what he was going to do. He might clear the first crevasse by jumping, only to fall into the second one. A third—100 feet deep and 20 across—would surely be his doom.

Werner's training as a jumper helped now. He'd studied the hill for days. He'd found a small rise in the middle, much like a real ski jump. Toward this one point he was steering now, teeth clenched, face gray with concentration. With a catlike lunge he took off, stuck his chest forward in the air, nose almost touching his ski tips, and soared across the entire glacier. He won the Inferno, of course. But no one—not even Field Marshal Montgomery, of Alamein, who was among the promoters—had seen anything comparable dating back to 1928, when the race was founded.

The year before the Squaw Valley Olympics, Werner blazed another new trail. He won the Hahnenkamm race at Kitzbühel, Austria, against Europe's best. He skied at great personal risk by taking the straightest line through unpacked snow. At 22 he was unbeatable in America, too. Yet he made the losers feel good, because he didn't brag.

He remained an amateur. He had offers to manage sporting-goods chains at fantastic salaries, offers to ski a little slower for $1000 so that a competitor's ski would be fastest and sell more pairs for the manufacturer. Every time ski makers asked him to lend his name to a product, he said no. Nor did he sell skis that were given to him, as many racers do. One day a Steamboat Springs brochure came out with his picture. Amateur officials hollered that it was against the rules. He immediately had the brochure destroyed.

To help pay for his trips, his parents didn't have a single vacation. They just worked overtime. Buddy didn't let them down. He perfected his style, eliminating the tiniest flaws in his technique. He was so good now that Coach Bob Beattie could help him very little. Werner had to help himself.

Would he win the Squaw Valley Olympics? All through the summer of '59 he prepared for it. He'd hit the trampoline daily, do long stints of calisthenics, dash for miles through the Colorado forests, often barefoot. He wouldn't touch liquor—even avoided beer—and wouldn't smoke. By the fall he was in unparalleled physical shape.

The first snow fell. The Olympics were only a few weeks away. Sailer was no longer competing. Many old-timers, past their peak, had dropped out. Werner was again the favorite.

On December 12, 1959, he counted the days to Squaw. His schedule had been a heavy one in Aspen: up the steep hill at daybreak, on foot. Dozens of tricky slalom gates. He flipped his way through, clawed his way up. One more run.

Suddenly his right leg got entangled in a bamboo flag. He strained against the crash, fought it with all his might. It was a mistake. He couldn't catch himself. A spectacular fall.

The break was a bad one. Compound fracture. The operation took hours, and they had to drill holes through Buddy's shin and drive in screws. It was a catastrophe for U.S. skiing. And a long winter for Werner.

But skiing was all he knew, and he could not get away from it. He needed the racing atmosphere as he needed air to breathe. You could see him in his cast on the slopes, crutches beside him, while the team trained. People would come up to Werner and shake his hand, and he would nod with those sad, soft eyes. But it was obvious that he hurt badly inside.

There was still physical pain when he went to the Olympics on his crutches. They'd given him a good seat on a platform, not far from a girl paralyzed by a ski accident years before. He would congratulate the winners. Sometimes he could not take it and disappeared to cry quietly in some corner. He must have taken a hard look at his future. The following summer he started to study in earnest. He picked economics. Should he finally accept one of the many juicy offers and cash in on his fame? He didn't. He remained an amateur. He abandoned only one training rule: No longer would he ignore women. A good-looking girl named Vanda Norgren made it easy.

The attraction of opposites worked its charm. He was broad-chested and sturdy. She was frail. Werner was comparatively unlearned and, despite his many years in Europe, still unable to speak anything but English. She was a linguist who taught French at a Denver school. He was taciturn, introverted; she was a bubbling extrovert. He came from plain, unmoneyed folks, she from glittering Colorado wealth. In June 1961 they married.

Werner's leg healed well. Before he knew it, he was in form again. He scored one victory after another: in raging blizzards, in thick fogs, in sub-zero temperatures. While other racers joined the professional circuit, which had become suddenly fashionable, Werner still couldn't bear to ski for money. He thirsted only for trophies. Just one Olympic medal!

One of his big years was 1963. "He has never raced better!" a coach exulted. The Olympics, to be held at Innsbruck, Austria, were imminent. In January *Sports Illustrated* featured Werner on its cover, goggles shielding his eyes, helmet with the U.S.A. insignia on his head. But again bad luck dogged him. It couldn't be otherwise. Disqualification for missing a gate in the giant slalom, a modest eighth in the slalom, a miserable 17th in the downhill. He'd fallen badly, ripping open an eyebrow. His younger team members—Billy Kidd and Jimmy Huega—won the medals instead.

There was one final race: the National Alpine championships. Buddy knew he would bow out after, and he gave it all he had. Someone else won. Sailing under a bad star, beset by bad breaks, deeply disappointed, he quit.

At 28 he finally devoted himself to earning a livelihood. He still had no sympathy for professional racing. But he gave time to a little Steamboat Springs ski shop his sister had opened. He also handled the national distribution of a line of ski boots and accepted the managership of a ski area. The money was finally rolling his way. In summer he would fish and play golf. He'd also complete his studies.

Life was at last treating him a little better. Perhaps that is why he hesitated a moment when Willy Bogner, Jr., called him from across the ocean about the movie. There would be famous skiers from all over, Bogner said: Fritz Wagnerberger, of Germany; Therese Obrecht, of Switzerland; Edda Kainz, of Austria; and Barbi Henneberger. There would also be a free trip to St. Moritz and a room at a luxury hotel. Plus a few dollars.

Werner left Denver on March 31. His wife kissed him at the airport. She would never see him again.

When Buddy arrived at St. Moritz, a front of nasty weather greeted him. The skiers sat in the Palace Hotel until it closed for the season. They moved to the Bernaseoni, in low spirits. Then the sky cleared abruptly, and the sun burst out, hitting the great mountains. They worked for a few days. When

Werner skied, he felt a little better. Soon his skin was peeling again.

On April 12 they were going to film two scenes. In the first one they'd all ski past a jagged line of rocks. Then Barbi would go as fast as she could, and Werner would execute a trick jump over her. Bogner explained it all at breakfast.

In the hotel lobby, while they talked, a radio blared out avalanche warnings. Later they walked past the ski-school shack just as a warning sheet was dumped on the director's desk. From the Swiss Institute of Snow Research, it advised skiers to use utmost care. "After the cold days, the sudden heat is bound to unleash *Lawinen*, avalanches," the paper read. "The snow contains too much water, and slopes over 2500 meters' altitude that lean from 25 to 60 percent are especially hazardous."

They reached Samedan, two miles from St. Moritz, around 9:00 A.M. The giant hills were still in the blue shade, which meant safety. At the ski lift Bogner was stopped by head patrolman Christian Tischhauser. "You're not filming up there, are you?"

Bogner looked at the huge frozen, unbroken expanse. "Why not?"

"The whole area is closed," Tischhauser said.

"Avalanches seldom go in the morning," Bogner said. He looked at Werner, who didn't speak. A moment later they were whirring upward. On the Trais Fluors station they stepped past a warning sign. It had a skull on it.

The cameras were set up on the proper slope, and Bogner took a test run. He shot down for a few hundred yards past the rocks. The snow held. The others tried it, too, then took the lift back up. By then, unfortunately, some tourists started to ski the same hill. The 15 people involved in the movie waited impatiently until the other skiers had made their awkward descent. Again the surface didn't budge.

Then, as they were about to begin, an avalanche cracked loose on the nearby Piz Nair peak. It rumbled to the valley with a ferocious racket as the sound of church bells pealed up from Samedan ten times, indicating it was ten o'clock.

"I'll take the lead," Bogner said. "Single file. First you, Barbi. Then you, Bud."

He tested the snow with his poles, and Werner did likewise. Hard. Underneath was a treacherous layer of soft snow. Bogner swung elegantly, and Werner looked his best. They had hardly started, when their ski edges brought the crashing, cascading, thundering mountain down. Out of reach, the cameras turned throughout the disaster.

The circle of bad luck had closed on Werner. In Colorado 62-mph gusts whipped dust across the fields when his wife got the news. She couldn't believe it. She called Switzerland, then broke down completely. They had been married less than three years.

Bogner was eventually tried for manslaughter by negligence. Inside the packed Swiss courtroom Bogner denied responsibility. He said he wasn't really in charge—it had all been teamwork. And how could he give orders to much older skiers, anyway? The attorney said, "It was the will of God."

The court deliberated until 8:30 P.M., then declared Bogner innocent.

At Buddy Werner's funeral people filed past the closed casket, then assembled outside in somber knots. Soon they drove off in their sports cars and station wagons.

The burial took place at Steamboat the next day. Flags flew at half-mast. Stores had closed. The minister delivered his eulogy to an overflowing church, and many who had come to pay their respects had to stand outside on the grass.

Finally the coffin was brought out; Buddy's teammates served as pallbearers. Buddy's wife had lost 30 pounds, and relatives had to support her.

There was one final sad touch. The funeral cortege received no flags, and the directors didn't indicate the route. Many cars got lost on the way to the cemetery. It's high above the town, where Bud Werner first learned to ski as a little boy.

ESCAPE FROM DEVIL'S ISLAND

By Henri Charrière

Henri Charrière, at age 25, was convicted in Paris of a murder he had not committed and sentenced to life imprisonment in the penal colony of French Guiana. A tattoo of a butterfly on his chest earned him the nickname of "Papillon" (French for butterfly). One thought obsessed him: escape. Forty-two days after his arrival in the islands he made his first break, traveling 1500 miles on the open sea in a tiny boat. There he was recaptured and sentenced to solitary confinement on the infamous Devil's Island. No one had ever escaped from this prison until Papillon did by flinging himself into the boiling sea with a makeshift raft made of two bags of coconuts. Eventually he found sanctuary in Venezuela, where he is now a citizen. His book, Papillon, *raised quite a furor in France when it was published a couple of years ago. Many authorities, perhaps not wanting to believe that the great Devil's Island could be breached, tried to discredit Charrière and his story. Charges flew back and forth for a while, but no one could prove Charrière didn't accomplish what he claimed, and the book became a best seller throughout Europe and then here in the United States. This, then, is the story of the most dramatic of his 12 escapes.*

Diable is the smallest of the three Iles du Salut. It is also the northernmost and the most exposed to wind and waves. From a narrow coastal flat it rises rapidly to a high plateau with a guardhouse and one small barracks for the few *bagnards*. Officially Diable was supposed to receive only those deported for political reasons. There were then about 30 of these men, each living in his own small house, and they would have nothing to do with the regular *bagnards* [nonpolitical prisoners].

I was greeted by the head guard, a brute named Santini. "Don't give me any trouble, Papillon, and I'll leave you in peace. I know you're a *cavale* [escape] man, but I'm not going to worry about it—escape from here is impossible. Go on up to the camp. I'll see you later."

There were six cons in my room: two Chinese, two blacks, a man from Bordeaux and another from Lille. One of the Chinese knew me from St.-Laurent. Chang had been a professional pirate, very dangerous, but he was a good man to live with; something about him inspired sympathy and confidence.

"It's OK here, Papillon," he told me. "You sleep there, next to me. I do cooking. You catch fish. Here many fishes."

Our job was feeding the pigs. Chang carried the coconuts and I split them open with a hatchet. The rest of the time we fished or wandered over the island.

The place I kept going back to was the stone bench where Dreyfus, maybe Diable's most famous political prisoner, had gazed out over the sea toward the France that had cast him out. There, on the northernmost point of the island, a good 120 feet above the sea, that innocent condemned man had found the courage to go on living. He never gave up. Nor would I. I would try another *cavale*.

During the long hours I spent on Dreyfus's bench staring at the sea, I came to know every quirk of the wind and waves. And that's how I made a very important discovery. Immediately opposite were some enormous craggy rocks that the waves broke against with particular violence. Two rocks formed a horseshoe about five or six yards wide, and a cliff rose directly above them, leaving the tons of water no exit except back out into the sea. Suddenly I saw that if, just as a wave was flinging itself into the chasm, I was to jump with the coconuts directly into its center, it would beyond the shadow of a doubt take me with it as it retreated.

I knew where I could find the jute bags for the coconuts; there were plenty of them in the pigsty. I would test my theory during the full moon, when the tides were higher, hence the waves bigger. I attached a rock to my carefully sewn bag of dry coconuts so that the total weight would be about the same as my own would be floating on two buoyant bags.

I was very excited. Nobody would ever suspect that this place would be used for an escape—it was the most dangerous spot on the island. It was also the only place from which one would be carried straight into the open sea without the hazard of cracking up on Royale.

The bag of coconuts and the rock were too heavy for me to carry alone; so Chang came to help me. We stood on one of the craggy rocks and watched a wave lunge at the base of the rock, and the moment it went into reverse, we threw in our sack. Like a straw, the bag was swept out to sea. "Chang! It works!"

"Wait and see if it comes back," he said. And sure enough, five minutes later, riding on the crest of a gigantic wave, it smashed against the rocks below us.

"No good, *cavale* from Diable. Royale better," Chang said.

"No. An escape from Royale would be discovered in an hour or two, and they have the boats. Here I have the whole night before they find out I'm gone, and then they'll think I drowned while fishing. And here there's no telephone and no boat."

I went back to Dreyfus's bench and took up again my study of the sea. It was then I discovered what an idiot I'd been. Only one wave out of every seven was a monster. The pattern was absolutely regular: There were six waves all about the same height—then, forming about 300 yards from shore, the big one, the great ground swell. It came in straight as a cannonball, growing in size and height as it approached. There was hardly any spray on its crest, and it had its special noise, like far-off thunder. When it broke on the two rocks, its great mass turned on itself in the passage between them. Then, after ten or fifteen seconds, the eddies would work their way out with a wild rumbling and churning.

Exactly as the ground swell broke, I threw in another sack. I saw it for a second as the water was sucked back to the sea. It did not return. The next six waves lacked the strength to throw it back onshore, and by the time the next great seventh had formed, the sack must have drifted beyond it, for I didn't see it again. Bursting with excitement, I went to tell Chang. I had it! I would wait for the 25-foot tide at the equinox— and then *cavale!*

Chang went back with me to watch another trial run, this time with two sacks tied together. "What was the name of little girl you tried save on St.-Joseph?" he asked.

"Lisette."

"We call wave that take you away Lisette, OK?" Lisette

arrived with the roar of an express train. She broke with such power that Chang and I were not only soaked but almost swept off our rock, and the sacks fell into the chasm. The sacks, though, were carried off—we could see them clearly far out from shore. We waited. Six waves and then Lisette again. But no sacks. They had gone beyond her reach. We climbed to Dreyfus's bench for a distant view. To our joy, we caught sight of them four different times riding the crest of the waves. And they were heading west!

Now we knew I could sail toward the great adventure on the back of Lisette. But I wanted a companion. The second stage of the *cavale,* alone in the bush, would be no picnic. A big, athletic guy named Sylvain looked like a good prospect. He was impressed with Lisette. He was pretty intelligent and had a lot of questions about the tides and ocean drift.

"It sounds all right," he said finally, "but once we're on the mainland, what then?"

"We have to find our way to the outskirts of a big fishing village called Kourou, where there's a Chinese *bagnard* camp, Inini."

"What do we do in a camp for Chinese?"

"My brother there," Chang said. "When you meet Cuic-Cuic, you got everything for *cavale.* He leave Guiana with you." Then he added, "Be careful. When you almost mainland, there's quicksand. Never walk on quicksand; it suck you up. Wait next tide to push you in bush so you grab branches. If not, you finished."

We spent the next ten days learning to ride our rafts. We soon realized that it would take a special effort to keep them from turning over. If we fell off, we might not be able to get back on. I found a chain about three yards long in a dried-up well and wove it in and out of the rope that held my sacks together. If I reached the point where I'd had it, I would chain myself to the sacks. That way I could sleep without falling into the water and losing my raft.

Chang made me a small waterproof bag to hang around my neck to keep my cigarettes and lighter dry. To take care of thirst as well as hunger, we would grate ten coconuts for each of us. We had our knives and two machetes we'd lifted from the toolhouse.

It was all set for Sunday at ten in the evening. With a full moon and a 25-foot tide, Lisette would be at full strength.

Chang was going to feed the pigs alone that Sunday morning, as I would sleep all of Saturday and Sunday. The guard Santini wouldn't discover we'd gone until Monday.

The wind was howling with hurricane force when Sylvain and Chang helped me push my raft to the top of the rock. I chained my left wrist to the raft. I was suddenly frightened at the thought of being carried off without it. Sylvain climbed up onto the rock opposite.

Chang hugged me around the neck and kissed my cheek. Then he stretched out flat on the rock and, wedged in a crack, prepared to hold my legs to help me resist the shock when Lisette broke.

"One more," Sylvain called out, "and then the good one!"

Lisette was coming straight for us, standing up like the spire of a church. With her usual deafening roar she broke over our rocks and swept toward the cliff.

I threw myself in a fraction of a second before my buddy, but we were close together as Lisette sucked us out into the open sea with dizzying speed. In less than five minutes we were more than 300 yards from shore. Chang had scampered up to Dreyfus's bench and, holding a white rag in his hand, was waving a last good-bye. Now we were a good five minutes beyond the dangerous area where the waves heading for Diable formed. We rose and fell from immense heights to great depths, all the while moving smoothly out with the ebb tide into the open sea.

As I rose to the top of one of the waves, I looked back and saw the white cloth in Chang's hand for the last time. Sylvain was perhaps 40 yards from me. He waved triumphantly.

The night went smoothly. Then we felt a powerful change in the direction of the sea. The tide that had drawn us out had turned and was now pushing us toward the mainland. I smoked a cigarette, inhaling in long, deep puffs. My fear was gone. There's no need to try to describe the agonies in my gut just before, during and after the leap. The real point is that I wasn't afraid any longer. In fact, after the cigarette I decided to eat a few mouthfuls of coconut pulp. Sylvain was quite far away, but we caught a glimpse of each other now and then when we crested a wave at the same time. The sun was roasting my skull with hell's own heat. I wet a towel and wrapped it around my head. Then I took off my sweater.

Suddenly, I didn't know why, my raft turned over! I took

in two huge gulps of seawater. Try as I could, I couldn't climb
back on. The chain I'd attached to my wrist was constricting
my movements. Furious, my nerves on edge, I tried to get free
of it, and finally I hoisted myself up. What a fool I'd been to
tie myself to the raft!

Sylvain was over 300 yards farther out to sea than I was.
He seemed to be rowing with his hands. Was he trying to slow
his raft? If he braked and I rowed, perhaps we could close the
gap between us. I'd chosen a good partner for this escape.
Sylvain had risen to the challenge 100 percent.

But I soon stopped rowing; it was tiring work, and I had to
conserve my strength. The sun was on the horizon, and I
hoped the night wouldn't be too rough. I downed two fistfuls
of coconut pulp, then lit a cigarette and smoked with deep
delight. Before night fell, Sylvain waved his towel and I mine
to say good night. I closed my burning eyes. "Don't sleep!"
Easy to say, but I was almost beyond caring. I was racked
with a fearful anxiety. What if I fell asleep? If I tumbled into
the water, would it really wake me up?

I became obsessed with the idea of locating my partner. I
dried my fingers in the wind and whistled through them with
all my might. Then I listened. No answer. I cupped my
mouth with my hands and yelled. The only answer was the
wind and the waves.

I smoked two cigarettes. It must have been about five
o'clock. I'd now been at sea 30 hours, and I had to admit
that for the moment things looked better rather than worse.
When the sun started cooking me again, it wouldn't be fun,
but burned or not, old pal, you're on *cavale*. The chances are
ninety to one you'll get to the mainland alive this very afternoon.

As the tropical sun loomed up behind me, I could begin to
see the bush clearly. An unusually strong wave lifted me high.
Hallelujah! Sylvain was less than 200 yards away. He was
looking around with his hand over his eyes, but he didn't
seem to see me. The next time a wave lifted me, I stood up
and whistled. He saw me this time and raised his sweater in
the air. We waved hello at least 20 times before we sat down
again. I was so overcome with joy that I wept like a child.
God is with you today, Papi! Here, in the midst of nature's
elements, you feel your infinitesimal smallness. Perhaps it's
here, without looking for Him, that you find God. I felt Him

around me, inside me. He even whispered in my ear. "You suffer, but you will be free. You will, I promise you."

By noontime my shoulders, back and arms were on fire. My eyes oozed pus, and the skin was gone from my nose and lips. Once in a while Sylvain turned around and waved. The shore was near now, and the waves raced toward it in long, straight lines. I could see the thicknesses of the various trees, and I made out one giant one that had fallen, its branches awash in the sea. Now, over the noise of the breakers, came the shrieks of thousands of wading birds.

Two or three yards more, then *ploof!* I had run aground in the quicksand. It was low tide. I had to hitch myself with the chain to avoid being swept off the raft when the breakers started to roll at the turn of the tide. It would take two or three hours of rising tide before I'd have draft enough to float. But by nightfall I'd be in the bush!

Sylvain was still about a hundred yards ahead on my right. He was making motions as if he were trying to shout something. What was the stupid ox doing? He was leaving his raft! Had he lost his mind? If he started walking, he'd sink in deeper with each step. I tried to whistle, but my mouth was too dry. The poor guy who got stuck in that quicksand was done for.

Sylvain kept making signs I didn't understand. I flung my arms about, trying to warn him. Suddenly I realized he was already being sucked in. The sound of a wail reached me. I lay down flat on my raft, dug my hands into the quicksand and pulled with all my might. The raft crept forward perhaps 20 yards. I could see Sylvain now, ten yards from his raft, buried up to his waist. Terror gave me back my voice, and I yelled, "Sylvain! Try to lie flat on top of it! Try to free your legs!" I clawed furiously at the sand. Rage gave me superhuman strength, and I moved another 30 yards. It must have taken an hour. I was now perhaps 50 yards away. I had trouble seeing him, though, because my arms and face were covered with mud and my eyes were weeping. Finally I saw him. He was up to his chest in quicksand.

The tide was turning. The first breaker passed over me and subsided ahead, covering the quicksand with foam. It swept over Sylvain. I had to reach him. I pulled and pulled against the sand. His eyes were wide open and glued to mine. A huge wave hit me, knocking the breath out of me. Forty yards. Sylvain was up to his armpits, still staring at me. He knew he was dying there in the muck, 300 yards from the promised land.

I kept on clawing at the now almost liquid sand. Our eyes stayed riveted on each other. Another giant breaker covered me with an avalanche of water and floated my raft five or six yards forward. When it had passed, I looked up. Sylvain was gone. The quicksand, covered with a thin layer of foamy water, was completely smooth. Suddenly I was seized with a shameful animal reaction: The instinct for survival swept all other feelings away. I said to myself, You may still be alive, but when you're in the bush all alone, your *cavale* will be in trouble.

A roller broke over my back—I was sitting now—and brought me back to reality. When I caught my breath, I saw the wave die beneath the trees. It was then that I wept for my friend: We were so near. If only you hadn't gotten off! Why did you do it? Too much sun? Did you lose the strength to endure? Why couldn't a man like you take the punishment a few more hours?

The breakers kept rolling me in, but I was not going to budge until I had a branch in my hand. Only 20 yards to the trees, but it must have taken another hour to get there.

Quickly, before the sun went down, I crept into the bush, half swimming, feeling for solid ground before I took a step. My first night was spent stretched out on the trunk of a fallen tree. I hung my sacks of coconuts high on a branch and, exhausted, fell asleep.

SHOT DOWN OVER RUSSIA

By Francis Gary Powers
with Curt Gentry

The year was 1960, and the cold war was still in full bloom. Eisenhower was in the White House and Khrushchev ruled the Kremlin. The divided city of Berlin was a major hot spot, and the Soviet premier was trying to make it hotter. A summit conference was scheduled, however—and perhaps, just perhaps, some easing of tensions would result. Then, with incredibly bad timing, an "incident" occurred. A U.S. high-altitude U-2 spy plane was shot down by a Russian antiaircraft rocket and the pilot, Francis Gary Powers, captured. Khrushchev had Eisenhower dead to rights, and he proceeded to make the most of it. The resulting brouhaha was to later influence the 1960 presidential election, and faint shock waves are still felt today whenever the subject of espionage is brought up in Washington. But perhaps the most dramatic part of the whole story was the experience of pilot Powers. Suddenly, and without warning or proper briefing, he found himself in a badly damaged aircraft spinning violently down toward the Russian countryside. That he managed to survive the readily apparent physical dangers and the mental rigors of KGB questioning and captivity that followed is a tribute to his indomitable courage.

After the single-click acknowledgment from Bob, only silence. A lonely feeling, knowing you'd broken radio contact.

Approaching the border, I could feel the tension build. It happened on every overflight. Once across the border, you relaxed a bit. For some reason you felt that anything that was going to happen would happen there.

The weather below was worse than expected. On the Russian side the clouds came right up to the mountains, a solid undercast. As far as intelligence was concerned, this wasn't important, there being little of interest in this area. But it didn't make the navigation easier. Without visual observations, I needed the sextant but couldn't use it, my celestial computations having been made on the basis of a 6:00 A.M. takeoff. Instead I had to rely on time and headings. The sextant was usable, however, as a check to see if the compass was working correctly. It was.

After about one and one-half hours I spotted the first break in the clouds. I was southeast of the Aral Sea. Slightly right of course, I was correcting back when some of the uncertainty came to an end.

Far below I could see the condensation trail of a single-engine jet aircraft. It was moving fast, at supersonic speed, paralleling my course, though in the opposite direction.

I watched until it disappeared.

Five to ten minutes later I saw another contrail, again paralleling my course, only this time moving in my direction. Presumably it was the same aircraft.

I felt relieved. I was sure now they were tracking me on radar, vectoring in and relaying my headings to the aircraft. But it was so far below as to pose no threat. Because of my altitude, it would have been almost impossible for the pilot to see me. If this was the best they could do, I had nothing to worry about.

Odd, but even before reaching the border, I had the feeling they knew I was coming.

I wondered how the Russians felt, knowing I was up here, unable to do anything about it. I could make a pretty good guess.

For four years the U-2s had been overflying the USSR. Much of this time, if not all of it, the Russian government had been aware of our activities. Yet, because to do so would be to admit that they could do nothing to stop us, they couldn't even complain. I could imagine their frustration and rage. Imagining it made me much less complacent.

Ahead, about 30 miles east of the Aral Sea, was the Tyuratam Cosmodrome, launching site for most of its important ICBM and space shots.

This wasn't our first visit to the area, nor was it a major objective of this particular flight. But since I was to be in the vicinity, it had been included. Due to the presence of some large thunderclouds, I couldn't see the launch site itself but could see much of the surrounding area. I switched on the cameras. Some intelligence was achieved, though not 100 percent.

The clouds closed over again and remained solid until about three hours into the flight, when they began to thin. I could see a little terrain, including a town. With my radio compass I picked up the local station. In regard to this particular station, intelligence had indicated that their information might not be accurate; the call sign, the frequency or both could be incorrect. The call sign was wrong, the frequency right. Again slightly off course, I corrected back.

About 50 miles south of Chelyabinsk the clouds disappeared. To my left I got a good view of the Urals. Once the traditional boundary between Europe and Asia, as mountains they were not very high. Still snow-topped, on either side the land was green. It was spring in Russia. It was also a beautiful day, and now that I was back on course, the clouds behind me, I began to relax a little.

Predictably, number 360 chose this moment to be unpredictable. The autopilot began malfunctioning, causing the aircraft to pitch nose-up. To correct the condition I had to disengage the autopilot, retrim and fly the plane manually for a few minutes. When I reengaged the autopilot, the plane flew fine for ten to fifteen minutes, after which the pitch controls again went to the full nose-up position. The aircraft couldn't take much of this. Again I went through the same procedure —with the same result. This time I left the autopilot disengaged.

Should I go on, I'd have to fly the plane manually the rest of the way.

It was an abort situation, and I had to make a decision: to turn around and go back or to continue the flight. An hour earlier the decision would have been automatic: I would have gone back. But I was more than 1300 miles inside Russia, and the worst of the weather appeared to be behind me, while ahead visibility looked excellent.

I decided to go on and accomplish what I had set out to do.

Normally, without this complication—having to navigate, compute ATAs and ETA, turn on the switches at the designated points, pay constant attention to the instruments to keep from exceeding the mach limitation on the high side and stalling the aircraft on the low side, the variance in speed also affecting fuel consumption—my work was cut out. Having to fly the plane manually called for an extra pair of hands.

Spotting a huge tank farm, I noted it on my map. Observing a large complex of buildings, which could have been either military or industrial, I marked them down, also, with the notation "big outfit" as a reminder for debriefing.

Sverdlovsk was ahead. Formerly known as Ekaterinburg, it was here, in 1918, that Czar Nicholas II and his family were assassinated by the Bolsheviks. Once a small village, isolated from the mainstream of Russian life, in recent years it and the surrounding area had grown as astronomically as southern California. Now an important industrial metropolis, Sverdlovsk was of special interest. I flipped the appropriate switches.

This was the first time a U-2 had flown over the area.

Once past Sverdlovsk, my route would take me northwest to Kirov, whence I would fly north to Archangel, Kandalaksha, Murmansk and, finally, Bodo, Norway.

About 30 to 40 miles southeast of Sverdlovsk I made a 90-degree left turn, rolled out on course and lined up on my next flight line, which would go over the southwestern edge of the city.

I was almost exactly four hours into the flight.

Spotting an airfield that did not appear on the map, I marked it down. My route would take me directly over it.

Following the turn, I had to record the time, altitude, speed, exhaust-gas temperature and engine-instrument readings. I was marking these down when, suddenly, there was a dull "thump," the aircraft jerked forward, and a tremendous orange flash lit the cockpit and sky.

Time had caught up with us.

Knocked back in the seat, I said, *"My God, I've had it now!"*

The orange glow seemed to last for minutes, although it was probably gone in seconds. Yet I had time enough to think the explosion was external to the aircraft and, from the push, probably somewhere behind it.

Instinctively I grasped the throttle with my left hand and, keeping my right hand on the wheel, checked instruments. All readings normal. Engine functioning OK. The right wing started to droop. I turned the wheel, and it came back up. Fine. Now the nose, very slowly, started to go down. Proper correction for that is to pull back on the wheel to bring it up. I pulled, but it kept going down. Either the control cable had severed or the tail was gone. I knew then I had no control of the aircraft.

As it kept nosing down, a violent movement shook the plane, flinging me all over the cockpit. I assumed both wings had come off. What was left of the plane began spinning, only upside down, the nose pointing upward toward the sky, the tail down toward the ground. All I could see was blue sky, spinning, spinning. I turned on the emergency oxygen supply. Sometime earlier—I hadn't felt it at the time—my suit had inflated, meaning I'd lost pressurization in the cockpit. The suit was now squeezing me, while the g forces were throwing me forward, out of the seat, up toward the nose.

I reached for the destruct switches, opening the safety covers, had my hand over them, then changed my mind, deciding I had better see if I could get into position to use the ejection seat first. Under normal circumstances there is only a small amount of clearance in ejecting. Thrown forward as I was, if I used the ejection seat, the metal canopy rails overhead would cut off both my legs. I tried to pull my legs back, couldn't. Yanking at one leg with both my hands, I succeeded in getting my heel into the stirrup on the seat. Then I did the same with the other heel. But I was still thrown forward, out of the seat, and couldn't get my torso back. Looking up at the canopy rails, I estimated that using the seat in this position would sever both legs about three inches above the knee.

I didn't want to cut them off, but if it was the only way to get out. . . .

Thus far I had felt no fear. Now I realized I was on the edge of panic. "Stop and think." The words came back to me. A friend who had also encountered complications trying to bail out had told me of forcing himself to stop struggling and just think his way out of his predicament. I tried it, suddenly realizing the obvious. The ejection seat wasn't the only way to leave the plane. I could climb out! So intent had I been on one solution, I had forgotten the other.

Reaching up—not far, because I had been thrown upward as well as forward, with only the seat belt holding me down—

I unlocked and released the canopy. It sailed off into space.

The plane was still spinning. I glanced at the altimeter. It had passed 34,000 feet and was unwinding very fast. Again I thought of the destruct switches but decided to release my seat belt first, before activating the unit. Seventy seconds is not a very long time.

Immediately the centrifugal force threw me halfway out of the aircraft, with movement so quick my body hit the rear-view mirror and snapped it off. I saw it fly away. That was the last thing I saw, because almost immediately my face-plate frosted over. Something was holding me connected to the aircraft; I couldn't see what. Then I remembered the oxygen hoses. I'd forgotten to unfasten them.

The aircraft was still spinning. I tried to climb back in to actuate the destruct switches but couldn't; the g forces were too great. Reaching down, I tried to feel my way to the switches. I knew they were close, six inches away from my left hand at most, but I couldn't slip my hand under the wind-screen to get at them. Unable to see, I had no idea how fast I was falling, how close to the ground. . . .

And then I thought, I've just got to try to save myself now. Kicking and squirming, I must have broken the oxygen hoses, because suddenly I was free, my body just falling, floating perfectly free. It was a pleasant, exhilarating feeling. Even better than floating in a swimming pool, I remember thinking. I must have been in shock.

I was thinking, I should pull the ripcord, when a quick jerk yanked me upward. The chute had opened automatically.

Suddenly my thoughts were sharp and clear. The chute had been set to open at 15,000 feet, which meant I was somewhere below that. And under 15,000 feet I didn't need the emergency oxygen in my seat pack and could take off my faceplate.

I was immediately struck by the silence. Everything was cold, quiet, serene.

The first thing to do when the parachute opens, I had been taught in air-force survival school, is to look up and make sure the chute has billowed correctly. This I was reluctant to do, since, having only one chute, I was not anxious to discover whether it had failed. But I looked up. The orange and white panels blossomed out beautifully. But against the vast expanse of sky, the chute looked very small.

There was no sensation of falling. It was as if I were hanging in the sky, no movement at all.

Part of the aircraft passed me, twisting and fluttering like a leaf. I thought it was one of the wings. Yet I had no way to estimate size or distance. It could have been a small piece up close or a large piece some distance away.

Looking down, I saw I was still quite high, probably 10,000 feet.

Below were rolling hills, a forest, a lake, roads, buildings, what looked like a village.

It was pretty country. A typical American scene, like parts of Virginia.

As if by wishing it I could make it so.

It was odd. Under other circumstances it would have seemed amusing. A country as large as the Soviet Union, so vast, with huge sections almost totally uninhabited, and I had to pick a populated area in which to go down.

Remembering a map in my pocket, which showed alternate routes back to Pakistan and Turkey, I took off my gloves, took it out, carefully ripped it into little pieces and scattered them. One piece of incriminating evidence was gone.

I also remembered the silver dollar and took it out. Looking at it at this point, I realized the coin cover wasn't such a good idea after all. What better souvenir of the capture of a capitalist American pilot than a bright, new U.S. dollar? It was one of the first things they would take. Unscrewing the loop at the end, I slipped out the poison pin and dropped it into my pocket, where there was a chance it would go unnoticed, then tossed away the coin.

I recall thinking, That's probably the first dollar I've ever deliberately thrown away.

I also recall wondering what some Russian farmer would think when he came upon this years from now—an American dollar in the middle of a Siberian field!

My mind seemed to be perfectly sharp and clear, though incapable of dwelling on a single thought for any length of time. It kept jumping from one thing to another.

Occasionally I would start to swing, but mostly I fell straight, without oscillation, without any real sense of falling.

I thought again of the pin, wondering whether I should use it. Recalling the crash of the C-118 and how the local populace had almost lynched one of the crew, for a moment

I seriously considered it. Yet I was still hopeful of escape.

The forest was to my right. I tried to maneuver the shroud lines in order to float down into the trees, thinking that if I could reach them, I might at least have a chance of getting away. But the winds were variable. I'd drift toward the woods, then back toward the lake. That worried me, since I knew that, tangled in the chute, with all the equipment I was carrying, swimming would be impossible.

Only a few hundred feet remained. I spotted a small car moving along a dirt road. It seemed to be following my course. I watched as it stopped near the village and two men got out.

I also saw, almost directly under me, a plowed field, a tractor and two men. One was on the tractor, the other standing alongside piling brush.

By now I was too far away to reach the trees. I had also missed the lake. But now a new worry emerged: power lines.

Suddenly the earth rushed up to meet me. I missed the lines by about 25 feet, coming down about an equal distance from the tractor, hitting hard, the weight of my seat pack causing me to fall, slamming my head against the ground.

While one of the men collapsed the chute, the other helped me to my feet. Soon joined by the pair from the automobile, they assisted in removing the parachute harness and helmet. My head ached and my ears rang from the sudden descent.

The village was less than 100 yards away. There must have been a school there, for suddenly there were 20 or 30 children running toward us, followed by almost as many adults.

Escape at this point looked impossible. I still had the gun, but the knife was attached to the parachute harness they had removed.

Everyone was questioning me at the same time. Because I couldn't speak Russian, I could neither understand them nor reply. They seemed solicitous but also curious. When I didn't answer—I didn't even know the words for "Thank you"—I could see that they were puzzled.

One of the men held up two fingers, pointed at me, then at the sky. Looking up, I could see, some distance away and very high, a lone red-and-white parachute. There had been no second chute on my plane. Unable to see whether there was a man below the chute, I guessed this to be in some way connected with the explosion. Had they used a rocket, it was possible this was the way they recovered the missile's first stage. I shook my head no, indicating I was alone.

With my continued silence I could see the puzzlement changing to suspicion. A man on either side, I was helped to the car. One, spotting the pistol on the outside of my suit, reached over and took it. I didn't try to stop him. By now the crowd numbered more than 50.

It was a small compact car. Loading my parachute and seat pack in the trunk, they motioned for me to slide into the front seat beside the driver. The man with the pistol slid in on my right. Three or four other men crowded into the back.

Driving through the village, I made motions indicating I was thirsty. It had been six or seven hours since I had had anything to drink, eat or smoke. Also, sure they were taking me to the police, I wanted to delay confrontation as long as possible.

It occurred to me that had I been able to speak Russian, I could have pretended to be a Soviet pilot and commandeered their automobile. I probably wouldn't have gotten far—knowing a plane had crashed and its pilot had bailed out, there would be search parties, roadblocks—but certainly it would have been better than my present situation.

Stopping in front of a house, one of the men went in and returned with a glass of water. Gratefully, I drank it, but my mouth remained dry. I suspected I was in a state of mild shock. I was terrifically tense, extremely tired. Pilots are unusually conscious of their hearts. Mine was racing, at well over 90 beats per minute.

I could only estimate this. Because of the difficulty of slipping the band over the pressure suit, I didn't wear a watch when I flew. I could only guess at the time. I had been four hours into the flight when the explosion occurred. Nearly a half hour had passed since then.

Too early for them to miss me at Bodo.

One of the men offered me a cigarette. I accepted, noticing the picture of a familiar dog on the package. "Laika," he said. I nodded, indicating understanding. The brand had been named for the Russians' *Sputnik II* passenger. A filter cigarette, it tasted very much like its American counterparts.

There was a package of Kents in my flight-suit pocket. I left them there.

The man who had seized my pistol now had it out of the holster and was examining it. I saw what he saw at exactly the same instant: on the barrel, the initials U.S.A. I hoped he didn't understand their meaning. But with one finger he traced the letters in the dust on the dashboard, asking in Russian what could only have been "Are you an American?"

Inside the trunk was my seat pack. In it, among other easily identifiable items, was the American-flag poster with "I am an American . . ." printed on it in 14 languages, including Russian. It seemed useless to deny it. I nodded, and the conversation around me suddenly grew very animated. Fortunately, it didn't seem hostile. Rather, they appeared to be congratulating themselves on having made such a prize catch.

The road was muddy, either from spring thaw or recent rains, and we bounced and slid over the ruts. It was important that I think clearly, decide what my course from this point should be.

The problem: I was completely unprepared. I presumed that once it was known I was missing, a cover story would be issued. Unfortunately, no one had ever bothered to inform us pilots what it would be.

I decided that, when questioned, I would say I had been piloting a weather plane, en route from Pakistan to Turkey, when my compass had gone out and that apparently I had accidentally flown in the wrong direction. I doubted that they would believe me—I was over 1300 miles inside Russia— but it was all I had to work with.

We were totally unprepared for the crash possibility. I could not speak Russian, had no one to contact. In the four years I had worked for the agency, only once had I received instructions on what to do in the event of capture. And that, brought out by my own questioning, had been the single remark of the intelligence officer: *"You may as well tell them everything, because they're going to get it out of you anyway."*

I was damned if I was going to do that. Although not sure how, or if, I could manage it, there were some things I was determined to keep from them at any cost.

After driving for about 30 minutes, we came to another village, larger than the first, with paved streets. Later I learned that I had landed on a large state farm. The second village was its headquarters; the building to which I was taken was the Rural Soviet. Pulling in front of the building, one of the men went in and brought out a man in uniform, whom I assumed to be a policeman. Making me stand alongside the automobile, he made a cursory search, finding and keeping my cigarettes and lighter but missing the poison pin.

Taking me to one of the offices in the building, they indicated I was to undress. This time the search was more thorough, even the seams of my clothing examined.

On completion, they kept the pressure suit but gave me back the outer flight suit. While putting it back on, I casually ran my hand down the outside of the pocket. And felt it. Again they had overlooked the pin.

Several of the men in the office wore military uniforms. As one took down the statements of the men who had apprehended me, another tried to question me in German. I shook my head. Apparently no one spoke English.

A doctor arrived, to my surprise a woman, about 30. She checked my heartbeat and pulse; noticing some scratches on my right leg, she painted them with antiseptic. When I indicated I had a headache, she gave me two small pills that looked and tasted like aspirin.

Perhaps I imagined it—perhaps I was so desperate for some hopeful sign that I created it in my mind—but I was sure the look she gave me was sympathetic, as if she understood my predicament and wished she could help me.

Individually and in small groups people began arriving bearing pieces of equipment or wreckage from the plane. I could see English lettering—manufacturers' names, maintenance instructions, serial numbers—on some of them.

I cringed inside. One man was carrying a reel of 70-millimeter film.

What little credibility my cover story possessed disappeared at that moment.

As the people came in, some took out small cards and proudly showed them to the officers. There was much examining and comparing. It was only a guess, but I thought they must be Communist-party membership cards, the lowest numbers perhaps indicating their owners had been party members longer than the others.

During all of this I seemed to be largely forgotten.

But I knew that was wishful thinking. There was also much telephoning. I didn't have to speak the language to surmise the subject.

After we had been there about two hours, I was escorted out of the building and placed in a military vehicle similar to, but a little larger than, the U.S. jeep. In the front seat were a military driver and civilian. I was in the middle of the back seat, between an officer and an enlisted man. Across the lap of the latter was an automatic weapon with a huge clip. It could have been a carbine but looked more like a submachine gun. He kept his finger in the trigger guard. A second car followed. Once on the road, a third car joined the procession.

Had my flight proceeded uninterrupted, I would have been about two hours from Norway.

Our destination was Sverdlovsk. From the flags, banners and crowds on the street, it was obvious something was being celebrated. Not until then did I recall the date and remember that May 1 is a Communist holiday.

The building in front of which we stopped—three-story, with a severe stone facade—was unmistakably a government building and would have been recognizable as such in either the United States or Russia. I was taken to a busy office on the second floor. There was no mistaking it, either. Although there were no bars on the windows and some of the men wore military uniforms and the others wore civilian clothes, they were far more authoritative and sure of themselves than any of the people previously encountered. They were police of some kind, presumably KGB. At this time I knew nothing about the KGB, other than its initials and that it was some form of Russian secret police. Later I would learn a great deal more than I wished to know. Its full name is *Komitat Gosudarstvennoi Bezopasnosti,* or Committee for State Security; it is the current descendant of the Cheka, NKVD and MVD.

These men were professionals. There was another search. And this time they didn't overlook the pin.

The man who found it, however, one of the civilians to whom the others seemed to defer, didn't seem greatly interested. Examining it cursorily, he slipped it into his brief-case.

I was determined to keep that briefcase within sight.

My ears were still ringing. I stuck my finger in one and shook my head, trying to stop the buzzing.

One of the men reached over and slapped my hand down.

It seemed uncalled for and made me mad, although I tried not to react.

A few minutes later I tried to clear my ears again, and again he knocked down my hand. Then I realized they were probably worried that I had a poison capsule in my ear and was trying to get at it.

From their careful examination of both my person and my clothing, it was obvious they expected to find some sort of poison on me.

"Are you an American?" one man asked.

Hearing English for the first time startled me. I admitted I was.

Apparently he was the only one who spoke the language, as he acted as translator whenever any of the others asked questions. His English was very poor.

As convincingly as possible I explained how I had lost my bearings and had flown over the border by mistake.

It was obvious they didn't believe a word of it.

I hadn't really expected that they would. Evidence indicated otherwise. As they brought in items from the wreckage, I had spotted my maps, which I'd hoped had been destroyed in the crash of the plane. Most hadn't. There were even maps I hadn't known were aboard, duplicates someone back at Peshawar had thoughtfully stuck in my pack or on the plane. My route, from Pakistan to Norway, was clearly marked on the set I had been using for navigation. And, from what I could see of them, these seemed to be intact.

Nor was this all. Not only did they have wreckage from the plane and contents of the seat pack, including the Russian rubles, gold coins, watches and rings, they also had my flight bag with my shaving kit, clothing and wallet.

Carrying that had been a mistake, I realized. It showed how complacent we had become. Thinking only of what I would need in Norway, I hadn't considered the possibility that I might not reach my destination. Nor had anyone else thought to stop me from carrying it.

I tried to recall exactly what the wallet contained. There was a Defense Department card, identifying me as a civilian employee of the Department of the Air Force, authorizing medical care and PX privileges and, I was sure, listing my outfit as Detachment 10-10; a NASA certificate (the National Aeronautics and Space Administration had succeeded NACA in 1958); instrument rating cards; U.S. and international driver's licenses; a selective-service card; a social-security card; American, German and Turkish currency; some U.S. postage stamps; pictures of Barbara; and I wasn't sure what else.

The social-security and selective-service cards had been issued in Pound, Virginia; the U.S. driver's license, in Georgia. Just from these items they could put together a pretty accurate profile, provided their intelligence didn't already know just about everything there was to know about the U-2 pilots.

I stuck to my story, untenable as it was.

Occasionally I'd glance at the unbarred windows. Always there was someone standing in front of them. When one man left, another replaced him. They were professionals. They knew the way a prisoner thought.

One thing about the questioning especially disturbed me: Again and again they tried to make me admit I was military, not civilian. I wondered why. Did they think the nature of my mission was something other than espionage? By trying to make me admit I was military, were they trying to establish that my purpose was not spying but aggression, that I was in fact the forerunner of an American invasion of Russia?

I now realized why the agency had hired civilians to fly the missions. It was important that I prove to them that I wasn't military.

Pointing out the card that identified me as a civilian employee of the Department of the Air Force didn't help. Ignoring the word *civilian,* they fastened onto *Air Force,* repeating it over and over. This was proof I was military!

Possibly it was a trick, but I thought not. The ramifications of what they were maintaining seemed to me far more dangerous than admitting the truth. I dropped my spur-of-the-moment cover story and told them I was a civilian pilot employed by the CIA.

They seemed aware of the organization, but it didn't change their thinking.

During the questioning there had been a number of incoming and outgoing telephone calls. Because the tone of voice used was becoming increasingly respectful, I assumed my case was being passed up the chain of command. After one call they stopped the questioning and held a hurried consultation.

One of the men took out a pair of handcuffs; after some additional discussion, however, he put them back in his pocket. Someone brought in a poncholike raincoat, and the interpreter told me to slip it on. Since it wasn't raining, I could only presume it was intended to cover my flight suit and make me less conspicuous.

We went downstairs, got into a large limousine and drove to an airport, stopping by a gate that led out onto the field. One of the men flashed his identification, the guard opened the gate, and we drove right onto the runway, where a jet passenger plane was waiting. From the car we ran up the ramp, one of the men prodding me in the back so I would move faster. As soon as we were inside, the door was shut, the ramp pulled away and the engines started.

Four men got on the plane with me: the interpreter, a major and two civilians, one with the briefcase that held the poison pin. There were no guards as such, although the major had a pistol strapped on his belt.

I asked the interpreter where we were going. He replied, "Moscow."

Although we were alone in the front part of the aircraft, with a curtain shutting off our compartment from the one behind it, there was a stewardess, and when she came through the curtain, I could see other passengers and presumed this was a regular commercial flight to Moscow that had been held up pending our arrival.

I was offered some fruit and candy but had no appetite. Two of the men passed the time playing chess. I eyed the major's pistol but gave up the idea. Even if I got it—and the holster was fastened—I could do nothing but complicate the situation.

There was no questioning on the plane, and I was grateful for that. I needed the time to plan.

It was while we were en route that I decided upon the

course of action I would follow in subsequent interrogations. It was entirely my own idea, and I was not at all sure it would work, but I had to try.

Although unsure of the time, I knew that more than nine hours had passed since my takeoff. They would give me another half hour, because I had carried that much extra fuel, but after that they would know beyond a doubt. I could imagine the panic among the crew at Bodo and, after the word was relayed, at Adana.

I wondered how and what they would tell my wife and parents. I had many worries, not only regarding Barbara but also regarding my mother, who had a heart condition.

I was exhausted, more so than I could recall ever having been before, but I couldn't sleep. My wife, my family, the people at Bodo and Adana occupied all my thoughts.

Worrying about them was, I suppose, an escape mechanism, preferable to thoughts of my own predicament.

As for what lay ahead, I knew for sure only one thing: Sooner or later they were going to kill me.

MANOLETE'S LAST DANCE WITH DEATH

By Vernon E. Pizer

Manuel Rodriguez was determined to escape the Spanish poverty he was born into, but the route he chose to travel was a tough one: bullfighting. At first he was awkward and clumsy, unable to master the theatrical fireworks of the romantic style of Spain's national sport. But he was brave, and his method of killing the bull brought gasps from the crowds. He would lunge straight in over the horns with his sword instead of the more usual twisting-away style favored by most matadors. But the kill was all he had. Then a promoter took him on and taught him to concentrate only on certain simple moves and forget the fancy stuff. He did, and his career blossomed. Soon he became the most talked-about bullfighter in Spain. Throngs went wild in city after city, their voices hoarse, as he calmly dispatched one fierce bull after another. By the 1940s he was recognized as the country's numero uno matador, *a worthy successor to the great Belmonte. Mexican and South American audiences began clamoring for him, and he traveled there. The audiences were huge and his performances flawless. The money rolled in, and his picture was plastered over all the papers. When he returned home, bone-weary and hoping for a long rest, however, he found a new challenge. Jealous Spanish matadors had been circulating stories that he was actually slipping, that his performances had come at the expense of inferior bulls. He decided to quiet his critics and embarked on a countrywide tour. Then, in a ring at Linares, near his Córdoba birthplace, he came up against a Miura, a huge, diabolical-looking black beast from a strain especially trained for fighting. Manolete, as he was now called, advanced to the center of the ring to begin yet another "dance of death." . . .*

It is easier to begin to understand the demon that rode Manuel Rodriguez's back if you have some idea of what it

117

means to be belly-rumbling hungry the way the Rodriguezes
were. When Manuel was born, in Córdoba in 1917, his
father, blind and ailing, was no match for the daily struggle
to keep the cooking pot filled, and the family's next meal
was always in doubt. Still, hunger and poverty were never
a novelty in Spain. In time Manuel might have learned to
accept the harsh facts of life. But there was more to it than
that. At an age when he should not have been old enough to
discover such things, he learned that his sister had been
forced to come to terms with hunger in the only way that
is always open to a desperate girl. And that was the point of
the spur that was driven into his flesh. That was the real
demon that rode his back.

Among the Spaniards there is a centuries-old conviction
that one can enjoy respect, prestige and wealth only by being
born into the aristocracy—or by becoming a successful bullfighter. Destiny had placed the Rodriguezes at the bottom of
the heap; so now he, Manuel, would bend destiny to his own
will by mastering the bulls. He would force life to make full
restitution for the hunger, the misery, the shame of his sister.
He would create honor and wealth in the bullring. He would
be a somebody, and his family would be somebodies along
with him.

Manuel had nothing going for him except his solemn, un-
shakable vow to conquer the bulls and, through them, to
conquer life itself. He was growing up spindly, awkward,
gaunt—the consequence of too many missed meals. He had a
long, thin face dominated by arrestingly sad black eyes.
When he was ten, he began bringing a few *pesetas* into the
house by working as a mason's helper. He said little, and he
never smiled as he did the mason's bidding. Outside he was
ice—inside he was on fire with his dream of the bullring
and of the honor and fortune he would find there.

Around Córdoba are a half-dozen ranches that breed
fighting bulls. Irresistibly drawn to those ranches, Manuel
seized every opportunity to trudge out to beg for a chance
to make a pass at one of the animals. The men who breed
bulls are themselves a special breed with almost religious
fervor for the great beasts. They can appreciate a new acolyte
begging for admission to the order; so they did not laugh at
the earnest, awkward beanpole of a youngster. But neither
did they accede to his pleas. Not, that is, for about two

years. Then one of the ranchers, worn down by Manuel's persistence, allowed him to take the cape to a small, young bull whose horns were still blunted knobs.

The bull charged. Manuel held his ground, fluttering the cape to draw the animal off to one side, and was bowled over hard. Scrambling to his feet, the boy tried another pass with the cape, and again he was hurled to the ground. For almost an hour, heedless of his accumulating bruises, he stood firm, trying determinedly and futilely to turn and dominate the yearling. Then a ranch hand climbed into the corral.

"You are not afraid, *chico,* and you are a stubborn one. However, you know nothing about a bull. Here, give me the cape, and I will teach you at least one little thing for all your effort." And so it started, the making of a bullfighter who had not been cut out by nature to fight the bulls.

Manuel had no natural grace for the stylized drama that is the epitome of grace. He had no instinctive talent for the ritualized, fluid movement of the bullfighter. He tended to knock-knees, and his feet turned inward in a pigeon-toed stance. He could almost have served as a model for a caricaturist. The ranchers around Córdoba saw all of these things, but they also saw the boy's unquenchable determination and his courage; so this one and then that one undertook to teach him something of the art of the bullring and something of the nature of the bulls.

By the time he was 17, Manuel had accumulated much knowledge of the ring, countless bruises and wrenched limbs and several horn scars on his upper thighs. His resolve to become a great matador had never wavered; if anything, it had become a fixation. He chafed to get out of the practice corral and into an actual ring. Adopting the professional name of Manolete, he went to see the fight promoters at Córdoba's Plaza de Toros. Something—perhaps the air of quiet brooding that seemed so odd in one so young, perhaps the tone of voice that conveyed the impression that refusal would be unthinkable—persuaded one of the promoters to give the newly christened Manolete a chance against a small bull.

Manolete was off to a poor start in his first professional fight. He was clumsy, and his inexperience showed in every move he made. He fell into the trap that yawns wide for every neophyte matador—attempting showy, fancy passes and twisting, gaudy pivots and exaggerating the sweep of the cape. Real bullfighting is all controlled movement, nuance and subtlety; Manolete's performance was as close to that as the bumps and grinds of burlesque are to a ballet. Until the time for the kill arrived. Then everything changed. For a moment Manolete stood immobile before the bull. In his left hand, close to his body, he held the muleta—the small red cloth that is draped over a stick. In his extended right hand he held his sword pointing ahead at the beast before him. There was nothing of the burlesque about Manolete now. He sighted down the length of his slim blade, aiming the downward-drooping tip at the narrow gap between the bull's shoulder bones. Then he lunged forward directly over the horns instead of twisting his body to the side in the more usual and safer approach. The tip of his blade struck true, and the sword plunged in to its hilt. The crowd yelled its approval, heedless now of the awkwardness Manolete had displayed earlier. Solemnly the novice matador left the ring with no hint in his hawklike face that the applause was his initial recovery of the debt he meant to collect from life.

Manolete was now accepted as a *novillero,* a fighter of bulls less than four years old. As a novice he embarked on a two-year barnstorming tour of the small, provincial rings that dot Spain, picking up a fight here, another one there. At the end of that time he had little to show for his efforts. He had been able to send some money home—nothing impressive, but it did put some food on the table. Otherwise, little was changed. He had grown taller, had picked up some additional experience, but he was still a gawky, lanky novice whose performance left the spectators dissatisfied and disdainful. Only when the moment for the kill arrived did the throng show any enthusiasm. In the final moment when Manolete and the bull confronted each other for the last, climactic act of the drama, the *novillero* made the audience forget the awkward prologue. But the kill alone was not enough; it alone could not carry him to the peak he meant to climb. By itself the sword would not make Manolete a somebody.

His clumsiness with the cape gnawed at Manolete. His thin face with its set expression masked the turmoil within as he strained to perfect the flamboyant passes he thought would excite the spectators. The harder he tried, the clumsier were his movements. He was resolved to be a great matador; so he continued to strain for greatness, and his goal continued to elude him. He might have ended up that way—a tragicomic *novillero*—had not José Camara become his manager.

Camara had all of the business enterprise of a typical manager, but he also had an almost uncanny knowledge of bulls and bullfighting. He was attracted to Manolete because he admired the youth's unrelenting purposefulness and his courage in the ring. The manager dismissed the *novillero's* awkwardness with a shrug and a wave of the hand. "He tries too hard and, worst of all, he tries the wrong things." It was a shrewd, accurate appraisal. Manolete was struggling to master what was never meant for him—the florid, exaggerated movements of the "romantic" style of fighting. Some matadors have the muscular physique, the stagy mannerisms, the dashing personality that romantic fighting calls for—not Manolete. He would always appear slightly ludicrous if he saddled himself with that style. As a matador in the classical tradition, Manolete could be quite another story; instinctively, Camara could recognize that. The tall, thin *novillero* with the pinched, sad face and the withdrawn, austere manner was made to order for the restrained elegance and purity of the classic style that had come to full flower with Belmonte, the idol of the "golden Twenties."

Camara withdrew Manolete from the second-rate fights in the second-rate rings in order to purge his technique of all that was wrong and then to create a new Belmonte. The manager was dictatorial and hard to please, but he knew his business; Manolete sensed that. The youth did not resent the long, grueling hours in the practice ring, because he, even more than his manager, was unwavering in striving to attain perfection—or as close to perfection as one can come when he is pitting himself against a wily bull with rage in his huge bulk and death riding his horns.

Under Camara's tutelage the young matador discarded all of the theatrical fireworks and instead concentrated on achieving mastery over only a few—no more than a half dozen—truly classical passes. He schooled himself to employ those passes with subtle artistry. Striding to his position in the ring, he stood erect, immobile, proud, feet planted close together, and stared at the bull haughtily. The only movement in his body was in his hands as he worked the cape in restrained, elegant, silky-smooth passes that drew the beast to him and past in a drumbeat of hooves. Manolete also learned to use the small muleta cape with a classic simplicity that required iron nerve as well as artistry. Disdaining the usual practice of keeping the cloth between himself and the bull, he held the muleta low on his left side, exposing his body to the bull defiantly. As the beast charged, Manolete remained statuelike, moving only his wrist to put a tremor into the cloth and so to divert the rushing bull to the muleta. Even at the ultimate moment, with the needle-sharp horns only inches from him, Manolete scorned any movement except for the magic of that wrist that could imbue the cloth with a life of its own. Then, as the horns ripped by his body, Manolete passed the cloth over the head of the charging beast. Only Manolete's swordwork remained unchanged—refined a bit, but essentially the same straight-in-over-the-horns lunge that had been the redeeming feature of the *novillero*'s earlier performances.

For months Manolete drilled himself relentlessly to achieve excellence as a matador in the classic tradition. Hour after hour, day after day, he practiced the techniques, working the bull in closer to himself than even the great Belmonte had dared. This brought a heightened thrill to his performance, because he allowed himself no margin for error. His life depended upon how accurately he judged the bull's peculiarities—which horn it hooked with, how quickly it shifted its eyes, whether it ran straight or tended to veer to one side. All of these things he had to study and assimilate quickly and precisely and then to make instant, fine adjustments in his fighting to compensate for them. The hangers-on around the practice ring shook their heads with a mixture of unbridled admiration and foreboding. "He is a genius, a master," they said, "and it will kill him. Nobody can fight the bull as he does and live for very long."

In 1937 Manolete returned to the bullring. At first Camara could book him into only the small provincial rings, because he was, as yet, an unknown. But he did not remain unknown for long. His style of fighting stirred the spectators, even the bellicose, hard-to-satisfy customers in the cheap seats on the sunny side of the ring. Before long the promoters were coming to Camara to offer bulls for Manolete to fight. By the end of the season Manolete was able to move his family into more adequate living quarters. For the first time in his life he had no crushing money problems. He had heard the applause of the crowd. He had seen his name up on posters. He was on his way to becoming somebody, and behind his withdrawn, dignified exterior he exulted.

At last on his way to achieving his goal, Manolete was impatient to continue the journey at an accelerating pace lest the ultimate success escape his grasp. He allowed himself no rest, insisting on fighting day after day, and each fight added to his growing reputation as a genuine phenomenon of the *corrida*. Soon he was fighting in the leading rings across the country, and the newspaper critics were referring to him with words of praise.

Two years after he had schooled himself in the classic style of fighting, Manolete was recognized as a full-fledged senior matador. In his position of seniority he was pitted against only prime bulls, the biggest and most dangerous in the ring. Now more than ever he had need for all of his skill and courage, for these were great animals especially bred for strength, for speed, for aggressive instinct and for craftiness, and they were at an age where they were at their peak. The matador made no concession to the greater hazards he faced. He remained the proud, dramatic figure rooted to his spot in the ring, feet planted together, matching his talent and bravery against the animal's rage, cunning and vastly superior strength. For Manolete there was no backward step, no cape held out timidly at arm's length from his body, no cautious dancing away from a rushing, slashing bull. The throngs went wild. In city after city they cheered until their throats were hoarse. In Madrid jaded big-city sophisticates acted like ecstatic schoolboys. At the annual Seville fair, a highlight of the bullfighting season, the reporters trotted out their most glowing phrases.

By 1945 Manolete was acknowledged throughout the nation as Spain's preeminent matador, the worthy successor to Belmonte. He had found all of the prestige and the fortune he had sought in the ring, and he had carried his family up with him, up to the heights from the very depths of poverty and hunger and family shame. His mother (his father had died a few years earlier) was living in luxury, lacking for nothing. His sister was sought after, respected, her friendship pursued. Nor was it only those close to Manolete who basked in the fruits of his stunning success.

The matador never forgot the abject poverty from which he had escaped, and he dispensed his funds with overwhelming generosity to aid those who were still caught in the trap. Hospitals for the poor, orphanages, schools, churches, clinics, as well as individual families by the hundreds, received financial support from Manolete.

But success has its price. Outwardly the matador was little changed—as icily calm, as remote and austere as ever. Within the shell that the world saw, he was worn, utterly exhausted, used up. Yet he still drove himself relentlessly, because he could not allow himself to falter now. He could risk no flaws, no weaknesses that might blemish what he had struggled so long and arduously to create. Nor would the fans, insatiable in their appetite for his performance, permit him any respite from the ring. Had his success been less complete, had his performance reached a lesser degree of magnificence, had his bravery in the ring been tempered with a measure of caution, the demands placed on him would have been less severe. But he was no longer Manuel Rodriguez—he was the great Manolete, who had become public property and a living legend.

After the season ended in Spain, it was the turn of the Mexicans, who set up a clamor for Manolete. They expected a brilliant display, but when the matador appeared in Mexico City, the fans got even more than they had bargained for. The city was infected with Manolete fever. At daybreak would-be spectators gathered outside the Plaza de Toros to offer ticket scalpers as much as $200 for a single admission. Federal troops had to be called out to maintain order. Inside the plaza 25,000 pairs of eyes were riveted on Manolete, savoring the marvel of his *derecho,* an elegant pass to the right, thrilling to his magnificent *natural,* a single-handed pass with the cape held limply that is the most dangerous move a matador can attempt. His work with the big cape and with the smaller muleta was perfection. His sensational, hazardous, straight-in-over-the-horns kill electrified the throng. Coats, hats, jewels, fur scarves showered down into the ring. The *presidente* of the *corrida* awarded Manolete both ears and the tail, the highest accolade he could grant. Regally holding them aloft as though they were marshal's batons, the tall, thin, proud and dreadfully tired matador circled the ring, gravely acknowledging the hysterics of the crowd.

After Mexico all of South America pressed for appearances by Manolete. Camara could, and did, name his own price, and the money rolled in in a great golden river. The matador earned it all, every penny, each day somehow finding the means to surpass his performance of yesterday. He was the hero of the continent. Police in Ecuador had to protect him from his delirious admirers. The citizens of Lima elected him honorary mayor of the Peruvian capital. Wherever he went, women threw themselves at him and men cheered. Manolete's tour of the New World was not so much a continuous round of bullfights as it was a triumphal procession. When the matador was at last ready to return home, he was an empty shell who had spent himself satisfying the demands placed on him by the excesses of his admirers. Before, there had been a hint of gray powdering his black hair; now it had become a silvery streak. On his thigh there was an ugly, fresh scar, a souvenir of a fight in Mexico, and his right cheek carried a T-shaped reminder of another horn on another day in another ring. But he was a somebody, of that there could be no doubt—a somebody in desperate need of a long rest.

There was no rest for the matador. As soon as he returned home, he found himself the center of a passionate controversy that had erupted in his absence. Spanish bullfighters, jealous of his fabulous success abroad and resentful of the vast sums he earned, argued that a matador must choose between Spanish or foreign rings and not be permitted to buzz among them all, lapping up the nectar like a greedy bee. To make it unmistakably clear that Manolete was the target of their attack, the dissident bullfighters circulated rumors that his performance had deteriorated and that he was coasting along on the ground swell of past successes. The bullring gossip that Manolete resented most was a malicious charge that he was covering up his faltering performance by fighting only inferior bulls that went to their slaughter docilely. Camara raged at the scurrilous attacks, but Manolete hid his anger behind his mask of icy pride. He permitted his manager only one reply to his detractors: to book him for a grueling nonstop tour through the nation's rings, where his skill and courage would speak for themselves. Camara knew how exhausted Manolete was, and he argued against the tour. The matador was adamant.

The tour of the bullrings began, and Manolete was brilliant. In ring after ring he demonstrated that he was still the reigning matador and that the bullfighters who carped about his performance were merely ambitious pretenders to his throne, bent on winning with their tongues what they could not win with their capes and swords. Manolete was as skillful as he had been; yet he was not precisely as he was before. Those who knew him best and observed him closest could observe a subtle change in him. He had always seemed so indifferent. He worked the bulls so close to his body that it brought gasps from the stands. Camara, deeply disturbed by this intensified exhibition of daring, remonstrated with the matador, but his words went unheeded.

During a benefit performance in Madrid, Manolete was gored in the left leg. The horn penetrated to a depth of three inches, ripping through the muscle and leaving him bleeding profusely. Disregarding his painful wound, the set expression on his face unaltered, Manolete remained in the center of the ring, proudly erect, and continued the fight, killing his bull cleanly. A medical bulletin issued later revealed that the muscle had been destroyed. Despite the injury, Manolete permitted Camara to cancel none of his scheduled fights.

On August 27, 1947, Manolete appeared in the ring in Linares in southern Spain, near Córdoba, his birthplace. The matador was entered into two fights that afternoon. His first encounter was typically Manolete—exquisitely controlled, classically graceful, confident, austere. The spectators cheered, but he seemed hardly aware of their shouts.

When Manolete's second bull of the day was loosed in the ring, those in the stands sucked in their breath audibly, for it was a huge, diabolical-looking, black beast—a Miura, the most dangerous, most feared strain of fighting bulls. The matador advanced to the center of the ring to commence the "dance of death." It was clear from the outset that the Miura was an especially wily and perilous animal. As the bull charged, it hooked its long, needle-tipped horns wickedly to the right. Coldly calm, Manolete drew the wild beast past him in a classic veronica, the slashing horn ripping by his body a hand's breadth away. The bull pounded to a halt and turned to gather itself for another attack. Manolete fluttered the cape gently to draw the animal's attention to it. The bull stood for a moment pawing the sand angrily, its eyes fixed not on the cape but on the man. This was a bad sign— a bull that can resist the enticement of the cape to fasten its malevolent eyes on the man himself is a bull to be feared. Manolete fluttered his cape once more, and it became a living thing in his skilled hands, forcing the animal's eyes to it. The Miura charged, and again Manolete swept it by in a beautifully executed veronica. Once more the bull stopped, turned and glared at the man.

The matador asserted his mastery over the bull in a half-dozen more thrilling passes that had the crowd yelling madly. Then he switched to the smaller muleta cape and brought the viciously hooking horns even closer to his body in a supreme display of artistry and courage. Again and again Manolete drew the wild beast thundering past him, and the spectators knew that they would never witness a fight to surpass this one. On his last pass with the muleta, Manolete raised his eyes from the charging beast and stared into the stands in a crowning demonstration of audacity, depending wholly on his instinctive reactions to maneuver the Miura by him. The audience was stunned.

Then the moment for the sword arrived. Feet planted classically close, muleta grasped in his left hand, sword in his right, Manolete drew himself up proudly, his "suit of lights" reflecting sparks of fire in the rays of the lowering sun. Anyone else would have taken the bull from the side to squirm away from those hooking horns—not Manolete, not the man who had made the straight-over-the-horns approach his indelible trademark. The matador extended his sword toward the great animal, sighting down the slim blade. The Miura charged. Simultaneously, the matador lunged straight ahead. His sword tip struck true, entering between the bull's shoulder blades. The sword buried itself up to the hilt in the massive body. At the very instant that the tip was piercing the beast's heart, the Miura hooked upward and to the right, driving a horn viciously deep into Manolete's groin. With a massive wrench of its head, the bull flung the impaled matador into the air, shaking him loose. Manolete thudded to the sand at the beast's feet. Twice more the Miura raked the matador's body before falling dead at his side, so that blood of the animal and of the man ran together in a single, spreading pool.

The unconscious matador was rushed to the infirmary under the stands. As the doctors worked on him frantically, even though they could see that there was no hope, Manolete roused. "Did I kill the Miura?" he asked. "*Sí, chico, you killed him,*" Camara answered. Someone pushed forward to hold up the two ears and the tail that had been awarded. A rare smile appeared on Manolete's thin, sad face. Ten hours later, as he was receiving his fifth blood transfusion, the 30-year-old matador died.

Later that day Manolete's body was carried to Córdoba to lie in state. Altars in private homes throughout the country were draped in black. Radio Madrid broadcast dirges in his honor. Generalissimo Franco sent a personal representative to pin a posthumous Order of Beneficence on the corpse. In Mexico movie theaters canceled their feature pictures and, instead, showed newsreels of Manolete over and over. In Peru and Ecuador street-corner gatherings spoke of the matador in hushed tones and many wept. In Córdoba, when the funeral procession commenced, 100,000 followed the bullfighter's bier.

In death Manolete extracted full and final restitution from life. Manuel Rodriguez of Córdoba had indeed created honor and fortune in the bullring. He had indeed become somebody.

BLOODY ROAD TO USUMBURA

By Jean-Pierre Hallet

Jean-Pierre Hallet was always aware of the pull of the Congo on his life. He had lived six years of his childhood there, where his father was known as "the painter of the Congo." So, after his studies were completed, he naturally looked for an assignment that would take him back. He was now an agronomist and a sociologist, and he was sent back by the Belgian government to live and work among the natives. He learned their languages (six aboriginal languages and seventeen dialects), taught them to cultivate the soil, build houses and schools. He was and is a big man at six feet, five inches and 240 pounds, and his acts of personal heroism endeared him to the people. He once wrestled a 450-pound lion to prove his bravery to the Masai tribe; another time he killed a leopard with a knife after it had attacked a terrified native. He was twice decorated by King Baudouin I of Belgium for his services. In 1955 he received word that some 1000 families in a section called South Mosso were facing starvation because of a drought. Hallet then risked his life day after day by dynamiting fish in Lake Tanganyika to provide food for the people. One day, as he was standing in a dugout canoe lighting and tossing sticks into the water, he noticed that some of the fuses were defective. Suddenly, without warning, a two-stick charge went off in his hand. . . .

The small yellow flame licked at the one-foot length of Bickford fuse cord attached to the two sticks of dynamite I held in my right hand. I waited for the spark and the little crackling noise that would come when the fuse caught, but nothing happened. Two or three seconds passed as I held the flame of my lighter to the end of the fuse. . . .

It was shortly before three o'clock in the afternoon of

Monday, October 24, 1955. I was standing in a dugout canoe about 300 feet off the eastern shore of Lake Tanganyika, at the southern border of Burundi. Three other canoes were positioned in a crude circle around me, about 100 feet away. Each of them held two Bagoma fishermen who were waiting, nets in hand, for me to drop the charge into the water. The dynamite would sink slowly and explode at a depth of 15 feet. Then a cloud of stunned silvery fish would float up to the surface, and my native helpers would scoop them into their nets.

Two or three seconds passed. Then, instead of a spark, there was a rapid, abnormal *hiss-s-s-s*. Something was wrong, and I knew it. Immediately I started to make the quick gesture that would toss the dynamite into the lake, but I was too late. The 200-gram charge of high explosives went off in my right hand.

Seconds later, when awareness returned, I found myself in the cold blue immensity of Africa's deepest lake, gasping for breath as I instinctively treaded water. I was half-blind and almost completely deaf from the blast. My face, neck and chest were laid open, my left hand was terribly wounded, and my right hand—I no longer had a right hand, only an abbreviated stub of arm that ended just above the wrist in two jagged bones and some tattered frills of skin.

My canoe was still floating about 20 feet away—upside down. I looked for the other boats and saw, with a feeling of rage, that the native fishermen were paddling furiously toward the shore. Frightened by the prospect of being involved in a white man's death, my helpers were deserting me. Then I looked in the opposite direction and saw four greenish-gray snouts about 100 feet in the distance. They moved toward me rapidly, with their ridged, scaly backs carving a wrinkled wake through the water. . . .

It began less than a week before, when I visited the Belgian colonial government's administrative center in Kitega. I had been working for the government for the past seven years as a sociologist and agronomist, both in the neighboring Congo and here in the mandated territory of Ruanda-Urundi (now two independent nations, the republic of Rwanda and the kingdom of Burundi). I had come to Kitega for a routine technical discussion, but the situation I found was very far from routine—it was tragic. There was famine in the South Mosso—severe, unrelieved famine that had already taken some 100 lives.

What was "the Mosso" and where? Imagine a scorched parallelogram 100 miles long and 20 miles wide, formed by the rolling plains and ramified valleys of the Malagarasi River, in the extreme southeast end of Burundi. Populate those lightly timbered savannahs and thickets of false bamboo with small herds of antelope, families of warthogs and bands of insolent baboons. Add lions, leopards, wild dogs, civets, genets, servals—and a few men.

In the past the human population had been far more dense. Then, as in much of Central Africa, sleeping sickness had decimated the area. The people died in droves until the Belgian government took over and launched a systematic program to stamp out the terrible disease. Now a few thousand human beings remained, a small, sturdy people almost like pygmies, called the Bamosso, who tried gamely to eke out a living on the worst farming land in Ruanda-Urundi.

Most of the time they succeeded. But this year the dry season, which usually lasted for two months, had stretched all the way from June to October. Corn, beans and sorghum had burned up during the drought; then the starving antelope and wild pigs, unable to find food on the parching savannahs, had raided the staple crops of sweet potatoes and manioc. Desperate, the people had eaten their precious reserves of seed. When there was nothing left, they simply starved and started to die.

When the Kitega officials learned of the tragic situation, they wired at once to the government's depot at Nioka, 400 miles away in the northeast part of the Congo. But the big warehouses at Nioka were almost empty; other famine-stricken areas had already depleted the available supplies. So, Kitega's urgent request for 15 tons of beans had gone on the waiting list—and the Bamosso continued to die.

That was the official situation when I decided to take some highly unofficial action. I found it impossible to stand by and shrug philosophically, like many of my colleagues, while thousands of human lives were drawing toward a slow, agonized end. But the possibilities were terribly limited. Hunting was out of the question: Game was scarce, to begin with, and now the Bamosso would certainly be too weak for me to organize them into effective hunting parties. It would be just as impractical to attempt bringing in hunters from the outside. Most of the people in Burundi had an almost superstitious fear of the strange, desolate Mosso country. They would refuse to enter, no matter how much I offered to pay them.

Hunting was out of the question—but fishing was an entirely different story. It would be relatively simple to drive my Studebaker pickup to the shore of Lake Tanganyika, hire some native helpers and gather immense quantities of fish—with dynamite. Then I could truck the life-giving food to the cooking pots of the Mosso, about 60 miles to the east. It was a sound, logical but thoroughly illegal plan. Dynamite fishing was strictly forbidden by the colonial government, for conservationist reasons. Usually I followed that philosophy myself, but now, when it was a question of saving human lives, the balanced ecology of Lake Tanganyika seemed trivial. Still, it was against the law, and I would probably lose my job if the government heard of my action. "The hell with it," I decided without further hesitation. "People are more important than fish—or a job."

Having reached that conclusion, I drove to my own official post, the territorial headquarters of Bururi, and loaded my pickup with axes and machetes, a 50-foot roll of Bickford fuse cord, detonators and a massive wooden box containing 50 sticks of 100-gram gelatin dynamite. Then I drove west toward Lake Tanganyika.

As far as fish were concerned, I was headed in the right direction. With a total of 233 species, including specialized forms for the surface, the depths and the shore, Lake Tanganyika possesses the richest and most diversified collection of freshwater fish in the world. Right now I had a particular interest in just one of those species: *Stolothrissa tanganicae,* a herringlike fish about two inches long that was known in these parts by the name of *ndagala.* Not only were they exceptionally rich in protein, calcium and phosphates, but the *ndagala* traveled in dense shoals that made them ideal prey for the dynamite fisherman.

I settled down for the night at Nyanza-Lac in a bungalow provided by the government for the use of occasional travelers. Then, early the next morning, I hired four pirogues and six fishermen in a little village about ten miles to the south. The men were members of the Bagoma tribe, who had emigrated originally from the northeast part of Katanga on the other side of the lake. We left the boats at the village, the six of them climbed into the back of my truck, and I drove two miles farther down the wretched little dirt road that had once led to Kigoma, in neighboring Tanganyika. At that point an old trail branched off from the road and headed west through the bush.

As I had expected, the trail was so heavily overgrown that I had to break out the axes and machetes and send my six helpers ahead to cut back the bush. Slowly, as they slashed a passage for us, my pickup and I crawled toward Lake Tanganyika. Finally, after excavating a green tunnel about three miles long, we came to a dead stop. The trail petered out and ended in a dense grove of sizable trees. It was impossible to force our homemade highway any farther toward the lake. It would have been a major project even to carve out enough space so that I could turn the truck around.

Then we hacked our way another mile along a small footpath until we reached the beach of Mwekarago Cove, a curved expanse of white sand almost completely overgrown with creeping lianas. We inspected the fishing site briefly, returned to the truck, reversed for three miles and drove back to the Bagoma village.

As soon as we arrived, I sent my fishermen to their boats with instructions to return at once to the cove. Then I negotiated with the chief to hire a large number of porters. Within a few minutes I had the back of my truck packed solidly with most of the young adults in the village, 15 muscular men and women armed with tightly woven baskets that would each hold about 40 pounds of *ndagala*. Once again I drove my truck back to the trail and led the long caravan of porters on the one-mile walk to the beach. The fishermen had already arrived on the scene. Then, while the entire crowd of natives watched from a respectful distance, I prepared my charges.

First I laid two sticks of dynamite parallel and taped them together, spiraling the tape up and down the entire length of the sticks to augment the force of the blast. When that part of the operation was finished, I attached a detonator to a one-foot length of Bickford fuse cord, crimping the hollow end onto the cord with my teeth. Then, after peeling back the heavy waxed paper at the end of one stick, I took an old lead pencil, poked a little tunnel in the gelatinous explosive and dropped the detonator into position. Afterward I pressed the sticky gelatin around the fuse cord, pushed the paper back into place and taped the joint securely.

Then we paddled out from the shore, fired the first series of two blasts, filled the boats with *ndagala,* unloaded and paddled back for the second. By the end of the day my truck was crammed well beyond capacity with 2500 pounds of shining, silvery fish. I smiled with satisfaction at that beautiful sight and drove 60 miles to the marketplace of Butana, in the South Mosso, to make the first distribution.

It had been a terribly hard and exhausting day, but it was worth it. I shall never forget the expressions on the faces of those weak, emaciated people when they saw me arrive at Butana with the truckload of fresh, shining *ndagala.* They were successively astonished, unbelieving and incredibly happy. They had resigned themselves to death, and now they knew that they were going to live.

During the next two days I speeded up the tempo, conducting both morning and afternoon blasting sessions at Mwekarago Cove, each of them followed by a long trip to the Mosso. Everything went off without a hitch, including the morning session of the fourth day, October 24, 1955. Even now I remember how I drove back to Lake Tanganyika from Butana exulting in the complete success of my plans. I had brought 7200 kilos of *ndagala*—more than seven tons of fish—to a thousand starving families of South Mosso. The famine was definitely licked.

Now I had only six sticks of dynamite left out of the original 50. I would use them this afternoon, and the great "fish safari" would come to a quiet, successful end. I stopped briefly at Nyanza-Lac, where I gassed up the truck from the Arab storekeeper's 200-liter drum. Judging from the position of the sun, it must have been about 2:30 when I got back to Mwekarago Cove and a little before three when I stood up in my pirogue, about 300 feet offshore, ready to drop the last three charges.

I lit the first one and tossed it overboard. It sank slowly, but there was no explosion. Apparently the fuse had been defective. That hadn't happened before during 22 drops. Now I had only four sticks left, two double charges. *"Nom de Dieu!"* I cursed softly. "The next one had better go off!"

I touched the flame of my lighter to the fuse, waiting for the spark and the familiar crackling noise, but nothing happened. Two or three seconds passed . . . and a vast, shattering moment of mindless oblivion. Then, suddenly, inexplicably, I found myself dazed and gasping for breath while my feet instinctively treaded water and my thoughts whirled around in complete confusion.

Desperately I tried to rub my eyes with the back of my right hand, but for some reason I couldn't manage to do it. I tried again and felt something sharp rake over my eyebrows. Something sharp—what the hell could it be? I ducked my head, hoping the water might bring back my vision. The simple maneuver worked, washing away the blood that had streamed down into my left eye. The right eye was apparently blind. Still, I felt immense relief being able to see again. Then I remembered the trouble I had trying to rub my eyes —something sharp—and I raised my right arm out of the water.

For an instant I stared at the mutilated stump without comprehension. There was no blood; the white, macerated flesh looked like the skin of a plucked chicken. . . . Abruptly I realized what I was looking at, and I grew terribly angry. *"Merde!"* I thought savagely. "I've lost my hand!"

Now I began to feel pain, a terrible burning pain that raged over my face, neck, chest, arms and hands. My *hands?* The right one was still full of fire, in spite of the fact that it no longer existed. The pain in the left was even more frightful —if I still had it. That thought really shocked me. I raised my left arm out of the water—and the hand was still there. The thumb and the first two fingers were badly injured; they were split open like burst sausages, and the bones of my forefinger gleamed whitely through the torn skin. But the hand was still there!

Another thought came, and I reached down with the mangled fingers to pass them over my belly, half expecting to find coils of dangling intestine. Nothing seemed to be wrong. Instinctively I explored a little farther down . . . intact, undamaged. I felt overwhelming relief. I relaxed for an instant, still treading water, and then, suddenly, I became aware of a strange new sensation in the stump of my right arm.

Only a few seconds before, the severed wrist had been dead white in color. Now it was spurting jets of bright-red arterial blood. Immediately I flexed the limb as hard as I could and pressed the flat inner surface of the stump against the upper part of my chest, squeezing the radial and ulnar arteries of the forearm against my rib cage. That slowed the pulsing stream down to a trickle.

Then for the first time I looked around me, trying to find the pirogues. Up until this moment I must have been expecting subconsciously to be caught by the back and hauled up into one of the dugouts. Now I saw my own overturned boat, my native fishermen paddling off into the distance and the white wakes of water made by the oncoming crocodiles.

That sight shocked me into action. I struck out toward the land with an awkward, left-handed Australian crawl, while I kept my flexed, mutilated right arm pressed tightly against my ribs. The pain was atrocious, but I rejected it—just as I rejected the inexorable logic of my situation. I knew that even if I reached the shore, I was a mile from my truck. Even if I reached the truck, I was three miles from the road. And even if I reached the road, where was I? Alone, terribly wounded, in the middle of nowhere. Everything proved conclusively that I was going to die—and yet, irrationally, I was determined to live.

I was still 100 feet from the shore when the crocodiles caught up with me. The big ones I had spotted first were almost at my heels, and as I turned my head, I saw a group of five more approaching from my blind right side. I'd swum in crocodile-ridden waters before—and even among them—so I knew what I had to do. Quickly I changed the angle of my body, assuming an almost vertical position in the water. Thus my awkward crawl stroke turned into an even clumsier dog paddle. That made it extremely difficult for the big reptiles to seize me: The anatomy of their jaws, skull and neck prevents them from turning their heads to the side, forcing them to seize their intended prey on a horizontal plane.

Now I moved toward the shore much more slowly, splashing as violently as I could. Undismayed by my tactics, two more crocodiles came toward me on the left. One of them was an enormous beast about 20 feet long—almost as large as a native pirogue. He shot forward like a ridged green torpedo, and an instant later I heard a hollow clack at my ear, like the beat of a large talking drum. It was the sound his jaws made as they snapped shut in the space I had occupied only a fraction of a second before.

Instinctively I moved toward the right—where his five colleagues were waiting. Another clack sounded near my right shoulder, and immediately after, I felt a crocodile pass behind me. His scutes scraped my back and tore off the tattered remnants of my shirt. Appalled, I sped up, summoning my final reserves of strength. Then, unbelievably, my feet touched the bottom. I swam the last few yards with a heart that seemed to be bursting and staggered out of the water, leaving behind me a fan-shaped flotilla of frustrated crocodiles.

I wanted desperately to rest, but I forced myself to walk at least 50 or 60 feet from the shore. At that distance I was safe. Then my knees buckled, and I sat down hard, right in the midst of the empty baskets my native crew had abandoned. They were all gone, the porters as well as the fishermen. I was alone.

I sat down, but I didn't really rest. The stump of my wrist was still trickling blood in spite of the pressure position. I knew that I'd somehow have to make a tourniquet in order to stop it. A tourniquet—out of what? My shirt was gone, and my khaki shorts were reduced to incredible tatters. But my socks remained, even though I'd lost both of my shoes and my Aussie-style campaign hat.

Using my injured left hand and my teeth, I took one of the cotton socks and managed to tie it around the upper part of my right arm. It was quite ineffective. I took the other one and knotted it just above my right elbow. The result was only a little better. Then I picked up a piece of liana from the ground and wound it tightly around my arm. The bleeding stopped—until the liana broke. I tried again, and the second liana broke.

Finally, only a few feet away, half-hidden by the creeping lianas, I spotted a short length of rope lying on the ground. It was a fragment of an old fishing net, some 18 inches long with a little loop at one end. I passed the free end into the loop, slipped it over my arm and tightened it. Then I took one of the socks, wadded it into a hard ball, and stuffed it beneath the rope where it would press against the brachial artery. As a final touch I wedged a small stick under the rope on the dorsal side of the arm. That slowed the bleeding down to a negligible ooze.

After that vital preliminary had been taken care of, I was able for the first time, using my two sound fingers, to make a systematic survey of the other damage. There was no way of telling how badly my right eye was injured, but the entire right-hand side of my face seemed to be a continuous expanse of burned lacerations. Those wounds had already clotted, but the blood still trickled down from a long, superficial slash on the top of my head that had apparently been made by the detonator. My jaw and neck were both badly torn. A big flap of skin hung down on my collarbone, and the blood from the large, shallow wound seeped down my chest. I tried to push the skin back into place, and it adhered, at least partially.

The rest of my injuries consisted of innumerable minor lacerations that covered my arms and the right side of my chest. The worst damage I had suffered, aside from my missing right hand, was undoubtedly the condition of my left. Only the pinkie and the ring finger were intact. As to the rest, it was possible that I might lose the first three fingers and perhaps the entire hand.

I thought about that for a moment as I watched the water-fowl flying overhead. They were strangely *silent*—and that bothered me. Then, for the first time, I realized that I was almost completely deaf. I had heard the drumlike clack of the crocodiles' jaws, but I couldn't hear the birds, and as I soon found out, I couldn't hear my own voice unless I came close to shouting.

What sort of future lay ahead of me—if I survived? No hands, one eye, deaf and a scarred face—those were the realities and possibilities I had to consider. It was an appalling vision, but still I wanted to live. I wanted to feel things, do things and make things, whatever the difficulty, no matter how demanding or impossible the challenge. So I forced myself to put aside my concern for the future and concentrate on the strange, unlikely present.

The fact that I was still alive was far more than I could have possibly expected. After all, the charge of high-grade dynamite that had exploded in my right hand was capable, if strategically placed, of destroying a 12-story building. It was only the complete instability of my position—standing up in a shaky canoe—that had saved me. Even dynamite has to work against some resistance. Then, after the blast had hurled me into the water, my continued consciousness and endurance were undoubtedly due to my top physical condition. I was big and rugged—six feet, five inches tall and 240 pounds—and I had been toughened by seven arduous years in the Central African bush. I was a hard man to kill, even with dynamite.

Now I knew that I would never be the same man again, but I refused to accept the idea that I might somehow be less. My life was in my own hands—or, rather, in my two unwounded fingers. If I succeeded in accomplishing the impossible—to survive—what obstacles could ever stop me in the future?

With that thought in mind, I struggled to my feet, ready to take the first step in the one-mile walk through the bush toward my waiting pickup. I rose, swayed and nearly fell to the ground, feeling an unbelievable pain and weakness in every part of my body. I closed my eyes for a moment, trying to adjust to the pain. It would have been so terribly easy if I never opened them again. . . .

The walk was interminable. I took step after step after step through a narrow green tunnel of bush that seemed never to change, and every step was a separate act of will, a triumph over my desperately wounded body. A hundred, five hundred, a thousand, two thousand painful steps—and then, with a feeling almost of disbelief, I saw a small patch of light blue up ahead. It was the fender of my truck.

I climbed into the cab, slowly and very awkwardly, and slid behind the familiar steering wheel. It was an immense relief to be off my feet. Now that I had made it to the truck, I felt that the worst physical exertion was behind me. I was filled with new confidence and an even stronger determination to survive. Then I caught sight of myself in the rearview mirror.

A strange and terrible face stared back at me, but I examined it with more curiosity than emotion. The entire right side was encrusted with coagulated blood, and the skin was pocked everywhere with peculiar little holes. The holes contained innumerable splinters of bone, the fragments of my pulverized right hand. The right eye was swollen shut, but at least it appeared to be intact. Both eyebrows were scored with long horizontal cuts: I had inflicted them myself with the naked bones of my arm.

I opened the glove compartment and rummaged through it until I found what I was looking for: a clean handkerchief and a strong rubber band for a new tourniquet. I wrapped the handkerchief carefully around my mutilated wrist and fixed it into place with the elastic, hoping that the cloth might aid in clotting the raw surface of the wound and keeping it as clean as possible. Then, feeling a little better, I decided that I was ready to start out on the three-mile journey to the road—in reverse.

The ignition key was still in the dash, where I'd left it. I turned the key, hit the starter button with the clutch pedal and fed the engine a little gas. It roared into life without hesitation, and I let out a sigh of relief. I put the truck in reverse, reaching around the wheel to pull the gearshift lever into position with my two working fingers. Then, as I started to move backward, I turned my head to the left to check my direction. When I did that, the tortured skin of my throat tore loose again, and I had to stop to tuck it into position. A moment later I was traveling backward, trying to hold my head rigid as I watched the rearview mirror with my left eye.

Three miles in reverse on a dark jungle trail, snaking my way around tree trunks . . . and then there was blue sky and brilliant sunlight. I was back at the dusty road that petered out to the south at the Tanganyika border and led north to the village of the Bagoma fishermen and the tiny trading center of Nyanza-Lac.

I paused for a moment to relieve the pressure of my jury-rigged tourniquet. The handkerchief covering the stump of my wrist swelled up like a blood-red balloon. Then I turned the truck around, excited by the thought that I could at last go forward. I shifted into second, skipping the lowest gear, gathered speed and shoved the lever down into third with my right elbow. The needle reached 50, and I felt better than I had since the moment of the blast. I was finally on my way —but where?

During the 12 miles between Mwekarago Cove and Nyanza-Lac I had to find the answer to that question. My ultimate destination, I knew, had to be the Hôpital Rodhain in Usumbura, the capital of Ruanda-Urundi at the northern tip of Lake Tanganyika. It was the only place where I could find qualified medical aid, the skill both to keep me alive and to save as much of my body as possible—especially my eye and my precious left hand.

But Usumbura lay far to the north, 80 miles from Nyanza-Lac at the end of a road that ran along the eastern shore of Lake Tanganyika. It was a smooth, easy road, but according to the latest official reports I had heard in Kitega, two bridges were down near the Usa end where the road crossed the Ruzibazi and the Karonge rivers. Meanwhile, much farther to the south, between Nyanza-Lac and Mutambara, the territorial public-works department was taking advantage of the fact that no traffic was coming from Usa to repair some shaky wooden bridges of its own.

The only crossing I could really count on was the metallic Bailey bridge over the River Nyengwe, about five miles north of Nyanza-Lac. Beyond that point, the condition of the bridges was pure conjecture.

For that reason the road that ran along the lake was obviously impossible. But the only alternative was a 200-mile circuit that wound through Makamba, Bururi, Ruzira and Kisozi before it finally reached Usumbura. It was almost a scenic railway, with more sharp curves and dangerous escarpments than any other road of comparable length in all of Central Africa.

It started at an altitude of 2531 feet near Lake Tanganyika. Then it swung out in a big arc to the east, climbing almost 1000 feet a mile to a peak of 5578 feet. Then it dived, only to climb again to over 7000 feet at Kitaba. Then it descended to 3000 feet, and after a series of wild undulations it rose to 7240 feet at Majejuru, about 30 miles east of Usa. Then it spiraled down dizzily toward the capital city and Lake Tanganyika nearly 5000 feet below.

There was a serious complication at the summit of Majejuru. After this point the road became so narrow and precipitous that two cars couldn't pass simultaneously. So the next 18 miles, ending at Buhonga, was a "one-way road," sectioned off by a system of barriers. Cars traveling to the west during the evening hours had to reach Majejuru by nine o'clock. At that time, punctually, the barrier was closed and no traffic could pass toward Usumbura until 8:30 the next morning.

The time limit made it a gamble, but the odds were in my favor. Yet, as I forced myself to realize, that serpentine road through 200 miles of mountains was difficult enough for a normal man to negotiate. It was obviously impossible for *me*. I knew that I would have to find help.

I considered the possibilities at Nyanza-Lac, only a few minutes away. There was a Greek trader there who might have been able to drive me, but he was convalescing from a severe illness. His wife, a nervous, haggard woman, would have been worse than useless. The Arab storekeeper, like most of his compatriots, didn't drive. As for the natives, I didn't even have to weigh that possibility before I rejected it. They would react just as my own fishermen and porters had done, with superstitious terror and fear of being involved.

Thus, Nyanza-Lac was out of the question. The nearest place where I could count on finding European aid was the Catholic Mission of the White Fathers at Makamba, 36 miles to the east, at the end of the great escarpment. There was no other alternative; so, when I reached the crossroads a moment later, I turned to the east without hesitation. I would have to chance the escarpment.

It was a wild, crazy and thoroughly hair-raising drive. I steered around those spectacular curves with two fingers, elbows and forearms, trying to make the maximum speed without going over the side. It was extremely painful holding and turning the wheel through all of those sudden changes of direction—but I made it. Then, as I descended to the great grassy plains on the other side of the escarpment, I stopped for a moment to loosen the tourniquet.

Right now, judging from the position of the sun, it must have been around 5:30. I had three and a half hours left to make the nine o'clock barrier at Majejuru, more than a 100 miles ahead. Nine o'clock was literally a deadline as far as I was concerned: Life lay on one side of it and death on the other.

That thought filled me with renewed urgency. I drove the 13 miles to Makamba at top speed. Then, when I reached my destination, turning off into the long driveway that led to a cluster of imposing red brick buildings, I felt almost at peace. Here among the White Fathers I was sure to find someone to take me to Usumbura, to complete successfully the long, arduous drive that a man in my condition could obviously never make.

I pulled to a stop and tried to get out of the truck. It was difficult. I found myself pasted into the driver's seat by a layer of dried blood. I was shocked by the terrible weakness I felt the moment I tried to walk. I leaned against the hood, gasping a little as I tried to overcome the waves of vertigo that threatened to sweep me under. Then a boy came running up, a sturdy little Muhutu native in a dark-blue apron. He stopped short, petrified with fear at the unexpected vision confronting him: a towering white man, nearly naked, atrociously mutilated and crusted from head to foot with coagulated blood.

"Padri iko wapi?" I asked—"Where is the father?"

He swallowed several times. He licked his lips nervously and managed to stammer an answer. The words were inaudible.

"Mi hapana sikia, sema ile tuzamisha," I said anxiously—"I can't hear you. Say it louder!"

"Padri Robert peke yake. Padri ingine yote iko ku safari," the boy repeated—"Father Robert is here alone. The others are all on safari." Then he backed away slowly until he collided with the wall.

I walked over to the massive wooden door of the refectory. I banged on it with the side of my right foot. Nobody answered. I banged again. A moment passed, and a white-robed priest opened the door, a slender man whom I had never seen here before. He stared at me with horror; his eyes widened and his face turned as white as his robe. He tried to speak, but the words never passed his lips. Instead he buckled and slid toward the ground. Instinctively I reached out to catch him with my right hand—and took most of his weight on the stump of my right wrist. The pain was unbelievable. I fought it for a long moment while I nearly bit through my lower lip. Then I poked at the fallen priest and called his name. Again there was no answer.

"Isn't there anyone else here?" I asked the trembling native.

"Hapana! Hapana!"—"No!"

I tried again to revive Father Robert. Then I realized how I was wasting my precious time. Even if he managed to compose himself enough to start out with me, he was obviously nervous and undependable—and probably a bad driver. "Take care of the *padri*," I told the frightened native. "Throw some water on him and he'll wake up. He'll be all right after a while."

The boy said something I couldn't hear, and I walked back to my truck. Each step took enormous, sickening effort, but once again I felt relief the moment I sat down. I loosened the tourniquet while I rested very briefly. Then I drove away at top speed toward the northwest.

Now that Makamba had failed me, I had to try to reach Bururi, my own territorial post, about 40 miles away. This stretch of road was relatively easy, but I felt much weaker since the incident at the mission, and the pain was more difficult to endure.

About 45 minutes later I pulled into Bururi, just as the last remnants of the sunset were fading out of the western sky. I felt tremendously happy when I saw the familiar little government headquarters and the *zamu*—the native night watchman—who was dozing on the front steps. Here in Bururi, there were three people whom I knew I could trust to make the rest of the long drive to Usumbura: either the territorial administrator, the sector veterinarian or Dandier, one of the territorial agents. Any of those three had enough emotional stability to remain calm and dependable and enough driving skill to make the Majejuru barrier by nine.

I stopped the truck in front of the little brick building and called out, very hoarsely, to the sleeping native. He didn't stir. I called out again, and he woke up with a start. He stared at me without comprehension. Then his eyes became almost circular with recognition, astonishment, shock and, above all, fear. A moment later, after an exchange of Swahili questions and answers, I found out that Bururi was just as hopeless as Makamba: The three men I had counted on were away on safari. The only European in the area was the *chef de poste* —a combination bookkeeper and "mayor" of the Bururi headquarters. He was a rookie, newly arrived from Belgium.

I knocked on the door with the side of my foot. After a moment it opened, and I thought at first that the *chef de poste* was about to follow Father Robert's example. He stared, whitened and seemed ready to faint at the sight of me.

Of course, he volunteered to take me to Usumbura, but to his astonishment, I turned him down. A short conversation had confirmed my instinctive decision, especially the fact that he had only recently learned how to drive. I thought of a nervous, newly hatched driver piddling along cautiously toward the nine o'clock barrier at Majejuru and finding it closed.

Before leaving Bururi, I drank five or six glasses of water but refused an offer of cognac. I didn't know exactly how much blood I had lost, but I felt sure that even a small amount of alcohol would have dulled my senses dangerously and weakened my self-control. The water was wonderfully refreshing. I gulped it down quickly, and then I asked for and received three very precious things from the frightened but helpful *chef de poste:* a khaki blanket to drape over my shoulders, a pair of woolen socks for my chilled feet and a cushion to support my back.

When I started my engine again, turned on my headlights and left Bururi, it was a little past seven o'clock. Four hours had passed since the explosion at Mwekarago Cove, and I had less than two hours left to travel some 80 miles to the Majejuru barrier.

Several times I felt myself starting to fall into a stupor. I fought back by singing and reciting classical French poetry. That kept me awake, but it tortured my wounded throat. Soon I was hoarser than ever and inconceivably thirsty. It wasn't only my throat; my whole body seemed to cry out for water with profound physiological urgency. . . .

After more than 70 miles of the thirst, the cold and the never-ending pain, I saw ahead, with a sense of shock, the crossroad that led to the agricultural research station at Kisozi. That meant I was approaching the Kitega-Usumbura fork at Nyakarago, a point that was only ten miles to the nine o'clock barrier.

What time was it now? I had no way of knowing, but it must have been well past 8:30—somehow, I felt sure of it. Perhaps it was already nine. . . . I pushed the throttle down to the floor, and the truck shot forward at 60 miles per hour, a dangerous speed for this type of road. The landscape shot backward in a green haze of banana plantations, and in less than five minutes I saw the Kitega-Usumbura fork loom up ahead.

I slowed down and started to swing into the left turn.

Then, at the last moment, I became aware of a truck on my blind right side—a big truck heavily loaded with produce—that was racing down the road from Kitega. I swung the wheel to the left, missing it by inches. The pickup skidded crazily, and I hung on to the wheel with my two sound fingers, fighting to keep control. I rocketed on the road, skimmed past a huge grevillea tree, ricocheted to the opposite shoulder and finally bounced back onto the road. Miraculously, I was still pointed in the right direction.

My fingers were bleeding badly after that session with the steering wheel, and I was shaken by the close call. But I speeded up again, feeling a strange mixture of relief and anxiety. The fact that a heavily loaded vegetable truck was traveling at that speed meant only one thing: The driver was trying to make the barrier at Majejuru before it closed. It wasn't nine o'clock yet, and I still had a chance to live.

I caught up with him. I hovered at his tail in the cloud of dust from his wheels. I started to pass, and then I fell back—the road at this point was a series of blind curves. I sounded my horn again and again, but the driver of the big truck refused to pull over. There was very little traffic here, but there was still the chance that a car might be coming toward me around the bend. And if I tried for the maximum speed on these curves, I might have trouble holding the road. But the big truck ahead had slowed me down at least 15 or perhaps even 30 miles an hour. That could cost up to five minutes in the race to Majejuru—five minutes that could save my life.

I swung out to the left with my gas pedal down to the floor. But the curve was sharper than I thought. The pickup skidded and nearly went off on the shoulder again. I clawed at the wheel with my bleeding hand and swung back to the right—almost too far. Then the big truck was behind me, and I was headed for Majejuru.

Those last ten miles to the barrier could never have been measured with a clock. I drove through an endless hour of motion that must have lasted only eight or nine minutes. For the first time since the blast I was able to forget completely the pain. All of my conscious thought was fixed on one frightful vision: a native guard placing a heavy padlock on a red-and-white striped wooden arm that stretched across the road. The lock clicked shut, and he mounted his motorcycle to start out on the scheduled inspection tour of the 18-mile strip to Buhonga. Then he disappeared around a big curve, and there was only a massive, unbreakable, striped barrier, locked immovably into place.

If that vision was a true one, I had three alternatives. I could sit in my truck and bleed to death, waiting for the road to open again at 8:30 the next morning. That was unthinkable. Or I could turn around and drive 40 miles to Kitega, which had a small, inadequate hospital, unprepared to deal with my case. Or, as a final possibility, I could set out on a long detour by way of Rubingo. In that case I knew that I would never make it, for two excellent reasons: The pickup was very low on fuel—and so was I.

In reality I had no alternatives. Either I made Majejuru by nine or I died. It was as simple as that.

I covered the remaining distance in an agony of doubt. Then I swung around the last curve and saw the native guard coming down from his hut on the hill, his motorcycle waiting on the shoulder, and the red-and-white arm of the barrier. It was still pointing to heaven. I drove past, stopped about 30 feet beyond, loosened the tourniquet and watched as the khaki-clad native reached the bottom of the hill. The striped wooden arm fell and the padlock clicked into place —behind me.

Now the barrier would remain closed for nearly 12 hours. The vegetable truck would arrive in a few minutes, and the driver would probably explode into angry Swahili curses. It wouldn't do him any good. Had I been too cautious and stayed behind him, I would never have made it.

But, of course, I hadn't made it yet. Usumbura lay ahead, only 30 miles away but 5000 feet below: 5000 feet of curves that spiraled down toward the lake in great looping jug handles and hairpin bends. The road was surfaced with crushed red laterite that made it very easy to slip and careen over the side into the jagged ravines that lay 3000 feet below.

The first 18-mile stretch was the narrow, precipitous and thoroughly notorious one-way road. Many people, including good drivers, were reluctant to cover those 18 incredible miles even after years in Urundi. In the past I had always enjoyed the dangerous trip, the knowledge of my own skill in handling a car or a truck and the wonderful feeling of risk. Now I breathed deeply, feeling my heart pound through all of my wounds, and began the long descent around those hundreds of sickening curves.

With two fingers, with elbows and forearms, I hung on to the wheel, peering through the gathering mist with one eye that was dazed with pain. The mist deepened—or was it the pain?—and I felt myself slipping away, sinking to the bottom of the lake and a beautiful, easy oblivion. The lake? Of course, I was in the lake, and the whole agonizing drive was only a dream. If I closed my eyes, I knew that I would awaken. "I am awake!" I shouted. "I *am* awake! And I won't close my eyes, I swear it!"

I drove on slowly, sick with thirst, cold and pain, fighting my way around mile after mile of curves. Then, gradually, I became aware of a new sensation: I had to urinate. Oddly enough, this single urge strengthened my confidence—it demonstrated that, in spite of all the blood I had lost, urine was still filtering through my kidneys. That proved my blood pressure was still above the critical level beneath which no urine could be produced. The obvious answer to my new problem was to follow my impulse without stopping the truck or to stop and aim at the far corner. But that idea outraged my dignity, and I suppose I felt a certain sense of loyalty to my faithful pickup. It deserved a higher tribute.

I pulled to a stop and eased out of the cab. My blanket flapped a little in the breeze, but I didn't have to hold on to it—it was pasted to my body. Slowly I inched my way toward the rear, holding the side of the truck as I went. That made me angry—I was revolted by my own weakness. I straightened up, removed my hand from the fender and took two steps toward the edge of the escarpment. I paused and surveyed the tremendous gulf. Then, with a gesture that I considered supremely defiant, I made an impressive trajectory that fell over the cliff for at least 2000 feet before, presumably, it splashed on the bottom. Afterward I grinned, staggered back to my truck, hauled myself into the cab and swung down into the next hundred curves.

Steadily, as I drove, I felt myself growing weaker and weaker. I was very close now to the absolute limit of my endurance, but I kept going on, clutching at life with my two fingers. I kept going on. . . . Then, suddenly, a pair of harnessed guib antelope loomed up in my headlights. I braked, stopped and stared at them with a sort of pantheistic emotion.

They were so beautiful, so innocent and so completely unaware of my own agony. They were wonder and youth and, above all, life—everything I was fighting to hold.

They stared back at me with huge, incredulous eyes. Then they leaped to the side and vanished into the bush. I started moving again, but now I felt stronger in spite of my pain and exhaustion. Without conscious volition I started to sing, and the words were those of an old song I had learned as a child in Belgium 20 years before: *"Route fière, De lumière, Route d'effort; Nous te suivrons, Jusqu'à la mort, Sainte route d'effort!"* I sang it again and again. Then I stopped, realizing for the first time the meaning of the words. "We follow you all the way to death. O road of pride and light. . . ."

I was determined that my road wasn't going to end in death, but still I continued to sing those same stubborn words until I reached Buhonga, at the end of the one-way road.

I stopped there for a moment and loosened the tourniquet for the last time. By now the severed ends of the blood vessels had probably clotted, since there was only a brief trickle of blood from my wrist. I felt terribly weak, at the point of fainting, but I forced myself to hold on. At this point I had already descended 4000 feet. Usumbura lay 700 feet below and only 12 miles to the northwest.

Those last 12 miles were an unbroken succession of smooth curves. The road itself was far less dangerous now, but the mist was thicker, and I had to watch for opposing traffic. After four or five miles the mist cleared, and I caught my first glimpse of Usumbura, a shower of golden lights next to the moonlit waves of Lake Tanganyika. It seemed like an impossibly beautiful vision. Then I saw another vision: a gas gauge that registered empty. I was outraged. It would have been too stupid, too meaningless to lose everything now—I refused to believe the possibility existed. I kept my eyes fixed on the road and the glorious lights of Usumbura, trying to ignore the ominous needle that pointed without wavering to the letter *E*.

I drove on, conscious of every tenth of a mile that registered on the speedometer. Then, with a feeling of incredulous relief, I saw the metal bridge that crosses the Muha River at the southern edge of Usumbura. The pickup and I rattled across, and a moment later I made a right turn onto the Avenue de la Limite. That name was wonderfully apt. I was indeed at the limit of my long ordeal through Burundi and, perhaps, at the limit of my life.

I drove half a mile. I turned to the left. I drove another half mile. I stopped the truck in front of the Hôpital Rodhain and turned off the engine. I sat in the cab for a moment staring at the crusted wheel, the dashboard and the streaks of blood on the windshield. I found it almost impossible to believe that the journey had finally come to an end. Then I struggled to get out of the cab and nearly fell to the ground. I swayed and caught the handle of the door with my two good fingers. I stayed there, trembling, trying not to buckle and fall.

The *infirmier de service*—a tall native in a white blouse—saw me standing next to the truck clutching at the door. His jaw dropped, and he started to run toward me. Then he rushed back into the hospital shouting for the doctors and nurses, calling for a *civière*—a light bed on wheels. When I saw him again, he was pushing the wheeled litter—and I was already in the main hall, walking along very slowly but without touching the walls. Something inside me had rebelled at the thought of being carried into the hospital. I wanted to finish my trip the way I'd started it, the way I'd been forced to continue it for eight terrible hours: alone and under my own power.

The tall native caught at my left elbow, trying to help. I pushed him aside gently. "I can walk!"

"Please let me help you!"

"I can walk!"

At that moment the White Sister on night duty came around the bend in the corridor. She stopped short and stared at me speechlessly, shocked by the unexpected vision of a walking dead man. Then she whirled on the native medical assistant. "Why aren't you helping this man?" she cried angrily.

"Leave him alone, Sister. I don't need any help."

She stared at me again with obvious disbelief. "Where did you come from? Who brought you here?"

"Nyanza-Lac. I drove here myself."

"*You drove?* But that's eighty miles!"

"No, two hundred. I came the long way around."

Just as I said that, one of the doctors arrived on the scene. He was successively astonished, clinically curious and extremely concerned. However, I continued to keep walking— under the eyes of a growing crowd and to refuse any aid. I had to do it that way. I was conscious of the strange drama I had lived, and I wanted to play the final scene with style. I'd come 200 miles, and now I was about to take the last steps in my odyssey through Burundi. I was going to take them *myself,* and no one was going to stop me.

I pushed my way through a swinging door into the treatment room, and the doctor moved quickly toward the opposite end, where another door opened into the surgery. He planted himself in front of it with outstretched arms, obviously intent on stopping me from violating the sterile domain. I looked around, resentful but terribly weary, and I saw a high metal bed covered with a clean sheet. I lurched toward it, and with a last dizzying burst of effort I managed to climb up and lie down. Then I closed my eyes and didn't open them again for 48 hours. October 24, 1955, had finally come to an end.

SURVIVAL IN BLACKETT STRAIT

By John Hersey

Survival in Blackett Strait *tells the story of a crucial episode in the life of John F. Kennedy, who, 17 years after these events, became president of the United States. It is a tale of a young man's discovery of his inner funds of resourcefulness, optimism and stamina, and it exemplifies the courage-giving force of a sense of community. Here the community was a small crew, Kennedy's own. As commanding officer of a patrol torpedo boat, he was responsible for the ten of his twelve who survived the precipitating accident, and the extent to which he grasped his duty toward them—so that his thoughts and anxieties and actions were all turned outward from himself—may well have been what saved both him and them.*

It seems that Kennedy's PT, the 109, was out one night with a squadron patrolling Blackett Strait, in mid-Solomons. [It was August 1943.] Blackett Strait is a patch of water bounded on the northeast by the volcano called Kolombangara, on the west by the island of Vella Lavella, on the south by the island of Gizo and a string of coral-fringed islets, and on the east by the bulk of New Georgia. The boats were working about 40 miles away from their base on the island of Rendova, on the south side of New Georgia. They had entered Blackett Strait, as was their habit, through Ferguson Passage, between the coral islets and New Georgia.

The night was a starless black, and Japanese destroyers were around. It was about 2:30. The 109, with three officers and ten enlisted men aboard, was leading three boats on a sweep for a target. An officer named George Ross was up on the bow, magnifying the void with binoculars. Kennedy was at the wheel, and he saw Ross turn and point into the darkness. The man in the forward machine-gun turret shouted,

"Ship at two o'clock!" Kennedy saw a shape and spun the wheel to turn for an attack, but the 109 answered sluggishly. She was running slowly on only one of her three engines, so as to make a minimum wake and avoid detection from the air. The shape became a Japanese destroyer, cutting through the night at 40 knots and heading straight for the 109. The 13 men on the PT hardly had time to brace themselves. Those who saw the Japanese ship coming were paralyzed by fear in a curious way: They could move their hands but not their feet. Kennedy whirled the wheel to the left, but again the 109 did not respond. Ross went through the gallant but futile motions of slamming a shell into the breach of the 37-millimeter antitank gun that had been temporarily mounted that very day, wheels and all, on the foredeck. The urge to bolt and dive over the side was terribly strong, but still no one was able to move; all hands froze to their battle stations. Then the Japanese crashed into the 109 and cut her right in two. The sharp enemy forefoot struck the PT on the starboard side about 15 feet from the bow and crunched diagonally across with a racking noise. The PT's wooden hull hardly even delayed the destroyer. Kennedy was thrown hard to the left in the cockpit, and he thought, "This is how it feels to be killed." In a moment he found himself on his back on the deck looking up at the destroyer as it passed through his boat. There was another loud noise and a huge flash of yellow-red light, and the destroyer glowed. Its peculiar, raked, inverted-Y stack stood out in the brilliant light and, later, in Kennedy's memory.

There was only one man below decks at the moment of collision. That was McMahon, engineer. He had no idea what was up. He was just reaching forward to wrench the starboard engine into gear when a ship came into his engine room. He was lifted from the narrow passage between two of the engines and thrown painfully against the starboard bulkhead aft of the boat's auxiliary generator. He landed in a sitting position. A tremendous burst of flame came back at him from the dayroom, where some of the gas tanks were. He put his hands over his face, drew his legs up tight and waited to die. But he felt water hit him after the fire, and he was sucked far downward as his half of the PT sank. He began to struggle upward through the water. He had held his breath since the impact; so his lungs were tight, and they hurt. He looked up through the water. Over his head he saw a yellow glow—gasoline burning on the water. He broke the surface and was in fire again. He splashed hard to keep a little island of water around him.

Johnston, another engineer, had been asleep on deck when the collision came. It lifted him and dropped him overboard. He saw the flame and the destroyer for a moment. Then a huge propeller pounded by near him, and the awful turbulence of the destroyer's wake took him down, turned him over and over, held him down, shook him and drubbed on his ribs. He hung on and came up in water that was like a river rapids. The next day his body turned black and blue from the beating.

Kennedy's half of the PT stayed afloat. The bulkheads were sealed; so the undamaged watertight compartments up forward kept the half hull floating. The destroyer rushed off into the dark. There was an awful quiet—only the sound of gasoline burning.

Kennedy shouted, "Who's aboard?"

Feeble answers came from three of the enlisted men, McGuire, Mauer and Albert, and from one of the officers, Thom.

Kennedy saw the fire only ten feet from the boat. He thought it might reach her and explode the remaining gas tanks; so he shouted, "Over the side!"

The five men slid into the water. But the wake of the destroyer swept the fire away from the PT; so after a few minutes Kennedy and the others crawled back aboard. Kennedy shouted for survivors in the water. One by one they answered: Ross, the third officer; Harris, McMahon, Johnston, Zinsser, Starkey, enlisted men. Two did not answer: Kirksey and Marney, enlisted men. Since the last bombing at base, Kirksey had been sure he would die. He had huddled at his battle station by the fantail gun with his kapok life jacket tied tight up to his cheeks. No one knows what happened to him or to Marney.

Harris shouted from the darkness, "Mr. Kennedy! Mr. Kennedy! McMahon is badly hurt." Kennedy took his shoes, his shirt and his sidearms off, told Mauer to blink a light so that the men in the water would know where the half hull was, then dived in and swam toward the voice. The survivors were widely scattered. McMahon and Harris were 100 yards away.

When Kennedy reached McMahon, he asked, "How are you, Mac?"

McMahon said, "I'm all right. I'm kind of burnt."

Kennedy shouted out, "How are the others?"

Harris said softly, "I hurt my leg."

Kennedy, who had been on the Harvard swimming team five years before, took McMahon in tow and headed for the PT. A gentle breeze kept blowing the boat away from the swimmers. It took 45 minutes to make what had been an easy hundred yards. On the way in Harris said, "I can't go any farther." Kennedy, of the Boston Kennedys, said to Harris, of the same hometown, "For a guy from Boston, you're certainly putting up a great exhibition out here, Harris." Harris made it all right and didn't complain anymore. Then Kennedy swam from man to man to see how they were doing. All who had survived the crash were able to stay afloat, since they were wearing life preservers—kapok jackets shaped like overstuffed vests, aviators' yellow Mae Wests or air-filled belts like small inner tubes. But those who couldn't swim had to be towed back to the wreckage by those who could. One of the men screamed for help. When Ross reached him, he found that the screaming man had two life jackets on. Johnston was treading water in a film of gasoline that did not catch fire. The fumes filled his lungs, and he fainted. Thom towed him in. The others got in under their own power. It was now about 5:00 A.M. but still dark. It had taken nearly three hours to get everyone aboard.

The men stretched out on the tilted deck of the PT. Johnston, McMahon and Ross collapsed into sleep. The men talked about how wonderful it was to be alive and speculated on when the other PTs would come back to rescue them. Mauer kept blinking the light to point their way. But the other boats had no idea of coming back. They had seen a collision, a sheet of flame and a slow burning on the water. When the skipper of one of the boats saw the sight, he put his hands over his face and sobbed, "My God! My God!" He and the others turned away. Back at the base, after a couple of days, the squadron held services for the souls of the 13 men, and one of the officers wrote his mother, "George Ross lost his life for a cause that he believed in stronger than any one of us, because he was an idealist in the purest sense. Jack Kennedy, the ambassador's son, was on the same boat and also lost his life. The man that said the cream of a nation is lost in war can never be accused of making an overstatement of a very cruel fact. . . ."

When day broke, the men on the remains of the 109 stirred and looked around. To the northeast, three miles off, they saw the monumental cone of Kolombangara; there, the men knew, 10,000 Japanese swarmed. To the west, five miles away, they saw Vella Lavella; more Japs. To the south, only a mile or so away, they actually could see a Japanese camp on Gizo. Kennedy ordered his men to keep as low as possible, so that no moving silhouettes would show against the sky. The listing hulk was gurgling and gradually settling. Kennedy said, "What do you want to do if the Japs come out—fight or surrender?" One said, "Fight with what?" So they took an inventory of their armament. The 37-millimeter gun had flopped over the side and was hanging there by a chain. They had one tommy gun, six 45-caliber automatics and one .38. Not much.

"Well," Kennedy said, "what do you want to do?"

One said, "Anything you say, Mr. Kennedy. You're the boss."

Kennedy said, "There's nothing in the book about a situation like this. Seems to me we're not a military organization anymore. Let's just talk this over."

They talked it over, and pretty soon they argued, and Kennedy could see that they would never survive in anarchy. So he took command again.

It was vital that McMahon and Johnston should have room to lie down. McMahon's face, neck, hands, wrists and feet were horribly burned. Johnston was pale, and he coughed continually. There was scarcely space for everyone; so Kennedy ordered the other men into the water to make room and went in himself. All morning they clung to the hulk and talked about how incredible it was that no one had come to rescue them. All morning they watched for the plane that they thought would be looking for them. They cursed war in general and PTs in particular. At about ten o'clock the hulk heaved a moist sigh and turned turtle. McMahon and Johnston had to hang on as best they could. It was clear that the remains of the 109 would soon sink. When the sun had passed the meridian, Kennedy said, "We will swim to that small island," pointing to one of a group three miles to the southeast. "We have less chance of making it than some of these other islands here, but there'll be less chance of Japs, too." Those who could not swim well grouped themselves around a long two-by-six timber with which carpenters had braced the 37-millimeter cannon on deck and which had been knocked overboard by the force of the collision. They tied several pairs of shoes to the timber, as well as the ship's lantern wrapped in a life jacket to keep it afloat. Thom took charge of this unwieldy group. Kennedy took McMahon in tow again. He cut loose one end of a long strap on McMahon's Mae West and took the end in his teeth. He swam breast stroke, pulling the helpless McMahon along on his back. It took over five hours to reach the island. Water lapped into Kennedy's mouth through his clenched teeth, and he swallowed a lot. The salt water cut into McMahon's awful burns, but he did not complain. Every few minutes, when Kennedy stopped to rest, taking the strap out of his mouth and holding it in his hand, McMahon would simply say, "How far do we have to go?"

Kennedy would reply, "We're going good." Then he would ask, "How do you feel, Mac?"

McMahon always answered, "I'm OK, Mr. Kennedy. How about you?"

In spite of his burden Kennedy beat the other men to the reef that surrounded the island. He left McMahon on the reef and told him to keep low so as not to be spotted by Japs. Kennedy went ahead and explored the island. It was only 100 yards in diameter, coconuts on the trees but none on the ground, no visible Japs. Just as the others reached the island, one of them spotted a Japanese barge chugging along close to shore. They all lay low. The barge went on. Johnston, who was very pale and weak and who was still coughing a lot, said, "They wouldn't come here. What'd they be walking around here for? It's too small." Kennedy lay in some bushes, exhausted by his effort, his stomach heavy with the water he had swallowed. He had been in the sea, except for short intervals on the hulk, for 15½ hours. Now he started thinking. Every night for several nights the PTs had cut through Ferguson Passage on their way to action. Ferguson Passage was just beyond the next little island. Maybe. . . .

He stood up. He took one of the pairs of shoes. He put

one of the rubber life belts around his waist. He hung the .38 around his neck on a lanyard. He took his pants off. He picked up the ship's lantern, a heavy battery affair ten inches by ten inches, still wrapped in the kapok jacket. He said, "If I find a boat, I'll flash the lantern twice. The password will be 'roger,' the answer will be 'wilco.' " He walked toward the water. After 15 paces he was dizzy, but in the water he felt all right.

It was early evening. It took half an hour to swim to the reef around the next island. Just as he planted his feet on the reef, which lay about four feet under the surface, he saw the shape of a very big fish in the clear water. He flashed the light at it and splashed hard. The fish went away. Kennedy remembered what one of his men had said a few days before: "These barracuda will come up under a swimming man and eat his testicles." He had many occasions to think of that remark in the next few hours.

Now it was dark. Kennedy blundered along the uneven reef in water up to his waist. Sometimes he would reach forward with his leg and cut one of his shins or ankles on sharp coral. Other times he would step forward onto emptiness. He made his way like a slow-motion drunk, hugging the lantern. At about nine o'clock he came to the end of the reef, alongside Ferguson Passage. He took his shoes off and tied them to the life jacket, then struck out into open water. He swam about an hour, until he felt he was far enough out to intercept the PTs. Treading water, he listened for the muffled roar of motors, getting chilled, waiting, holding the lamp. Once he looked west and saw flares and the false gaiety of an action. The lights were far beyond the little islands, even beyond Gizo, ten miles away. Kennedy realized that the PT boats had chosen, for the first night in many, to go around Gizo instead of through Ferguson Passage. There was no hope. He started back. He made the same painful promenade of the reef and struck out for the tiny island where his friends were. But this swim was different. He was very tired, and now the current was running fast, carrying him to the right. He saw that he could not make the island; so he flashed the light once and shouted, "Roger! Roger!" to identify himself.

On the beach the men were hopefully vigilant. They saw the light and heard the shouts. They were very happy, because they thought that Kennedy had found a PT. They walked out onto the reef, sometimes up to their waists in water, and waited. It was very painful for those who had no shoes. The men shouted but not much, because they were afraid of Japanese.

One said, "There's another flash."

A few minutes later a second said, "There's a light over there."

A third said, "We're seeing things in this dark."

They waited a long time, but they saw nothing except phosphorescence and heard nothing but the sound of waves. They went back, very discouraged.

One said despairingly, "We're going to die."

Johnston said, "Aw, shut up. You can't die. Only the good die young."

Kennedy had drifted right by the little island. He thought he had never known such deep trouble, but something he did shows that unconsciously he had not given up hope. He dropped his shoes, but he held on to the heavy lantern, his symbol of contact with his fellows. He stopped trying to swim. He seemed to stop caring. His body drifted through the wet hours, and he was very cold. His mind was a jumble. A few hours before, he had wanted desperately to get to the base at Rendova. Now he only wanted to get back to the little island he had left that night, but he didn't try to get there; he just wanted to. His mind seemed to float away from his body. Darkness and time took the place of a mind in his skull. For a long time he slept or was crazy or floated in a chill trance.

The currents of the Solomon Islands are queer. The tide shoves and sucks through the islands and makes the currents curl in odd patterns. It was a fateful pattern into which Jack Kennedy drifted. He drifted in it all night. His mind was blank, but his fist was tightly clenched on the kapok around the lantern. The current moved in a huge circle—west past Gizo, then north and east past Kolombangara, then south into Ferguson Passage. Early in the morning the sky turned from black to gray, and so did Kennedy's mind. Light came to both at about six. Kennedy looked around and saw that he was exactly where he had been the night before when he saw the flares beyond Gizo. For a second time he started home. He thought for a while that he had lost his mind and that he only imagined that he was repeating his attempt to reach the island. But the chill of the water was real enough, the lantern was real, his progress was measurable. He made the reef, crossed the lagoon and got to the first island. He lay on the beach awhile. He found that his lantern did not work anymore; so he left and started back to the next island, where his men were. This time the trip along the reef was awful. He had discarded his shoes, and every step on the coral was painful. This time the swim across the gap where the current had caught him the night before seemed endless. But the current had changed; he made the island. He crawled up on the beach. He was vomiting when his men came up to him. He said, "Ross, you try it tonight." Then he passed out.

Ross, seeing Kennedy so sick, did not look forward to the execution of the order. He distracted himself by complaining about his hunger. There were a few coconuts on the trees, but the men were too weak to climb up for them. One of the men thought of seafood, stirred his tired body and found a snail on the beach. He said, "If we were desperate, we could eat these." Ross said, "Desperate, hell. Give me that. I'll eat that." He took it in his hand and looked at it. The snail put its head out and looked at him. Ross was startled, but he shelled the snail and ate it, making faces because it was bitter.

In the afternoon Ross swam across to the next island. He took a pistol to signal with, and he spent the night watching Ferguson Passage from the reef around the island. Nothing came through. Kennedy slept badly that night; he was cold and sick.

The next morning everyone felt wretched. Planes that the men were unable to identify flew overhead, and there were dogfights. That meant Japs as well as friends; so the men dragged themselves into the bushes and lay low. Some prayed. Johnston said, "You guys make me sore. You didn't spend ten cents in church in ten years; then all of a sudden you're in trouble and you see the light." Kennedy felt a little better now. When Ross came back, Kennedy decided that the group should move to another, larger island to the southeast, where there seemed to be more coconut trees and where the party would be nearer Ferguson Passage. Again Kennedy took McMahon in tow with the strap in his teeth, and the nine others grouped themselves around the timber.

This swim took three hours. The nine around the timber were caught by the current and barely made the far tip of the island. Kennedy found walking the quarter mile across to them much harder than the three-hour swim. The cuts on his bare feet were festered and looked like small balloons. The men were suffering most from thirst, and they broke open some coconuts lying on the ground and avidly drank the milk. Kennedy and McMahon, the first to drink, were sickened, and Thom told the others to drink sparingly. In the middle of the night it rained, and someone suggested moving into the underbrush and licking water off the leaves. Ross and McMahon kept contact at first by touching feet as they licked. Somehow they got separated, and, being uncertain whether there were any Japs on the island, they became frightened. McMahon, trying to make his way back to the beach, bumped into someone and froze. It turned out to be Johnston, licking leaves on his own. In the morning the group saw that all the leaves were covered with droppings. Bitterly, they named the place Bird Island.

On this fourth day the men were low. Even Johnston was low. He had changed his mind about praying. McGuire had a rosary around his neck, and Johnston said, "McGuire, give that necklace a working over." McGuire said quietly, "Yes, I'll take care of all you fellows." Kennedy was still unwilling to admit that things were hopeless. He asked Ross if he would swim with him to an island called Nauru, to the southeast and even nearer Ferguson Passage. They were very weak indeed by now, but after an hour's swim they made it.

They walked painfully across Nauru to the Ferguson Passage side, where they saw a Japanese barge aground on the reef. There were two men by the barge—possibly Japs. They apparently spotted Kennedy and Ross, for they got into a dugout canoe and hurriedly paddled to the other side of the island. Kennedy and Ross moved up the beach. They came upon an unopened rope-bound box and, back in the trees, a little shelter containing a keg of water, a Japanese gas mask and a crude wooden fetish shaped like a fish. There were Japanese hardtack and candy in the box, and the two had a wary feast. Down by the water they found a one-man canoe. They hid from imagined Japs all day. When night fell, Kennedy left Ross and took the canoe, with some hardtack and a can of water from the keg, out into Ferguson Passage. But no PTs came; so he paddled to Bird Island. The men there told him that the two men he had spotted by the barge that morning were natives, who had paddled to Bird Island. The natives had said that there were Japs on Nauru, and the men had given Kennedy and Ross up for lost. Then the natives had gone away. Kennedy gave out small rations of crackers and water, and the men went to sleep. During the night one man, who kept himself awake until the rest were asleep, drank all the water in the can Kennedy had brought back. In the morning the others figured out who was the guilty one. They swore at him and found it hard to forgive him.

Before dawn Kennedy started out in the canoe to rejoin Ross on Nauru, but when day broke, a wind arose and the canoe was swamped. Some natives appeared from nowhere in a canoe, rescued Kennedy and took him to Nauru. There they showed him where a two-man canoe was cached. Kennedy picked up a coconut with a smooth shell and scratched a message on it with a jackknife: "ELEVEN ALIVE NATIVE KNOWS POSIT AND REEFS NAURU ISLAND KENNEDY." Then he said to the natives, "Rendova, Rendova."

One of the natives seemed to understand. They took the coconut and paddled off.

Ross and Kennedy lay in a sickly daze all day. Toward evening it rained, and they crawled under a bush. When it got dark, conscience took hold of Kennedy, and he persuaded Ross to go out into Ferguson Passage with him in the two-man canoe. Ross argued against it. Kennedy insisted. The two started out in the canoe. They had shaped paddles from the boards of the Japanese box, and they took a coconut shell to bail with. As they got out into the passage, the wind rose again, and the water became choppy. The canoe began to fill. Ross bailed and Kennedy kept the bow into the wind. The waves grew until they were five or six feet high. Kennedy shouted, "Better turn around and go back!" As soon as the canoe was broadside to the waves, the water poured in, and the dugout was swamped. The two clung to it, Kennedy at the bow, Ross at the stern. The tide carried them southward toward the open sea; so they kicked and tugged the canoe, aiming northwest. They struggled that way for two hours, not knowing whether they would hit the small island or drift into the endless open.

The weather got worse; rain poured down, and they couldn't see more than ten feet. Kennedy shouted, "Sorry I got you out here, Barney!" Ross shouted back, "This would be a great time to say I told you so, but I won't!"

Soon the two could see a white line ahead and could hear a frightening roar—waves crashing on a reef. They had got out of the tidal current and were approaching the island, all right, but now they realized that the wind and the waves were carrying them toward the reef. But it was too late to do anything, now that their canoe was swamped, except hang on and wait.

When they were near the reef, a wave broke Kennedy's hold, ripped him away from the canoe, turned him head over heels and spun him in a violent rush. His ears roared and his eyes pinwheeled, and for the third time since the collision he thought he was dying. Somehow he was not thrown against the coral but floated into a kind of eddy. Suddenly he felt the reef under his feet. Steadying himself so that he would not be swept off it, he shouted, "Barney!" There was no reply. Kennedy thought of how he had insisted on going out in the canoe, and he screamed, "Barney!" This time Ross answered. He, too, had been thrown on the reef. He had not been as lucky as Kennedy; his right arm and shoulder had been cruelly lacerated by the coral, and his feet, which were already infected from earlier wounds, were cut some more.

The procession of Kennedy and Ross from reef to beach was a crazy one. Ross's feet hurt so much that Kennedy would hold one paddle on the bottom while Ross put a foot on it, then the other paddle forward for another step, then the first paddle forward again, until they reached sand. They fell on the beach and slept.

Kennedy and Ross were wakened early in the morning by a noise. They looked up and saw four husky natives. One walked up to them and said in an excellent English accent, "I have a letter for you, sir." Kennedy tore the note open. It said, "On His Majesty's Service. To the Senior Officer, Nauru Island. I have just learned of your presence on Nauru Is. I am in command of a New Zealand infantry patrol operating in conjunction with U.S. Army troops on New Georgia. I strongly advise that you come with these natives to me. Meanwhile I shall be in radio communication with your authorities at Rendova, and we can finalize plans to collect balance of your party. Lt. Wincote. P.S. Will warn aviation of your crossing Ferguson Passage." [1]

Everyone shook hands, and the four natives took Ross and Kennedy in their war canoe across to Bird Island to tell the others the good news. There the natives broke out a spirit stove and cooked a feast of yams and C ration. Then they built a lean-to for McMahon, whose burns had begun to rot and stink, and for Ross, whose arm had swelled to the size of a thigh because of the coral cuts. The natives put Kennedy in the bottom of their canoe and covered him with sacking and palm fronds in case Japanese planes should buzz them. The long trip was fun for the natives. They stopped once to try to grab a turtle and laughed at the sport they were having. Thirty Japanese planes went over low toward Rendova, and the natives waved and shouted gaily. They rowed with a strange rhythm, pounding paddles on the gunwales between strokes. At last they reached a censored place. Lieutenant Wincote came to the water's edge and said formally, "How do you do. Leftenant Wincote."

Kennedy said, "Hello. I'm Kennedy."

Wincote said, "Come up to my tent and have a cup of tea."

In the middle of the night, after several radio conversations between Wincote's outfit and the PT base, Kennedy sat in the war canoe waiting at an arranged rendezvous for a PT. The moon went down at 11:20. Shortly afterward Kennedy heard the signal he was waiting for—four shots. Kennedy fired four answering shots.

A voice shouted to him, "Hey, Jack!"

Kennedy said, "Where the hell you been?"

The voice said, "We got some food for you."

Kennedy said bitterly, "No, thanks, I just had a coconut."

A moment later a PT came alongside. Kennedy jumped

[1] The wording and signature of this message are as Kennedy gave them to me in Boston in 1944. The message was in fact slightly, though not substantially, different, and many years later, after Kennedy had become president, the identity of the actual signer was uncovered—A. Reginald Evans. Wherever the name Wincote appears in the rest of this story, the reader will understand that that of Lieutenant Evans should be substituted.

onto it and hugged the men aboard——his friends. In the American tradition, Kennedy held under his arm a couple of souvenirs: one of the improvised paddles and the Japanese gas mask.

With the help of the natives, the PT made its way to Bird Island. A skiff went in and picked up the men. In the deep of the night the PT and its happy cargo roared back toward base. The squadron medic had sent some brandy along to revive the weakened men. Johnston felt the need of a little revival. In fact, he felt he needed quite a bit of revival. After care of that he retired topside and sat with his arms around a couple of roly-poly, mission-trained natives. And in the fresh breeze on the way home they sang together a hymn all three happened to know:

> Jesus loves me, this I know,
> For the Bible tells me so;
> Little ones to him belong,
> They are weak, but He is strong.
> Yes, Jesus loves me; yes, Jesus loves me. . . .

A HOLE IN THE CLOUDS

By Ernest K. Gann

Ernest K. Gann is a pilot who has written extensively of his experiences in the air. This episode details one of his more harrowing moments while trying to fly a four-engine C-54 cargo plane from Newfoundland to Scotland just after World War Two. First the hydraulic system controlling the flaps and landing gear went out. Then a fire started in the cargo bin. Finally the weather closed in. The crew's chances of getting back to earth safely were rapidly diminishing. . . .

To suggest, even by inference, that captains should be given sole credit for moving a multiengine airplane from one place to another would be the ultimate in strutting dishonesty. Each man in the crew has his manifold duties, and unless he performs them well, the captain is sorely tried.

A captain of any aircraft was, and is, exactly what the ancient and honorable term has always defined. Regardless of the circumstances, regardless of whatever human temptations may invite this man to shift or even share blame and responsibility, he must refuse them. Otherwise he is a man moving in hypocrisy, thieving the respect with which he so freely adorns himself and betraying the very basis of the faith which is always offered to him.

It is a rare captain who is not heavily conscious of his duty; even the most lighthearted recognize that theirs is a special appointment and jealously guard the tradition that whatever misfortune occurs on any flight is fundamentally their fault.

Even so, this maxim has been twice denied. In the one case it was sheer deception bordering on insanity, and in the other an incredible and shameful attempt to shift the blame for a disaster upon others of the crew. The eventual results were satisfying to those who felt obligated to live and fly by the code. Mercy had no place in our thinking, because it has no place in such a potentially lethal instrument as an airplane. The first man died in disgrace and by his own hand, and the second was repudiated forever, through permanent loss of his license.

As the C-54s became more abundant and the whole enterprise of flying the oceans matured, the stature and line of command became ever more pronounced. A good crew was treasured by any captain, and each did his utmost to assemble a group of aides whom he could trust. There was open competition for skillful copilots, navigators who could work with accuracy and calm, radio operators who would stay alert through a long flight and engineers who would turn the proper valves at the right time. In this internecine and sometimes amusingly petty warfare the seniority numbers played no part. The most junior captain was entitled to connive, cajole and maneuver at will in capturing the best of men.

For various reasons there were always substitutions in any crew and inevitably a certain amount of subtle trading. Captains and crew members tried to achieve what they hoped would become the ideal unit. However, it was sometimes possible for crews to stay together for long periods of time. The result was that a navigator was known as one of so-and-so's crew or a copilot as having been long with so-and-so. They were accordingly either envied or pitied.

On our line Robbins was still charged with this sort of thing and, in the process of making his constant deals of assignment, lost even more of his hair. I continued to seek his counsel and shrewd aid, contriving by flattery, which he saw through instantly, and pleas, which he professed touched him deeply, to gather and hold excellent men. Thus, the only crew member of whom I ever had true complaint was the hapless copilot on the flight to China.

My usual comrades aloft were such men as Robertson, who soon became as trustworthy a copilot as Johnson had been.

Robertson was an extraordinarily powerful and darkly handsome man. His features were classic Greek in line and his forbearance almost unbelievable. He patiently tolerated a continuous needling from all of us on the subject of his masculine beauty and never mentioned that should we prod him too hard, he could have easily broken any one of us into small pieces. In contrast to his physique, his voice was soft and melodious.

And there was LaFrenier, who became one of the finest and most versatile navigators I would ever know. Perhaps it was because of Robertson's muscular presence that LaFrenier seemed frail, but he was in fact a slight man with strangely delicate hands. He was cheerful almost to the point of exasperation, and if he was not whistling merrily, he was singing popular songs—the saccharine lyrics of which he was devoted to memorizing. He was never discouraged by our sour reception of his efforts when he persisted in whistling through a thunderstorm or sang through a blizzard at four o'clock in the morning. LaFrenier was nearly fearless and in several situations displayed an *élan* and faith in our continued future that was heartening to behold. He was a devout Catholic, observing all the rites of that demanding religion. We all envied him a little in his unswerving belief.

To my regret, Summers, the radio operator, had somehow been stolen or lured away during one of the many shifts of scene. He was eventually replaced by Bradford, who was equally proficient with his key. Bradford was a big man, often silent for extended periods. But, then, he was in love, and we knew he was in love and did not cease our chiding of him until he finally married the girl.

Our flight engineers were more difficult to keep in the family, and so we were never able to know them well. They would make one flight and then perhaps another, after which they would be gone. Millington was an exception and somehow managed to stay with us for many flights. He was even darker of complexion than Robertson, enthusiastic and ambitious—and, more important, possessed a thorough mechanical knowledge of the airplane.

Every crew, eating together, sleeping within a few feet of each other and flying together, naturally developed certain special methods and customs within their family unit. These were the trifles and rather pathetic little trimmings that eased friction between those compelled to live so closely. They offered amusement when physical weariness and the instinctive urges for a more stable existence disturbed us. One crew disdained the tedious box lunches normally furnished on flights and carried a special commissary bag in which they stored whatever delicacies they could buy or steal. The engineer made an ingenious stove that could be plugged into the airplane's electric system, and while others breakfasted on limp sandwiches, the members of this crew enjoyed ham and eggs, hot rolls and really fresh coffee. In our envy we developed a new hatred for their cleverness.

Our own crew was more given to personal eccentricities. Perhaps LaFrenier sang so lustily because he had survived 63 flights across the Hump in C-87s, which was reason enough. Bradford was a storehouse of cookies, always replenished on those occasions when he returned to his love. He was generous but also a careful rationer, so that the supply often lasted two weeks. The crumbs mixed nicely with the droppings of the cigarettes that I now affected to roll by hand.

Our pretakeoff ceremonies had become rather elaborate and were strictly observed. A movie star of great natural beauty had presented us with her photo, on which she had written sentimentally of her desire for our safety and well-being. As we started the engines, LaFrenier would thumbtack the photo above his navigation table and carefully adjust the nearest flight-deck light so that the picture would be advantageously illuminated. A chance meeting with a great theatrical personality had produced a black garter, having upon it a colorful rosette. This, Robertson would solemnly hang on the knob that was normally used to set one of our horizon instruments. At the end of the runway, when all of this nonsense was done and the engines had been checked, I would take the concertina from beside my left foot and quickly render "You take the high road. . . ." It made no difference that LaFrenier might be singing some other tune at the same time. The sound of the engines mercifully subdued everything.

It was after such embellishments to our technical preparations that we were ready for takeoff from Stevensville, Newfoundland, on a gloomy August morning. We were all in excellent humor in spite of a certain strangeness created by the absence of two of our regular family members. Ditmeyer sat at Bradford's place behind the radio, and Braseman had taken over as engineer. We had slept well, the weather forecast for our arrival time in Scotland was encouraging, and the winds throughout the flight were predicted as most favorable.

Hence the rotten weather at Stevensville itself could not depress us. The cloud ceiling was a bare 400 feet, and the visibility somewhat less than a mile in the intermittent rain squalls that were typical of the season. We knew that we would leave all of this behind in an hour or two, because the condition did not extend far over the ocean. We did not know that in a much shorter time we might question the authority of those little trophies now set up as household gods.

Stevensville airport is situated at the end of a long, finger-like bay that is confined between a considerable peninsula of rolling hills and a wide arm of the Newfoundland mainland. The barren hills on both sides of the bay are of like design but somewhat higher to the east. The bay extends in a northerly direction for several miles, where it is eventually cut off by the land. Here, at first, the upward slope is gentle from the shore, so that an airport could be built. The whole establishment tilts toward the sea, and the runways at their northern ends are higher than their southern extremities. Because the normal approach to the airport is from the bay, this lack of plumb is more aid than handicap to aircraft. Beyond the fringes of the airport the rock-speckled hills rise abruptly and finally achieve the full dignity of mountains.

These mountains extend toward the north and east and after a time diminish gradually until they melt into the glacial terrain that prevails to the coastline. Because of the mountains the minimum instrument-flight altitude in the vicinity of Stevensville is 6000 feet. And descent below that altitude must be accomplished when the pilots can see, unless they are actually flying the approach leg over the bay.

This did not concern us. We were bound for Scotland and had no intention of returning to Stevensville. There were 34 military passengers sitting on bucket seats in the cabin.

We took off in a squall, and the rain instantly found its way through the framing of the windshield and dribbled on my left knee. We plunged into the solid overcast only a moment after we left the ground. I was at once much occupied with the flight instruments and trying to kick my concertina box to a dry place beside the rudder pedals. I could hear LaFrenier singing of some unrequited love and knew that his vocalizing was only an accompaniment to his recording of our takeoff time, course and the laying out of his charts and graphs. Robertson nursed the throttles with his big hands, keeping the engines at proper climb power. Braseman, the engineer, eased the flaps up a few degrees at a time. Thus all was pleasantly normal, and the whine of the Stevensville radio range faded rapidly in my earphones. We were on our way, another morning, another flight over the ocean, another entry in our logbooks.

The airplane was new and climbed well, so that proceeding upward through the heavy overcast became an exhilarating business. Like any craftsman whose tools seem to have a sharper edge than usual, I indulged in a certain smugness and self-appreciation—in this event because I could so casually hold exact course and rate of ascent when the visibility was nil. I could even feign temperament, using the dribbling rivulet of rain as a foil and cocking half around in my seat to escape it.

After a little time I noticed that Braseman had not yet settled down to his bookwork of recording engine temperatures and pressures. Instead he was tinkering with the lever controlling the hydraulic system. The lever was on the floor beside Robertson's seat and could be pulled up and back by inserting two fingers in the faceplate. I glanced at Braseman.

"What's going on?"

"I don't know. I can't budge it."

"Let Robertson try."

Braseman relinquished his grip and stood back.

Robertson placed his fingers in the hole and heaved until his face flushed. We laughed at his mighty struggles, because the relatively weak must always relish the physical defeat of the very strong. But soon our laughter subsided. If the lever could not be moved, the entire hydraulic system that controlled the raising and lowering of the flaps and landing gear must remain in continuous operation until the engines were shut down. The hydraulic oil would circulate all through the maze of piping at high speed and under great pressure. We were not certain if this was bad, but since it was abnormal, we were reasonably sure it was not the best way to start out on a long flight.

"Maybe if we put the flaps down and then bring them up again, it will help. The pressure should be released long enough. . . ."

We put the flaps down and brought them up again. Neither Robertson nor Braseman could move the lever.

"Let's try putting the gear down and then retracting."

I resented these diversions, because they would interrupt

the smoothness of my flying, but we put the gear down and brought it up again. In spite of our combined efforts, the lever remained flush with the floor.

LaFrenier stopped singing.

We were 11 minutes out of Stevensville and had just reached 7000 feet, which was to be our cruising altitude. A bitterness had stained the morning. As I leveled out and settled the plane on course, it seemed to me that a flying man had enough to do without concerning himself with a complicated mess of hydraulics. Well enough, I thought, to understand its principles, but the intricacies of valves, poppets, pipes should be classed as *et cetera*. My business was to set the plane smoothly and surely on the west leg of the Gander Range as soon as it could be heard and thus send us nicely on a fixed departure from shore. Yet secretly, guiltily, I knew that the hydraulic system was also my business, and I should be able to correct the fault.

I tried to recall what I had learned about hydraulics in Lester's school, but the fragments of ignorance outweighed those of knowledge, and I could not think of a thing to do other than what we had already done. I fell back on reasoning that Braseman was the engineer and would eventually come up with the solution. Meanwhile the intensity of the rain had increased, which brought on so much static I could not surely identify the signals of Gander Range.

LaFrenier started singing again.

Robertson glared at the lever, gave a final hopeless tug and then appeared to forget about it. We passed out of the squall, and I was pleased to see the needle on the direction finder swing around on the Gander signal and point straight ahead. Now, if Braseman would only fix the confounded hydraulic system, we should be well on our way.

Where *was* Braseman? I suddenly realized that he was gone and had been absent for several minutes. I glanced over my right shoulder, intending to say something about first things first if he was back in the crew compartment having a cup of coffee. Braseman?

In turning, my eye caught a dull red glow at the top of the instrument panel. I forgot about Braseman momentarily. Now one of the fire warning lights was misbehaving, which was so common an occurrence in a C-54 that we had all long lost faith in their dire reports. They were small red glass boxes behind which a bulb was supposed to light up if a fire developed in any of the engines or various compartments in the airplane. But they cried wolf too often. Some malfunctioning, which the engineers had so far been unable to correct, caused them to light up across the instrument panel like a crazy pinball machine and sometimes report fires in all four engines when absolutely nothing was wrong. Occasionally the lights would flicker and then go out, or they might remain on for hours—in which case we would remove the bulbs to avoid the glare. We were certain our senses, supplemented by the regular engine instruments, would inform us of any fires quite soon enough.

But this red light was marked "B," which meant that the alleged fire was in the cargo bin beneath the floor of the crew compartment. Robertson frowned at the light and said, "Now, what. . . ."

I was disgusted. Where was Braseman, and what about the hydraulic system? Then I remembered that a considerable assembly of the system was located in cargo bin B. Perhaps if Braseman was down there working, he might have bumped against the heat-sensitive switch and somehow set off the warning light.

I had just resolved to turn the flying over to Robertson and investigate when Braseman came running forward.

"There's a hell of a lot of smoke back in the passenger cabin! And it's starting to come up through the floor in the crew compartment! I think we'd better——"

Whatever it was that Braseman thought was lost upon us, for he brought smoke with him like a devil's veil. But it was thin smoke still, and I believed Braseman must be exaggerating—until I turned in my seat to look back at the crew compartment. LaFrenier had pulled back the curtain. Smoke, becoming heavier by the moment, gushed into the flight deck.

And fright took instant command of us all.

Braseman was tugging at the hydraulic control lever. "We've got to stop it working. . . ."

I saw the fire signal light marked "B." It was now a bright red. I pulled the extinguisher lever, which would flood the compartment with CO_2. The red light continued to burn and, if anything, the smoke seemed to become heavier.

Fright alone instructed me. I put the ship in a tight left bank, holding it until our course was reversed and we were headed back for Stevensville.

"Ditmeyer! Get an emergency clearance. Six thousand. Returning Stevensville."

LaFrenier called to me. "Twenty minutes back to Stevensville!" His voice was unnatural in its gravity, but then he had the wit to add a refinement: "Twenty minutes . . . *mais ou menos!*"

Mais ou menos—an old Natal way of expressing almost anything in doubt, from the price of mosquito boots to hopes of transfer. LaFrenier said it exactly right, as if he really didn't care.

The smoke was thickening but was still no worse than in a crowded barroom. Now it had taken on a faintly acrid smell.

Braseman and Robertson were alternately tugging at the hydraulic lever. There were many profanities.

I saw the hydraulic pressure gauge beyond Robertson's right arm. It read 3700 pounds! Something was going to give.

Twenty minutes—nineteen, maybe eighteen now.

We were on instruments. We could not descend, because of the terrain. This was suddenly the slowest airplane in the world.

I cranked Stevensville on the direction finder. The needle swung around and held steadily. I saw my hand tremble when I took it away from the instrument. Where the hell was our clearance?

Ditmeyer seized the back of my seat and pulled himself forward.

"Cleared to cruise six thousand. Stevensville weather, three hundred feet variable . . . one mile . . . light rain . . . field closed."

I saw the field in my mind too clearly. It would be exactly as when we had left, with the lower cloud base enveloping the rock hills and the runway ends dissolving into vapor. We would have to go through a long approach procedure—out over the western peninsula, turn and back up the bay, thence creeping toward the sea edge of the field. Allow eight minutes as a minimum for the whole business. Eight minutes' more pressure to build and a fire to smolder.

"Braseman, lift the hatch. See if the fire is out."

He went back to the crew compartment. LaFrenier held the curtain aside. We watched Braseman pry at the hatch in the floor. He raised it an inch or so and slammed it shut again. Smoke spewed up at him. He began a fit of coughing.

LaFrenier, pray in your special way. Pray hard, if you will.

Now the smoke rushed forward. My whole body began to shake. My feet would not stay still on the rudder pedals. I coughed to conceal my trembling. My thoughts were a wild, whirling mixture of frantic possibilities and technical demands. Should I chance a descent, hoping we might find a break down below? Land wheels up along the side of a hill or perhaps in a swamp? Suicide. Not a chance in a million. But anything was better than fire in the air.

Fright had passed. Fear, true fear, now possessed me. I felt it throughout my body like a devouring ague, and I saw myself beginning to flounder, as if I were utterly detached. Our altitude had slipped 200 feet. We were 15 degrees off course. I thought I heard the others talking, or perhaps they were shouting. Their voices were without intelligence—mere sounds in the smoke.

It was suddenly much thicker. We were all coughing, and our eyes wept. I could no longer see the instruments clearly or even Robertson, who sat so near. . . .

I yanked open my side window. Doing so would create a draft in the ship, I knew, but we had to see and breathe. Smoke rushed past my face, and my eyes protested. After a moment I closed the window.

Twelve minutes to go.

Looking at the red light, Braseman asked me if he should shoot some carbon tetrachloride into compartment B, since the CO_2 had apparently failed. I rejected the idea, fearing the creation of poison gas.

Robertson opened his window, breathed deeply and shut it again.

The army sergeant in charge of the cabin appeared at my side. I asked him how the passengers were behaving.

"They're scared. What shall I tell them?"

"Anything."

Nine minutes.

I asked LaFrenier if he was certain of his estimate.

"Mais ou menos. . . ."

Stalwart LaFrenier.

We could no longer tell if the smoke was getting better or worse. We endured it as long as we could and then opened the windows just long enough for quick relief. We were drowning in smoke, but so far there was no flame visible.

I tried to visualize compartment B. It could be entered from the belly of the ship, which was impossible in flight, or it could be entered through the floor hatch, which now seemed quite as impossible. The compartment was not very large and was used for stowing either cargo or baggage. It seemed an unlikely place for a fire.

Six minutes. The direction-finder needle was steady now. When it began quivering, we should be almost over the Stevensville range station. Six minutes, and add eight more for the approach. I knew the last eight were going to be very long minutes.

My intestines were seething. For a moment I thought I would soil my pants.

I forced myself to explore B compartment again mentally. There was a mess of hydraulic pipes running through it. Because we could not disengage the system, the oil would be passing through the pipes at tremendous speed and under increasingly greater pressure. The result would be heat— also of increasing intensity. There was a blockade somewhere. A very small poppet valve could set us aflame.

The compartment was lined with a heavy cloth padding. The pipes ran between the padding and the aluminum skin of the ship. If the overheated pipes set the padding afire, then the skin would go next. And aluminum burned like a torch.

How silly to die because of a bit of metal I could hold in the palm of my hand.

Time could be our final enemy on this morning. How long did it take a smoldering piece of cloth to ignite and serve as kindling for aluminum? Two minutes? Ten minutes?

There was a hand bottle of CO_2 hanging between the crew bunks. I told Braseman to pry up the hatch again and shoot the contents into B compartment until the bottle was exhausted.

When he had done this, the smoke became unbearable. Yet if we opened the windows, a terrific draft would be created.

We needed three more minutes to the range station and then those eight for an approach. I resolved to cut some corners and make the approach in four.

We coughed, sucked at our cupped hands and writhed in our seats.

Robertson had the sense to clamp on his oxygen mask.

I imitated him at once, pressing the mask hard against my face. The result was extremely painful. Somehow the smoke seemed more concentrated in the mask. Two daggers probed my nostrils. I threw the mask on the floor.

Robertson and Braseman had abandoned their efforts with the control lever. I could not blame them. Physical effort was intolerable with suffocation so near.

But I *had* to concentrate. Ross was holding the match.

The direction-finder needle began to quiver. Even our gasping subsided. We lived on little half breaths.

Now, at best, another minute.

A spasm of rain lashed the windshield, and we passed into moderate turbulence. I wanted very much to hit the range station exactly. It was very important.

The turbulence ceased, and suddenly a lightening in the overcast caused me to glance out my side window. And that instant I believed in miracles, for there was a hole in the overcast that shafted almost straight down. And at the bottom of the hole I saw the crisscross design of the Stevensville runways. The hole was of no greater dimensions than our wingspread, and optics caused it to appear even smaller at the bottom. But there, 6000 feet below, was our salvation.

Under ordinary circumstances I should have ignored such a sucker hole. They were snares for the foolish. The hole could close as quickly as it had opened. If we were caught circling blind between the rock hills, we would be in an even worse situation.

I had only a few seconds to accept or reject the invitation. I saw it as an offering of time.

So I impulsively chopped the throttles full back, wrapped the ship in a near-vertical bank and tried to stay within the vaporous confines of the hole. I yelled at Robertson to slam the landing gear down and shoved the nose over in a steep dive. It was a crazy maneuver in a big, heavily loaded four-engine airplane. Such violent acrobatics belonged in an air circus, but we needed minutes.

We spiraled down in a near-vertical bank. Our high right wing sliced continuously through the walls of the hole. But I could see from my side—straight down. And the crisscross pattern of the runways revolved like the spokes of a slow-turning wheel.

The only sound was the erratic backfiring of our engines

and the rumbling of our slipstream. Somehow our steep angle of attack seemed to reduce the smoke. I could see that the runways were wet with rain.

Robertson called for an immediate clearance to land.

We were descending at 2000 feet per minute. The airplane was extremely stiff on the controls; yet it behaved like a fighter. I renewed my love affair with Douglas airplanes though a two-headed monster now arrived on the scene.

We could not use any power and stay within the confines of the hole. The engines were cooling far below prescribed limits. We could only hope they would catch again and give us power when most needed.

Passing through 3000 feet, I saw that the hole extended only to the perimeter of the field. The adjacent buildings were hidden beyond the misty lips of the shaft. How much room would there be *underneath* the cloud mass? We needed maneuvering room to break away from our spiral and execute a landing.

We could not see the bay or the hills or anything else except the very center of the field. It was a beautiful target, but we had no wish to make a bull's-eye.

I tightened the spiral until our cheeks sagged.

I now was so involved with these problems I almost forgot about the smoke or what might be happening in compartment B.

Not a word passed between us as the earth rose swiftly.

I wished LaFrenier would sing.

At 400 feet there were tatters in the mouth of the hole. I eased the bank and gunned the engines twice. They protested in a long series of backfires, but they caught.

At 300 feet I saw a dim division in the overcast, then a faint scraggly line that marked the shore of the bay. If we could make the water, we could make the field on a level approach, though the ceiling might be almost nil.

I rolled the ship out of the bank and made a final dive for the scraggly line. We held our breath until it became a definite reality.

Robertson handled the throttles, for I had no time to consider engine pressures. We were at 200 feet, heavily loaded, and the gear was down. There was no horizon, and the smoke in the cockpit remained. The field was now behind us, and we were over the bay. My sole devotion was air speed. Too little and we would stall, too much and we would overshoot the field when we reversed the course. As I began the final turn, Robertson called out continuously.

"One sixty . . . one sixty . . . one fifty-five . . . one fifty-two . . . one *forty-five*. . . ."

We were headed back in the direction of the field. I called for 15 degrees of flaps.

"One forty . . . one forty . . . one *thirty*. . . ."

Where was the shore again?

There . . . and the end of the northeast runway. Both loomed very suddenly ahead.

"Full flaps!"

We swooped down, and as the wet runway slithered beneath our nose, I saw fire trucks waiting in line. Before the landing roll was completed, we had yanked open the windows and gulped at fresh air.

There were several curious things about this morning, one of which had to do with the almost instant deterioration of some men's judgment when pressure is relieved. There was also a seriocomic display of the acumen characteristic of crowds in fear.

And there were other things we could not analyze so blithely.

In the first instance, I was so grateful to be alive and on the good ground that whatever thinking processes had so far compelled me ceased altogether and at once. For what I did automatically, with the fire trucks trailing uselessly behind, was to taxi the airplane at high speed to its usual loading position and there stop it. This position was directly over underground tanks that contained many thousands of gallons of high-octane gasoline. Fortunately, the fire crews extinguished the still-minor conflagration in compartment B before my stupidity could create a holocaust.

Next, the heavy smoke in the cabin created understandable concern among the passengers. When it seemed they were very near panic, the sergeant in charge of the cabin told them there was really nothing to worry about, since what they saw was only *carbon monoxide*.

This statement, incredibly, broke the tension, and the passengers relaxed.

Finally, there was the weather. The hole through which we had descended closed completely five minutes after we were on the ground. Whether the minutes saved prevented a full fire and an inevitable midair explosion remained conjecture—but this fact was undeniable.

In the weather office we learned that our blessed hole that was so precisely over the airport had been the only known break in the cloud mass for 700 miles.

back vertical wing at bottom. will reach, ac other,
up the midget. saddleback will reach the saddle-shaped
and either. Only "T will pull and then. the tree. on the
opposite side because their middle line. 182. forward as

182

SHOWDOWN ON
THE ONE-FOOT LINE

By Jerry Kramer with Dick Schaap

The 1967 National Football League season was climaxed by the now-famous "frozen game" at Green Bay, Wisconsin, between the Green Bay Packers and the Dallas Cowboys. Jerry Kramer, Green Bay's great offensive guard, kept a diary of that season. Here are his excerpts for the days preceding the game and the game itself, a contest played in 13-degree weather and decided by one momentous play—a play that required superhuman effort on the part of Kramer and his teammates.

Coach Lombardi talked to us this morning about the third world championship, about how much it would mean to all of us all our lives. He mentioned that Green Bay had won three straight championships in 1929, 1930 and 1931, in the days before playoff games, but he said that those years didn't count. "The Little Sisters of the Poor could have won then," he said.

"I want that third championship," Vince said, "AND I DESERVE IT. WE ALL DESERVE IT."

Then he lowered his voice and talked about the type of men who play for Green Bay. "Lots of better ballplayers than you guys have gone through here," he said, "but you're the type of ballplayers I want. You've got character. You've got heart. You've got guts." He got worked up, very emotional, and then, abruptly, he stopped. "OK, that's it," he said. "That's my pregame speech. Let's go."

We went out on the field, and he gave us two new plays to use against Dallas. One looks particularly good. The fullback, either Wilson or Mercein, will lead the halfback right up the middle. The fullback will go for the middle linebacker, and either Gilly or I will pull and block the tackle on the opposite side. Because their middle linebacker, Jordan, is so fast, we're hoping that he'll be moving, following the guard, and our fullback will be able to handle him.

"You'd better not miss that block, Gillingham," Vince yelled before we even tried the play. "You'd better not miss it."

"Damn," said Gilly. "That's the first time I ever got chewed out for a block before I got a chance to make it."

Most of the time Vince was in a good cheerleading mood. He kept smacking his hand and saying, "We're ready, we're ready." And he kept looking to Paul Hornung, who watched the whole practice, for his approval. Paul was having fun. He asked Max, "What kind of year have you had?" And Max said, "Coach Schnelker and I have had about the same kind of year. We've both kept real warm and haven't had too much contact."

After the workout we watched movies of our 1966 championship game with Dallas and half of their game with Cleveland. Everybody still seems to have that confident feeling, no tightness, no real strain. Chandler's a little concerned, and so am I. The guys can't possibly be thinking of anything but the game. I know I can't think of anything else.

I'm not daydreaming about Jethro Pugh, the way I did about Merlin Olsen. My thoughts are of a more precise nature: What am I going to do on pass protection? Head up, keep moving, keep his hands off me.

I noticed something about Jethro in the movies today, and I mentioned it to Lombardi when we were talking about our goal-line plays. "Pugh's high, Coach," I said. "He doesn't get down. He doesn't bury himself the way Bob Lilly"—their other tackle—"does. If we're gonna wedge, we should wedge Pugh."

I'm thinking about Jethro all the time. This morning, in fact, I started calling my wife Jethro. "C'mon, Jethro," I yelled at Barbara. "Get me breakfast, Jethro. Get me my coat, Jethro. Get me my car keys, Jethro." I don't know if it's going to help me much Sunday, but it's kind of fun today.

December 30

The tension really hit me last night. I went to bed at 6:15, slept a few minutes, woke up, slept, woke up, slept, woke up, finally had to take two sleeping pills, a little one, then a big one, to knock me out. I had a wild dream about the game. I dreamed I suffered a concussion and woke up three days after the game and asked who won, and my daughter, Diane, said we won 60–4, and Barbara said we lost 17–7. And then I started remembering the game, and Dick Modzelewski, the old Cleveland tackle who hasn't played in years, was opposite me, and he and Forrest Gregg started fighting over a fumble. They both bobbled it, and I recovered the ball, and something hit me, and I staggered off the field and asked someone, "Who's the coach?" Then I told the coach that I didn't feel I should continue to play.

I've never had a dream quite that wild. I don't know how Dick Modzelewski got in there, and I never heard of a game anywhere ending with a score like 60–4.

We played a world-championship volleyball game this morning, and we used a real volleyball for the first time all year. My team, the Cicero Sissies, was beating the King Ranch Bullies 5–4 when the commissioner, Tom Brown, made an extremely bad call. The call totally demoralized our team, and we lost 9–6. We filed a protest against the commissioner with the commissioner, but we don't expect it to be acted upon favorably.

I suggested to Coach Lombardi that we have Paul Hornung sit on our bench tomorrow. I said it would help the team and make us play better. Vince said he'd check to see if it was OK with the commissioner. He meant Pete Rozelle, the commissioner of the National Football League, not Tom Brown.

Just before we left the field today, Coach Lombardi gave us a brief talk. He simply said that this is for the NFL championship and that we all know what it means. I know. The championship game was the biggest game of my life the first time I played in it, and the second time and the third time. This is the sixth one for me—the ninth one for Don Chandler—and the more you play in it, the more you realize how much it means, especially if you lose. We lost the title game to Philadelphia in 1960, and the defeat obsessed me for six months. I thought about it almost every night. Over and over and over I kept seeing a play I had blown. I had one of the most miserable winters of my life.

The Cowboys have just gone through a terrible winter remembering the game they lost to us. I was in Dallas last spring to set up their participation in the portrait program, and I visited Bob Lilly and his wife. She didn't know quite what to think of me. She was still hating the Green Bay Packers. To break the strain—or maybe to increase it—I said, "Katsy, if you like, I could leave this package of Green Bay Packer portraits with you. Maybe you'd like to put them up around the house." She wasn't too amused. "I've heard enough about the Green Bay Packers," she said. "That's all I've heard all winter." When I left the Lillys' house, Katsy Lilly said, "We'll see you in Green Bay in December."

I guess she's here for the game.

I thought I wasn't too nervous today, but when I got home this afternoon, I discovered that, in the dressing room, I'd put my shorts on backward.

December 31

When I woke up this morning, after a good night's sleep, I knew it was cold. "It must be ten below zero," I told Barbara. I thought I was kidding.

During breakfast I found out the temperature was 16 degrees below zero, the coldest December 31 in Green Bay history, and I started to shiver. Still, I figured it would warm up a little by noon. It warmed all the way up to 13 below by game time.

Chandler and I bundled up driving over to the stadium, and we didn't realize quite how bitter the cold was. As we ran into the dressing room, we saw a helicopter hovering over the stadium blowing snow off the seats.

When I got inside and began dressing, Gilly came over to me and said, "You gonna wear gloves?"

I hadn't thought of it. I'd never worn gloves before in a football game. I was about to say no, and then I thought, "Who the hell am I kidding? I don't use my hands out there."

"Hell, yeah," I told Gilly.

Maybe if it were five above zero or ten above, I would have passed up the gloves and tried to psych the Cowboys into thinking that the cold wasn't bothering me. But at 13 below I wasn't going to be psyching anyone. Everybody in the whole United States was going to know I was cold.

Gilly, Forrest, Ski and I—the interior linemen—got gloves from Dad Braisher, the equipment manager. We're the only ones who don't have to use our hands in a game. We decided we'd wear the gloves outside to loosen up and see if we needed them for the game.

"With this cold," Ron Kostelnik mentioned to me, "it's gonna hamper us on defense. We won't be able to grab, to use our hands too well. You won't have to be afraid of popping people, Jerry. They won't be able to throw you with their hands." The thought warmed me up slightly.

We got dressed in our long stockings and our silk pants, and when we stepped out on the field—I was wearing my thermal underwear, but only knee-length and elbow-length, so that it wouldn't restrict my mobility—icy blasts just shot right up our skirts. It took Gilly and Forrest and Ski and me about three seconds to decide we'd keep on the gloves. "Hell, let's get another pair," I told Gilly.

I looked over at the Dallas Cowboys, and I almost felt sorry for them. As bad as the cold was for us, it had to be worse for them. We were freezing, and they were dying. They were all hunched over, rubbing their hands, moving their legs up and down, trying to persuade themselves that they weren't insane to be playing football in this ridiculous weather.

We kicked off, and our defense held, and when I came out on the field for the first time, we had the ball around our own 20-yard line. Bart started right off with the 41 special, the new play we'd put in for the Cowboys. Gilly pulled out to his right, faking Lee Roy Jordan, the middle linebacker, into thinking the play was going that way, and Bob Hyland blocked on Gilly's man, and I blocked on Jethro Pugh, and Chuck Mercein, at fullback, leading Donny Anderson into the line, blocked Lee Roy Jordan trying to recover. The play worked just the way we hoped it would. Donny picked up five yards before he got hit. He fumbled, which wasn't part of our plan, but Mercein recovered for us. With Bart calling that 41 special a couple of times, and with the aid of a few penalties, we marched all the way down the field for a touchdown. Bart passed to Dowler in the end zone, and midway through the first period we were leading 7–0.

The cold was incredible, cutting right through us, turning each slight collision into a major disaster, but for me the footing on the field wasn't too bad. The ground was hard, but by putting most of my weight on my toes, I could dig in and get a foothold. I handled Jethro pretty well, popping him more than I would under normal conditions, keeping his cold hands away from me, moving him on running plays and checking him on passing plays. We didn't say a word to each other; even if we'd had anything to say, it was too cold to talk.

The only conversation I had all day was with Lee Roy Jordan. When we tried a screen pass, Bob Lilly or one of their linemen read the play and grabbed the back, the intended receiver, by the jersey. Bart had no one to throw to. "Look, he's holding, he's holding," I screamed at the referee. But the referee didn't see the infraction, and Jordan smiled and said to me, "He wasn't holding, Jerry. Your guy just slipped and fell down, and we were just helping him up."

We had more conversation on our own bench, mostly over who'd get the good seats by the warmer. Hornung usually had one of them; the commissioner had said he could sit on our bench. At one point the warmer ran out of fuel and started to smoke, and we all jumped off the bench. Another time Donny Anderson was sitting on the bench freezing, and when he saw the CBS sidelines microphone, sponge-covered to kill the wind sound, dangling in front of him, he reached up and put his hands around the microphone, thinking it was some new kind of heater.

Early in the second quarter, when we had the ball on a third-and-one situation just past midfield, Bart crossed up the Dallas defense, faded back and threw a long touchdown pass, again to Dowler. We were ahead 14–0, and I felt warmer. I was only worried about our tendency to let up when we get a few touchdowns ahead.

Less than a minute later Herb Adderley intercepted one of Don Meredith's passes and returned the ball almost to the Cowboys' 30-yard line. If we can get this one now, I thought, we can forget it, the game's over, the whole thing's over. I had a beautiful feeling about the ball game—until we didn't score. Bart lost some yardage eating the ball when he couldn't find an open receiver, and we had to punt. I felt frustrated, terribly let down. I'd been so certain that we were going to get at least something, at least a field goal.

Then, late in the second period, deep in our own territory,

again Bart faded to pass and again he couldn't get rid of the ball, and Willie Townes, their big defensive end, hit Bart and knocked the ball loose, and George Andrie, their other defensive end, swooped in and picked up the ball and charged to the end zone for a touchdown.

Forrest Gregg tackled Andrie just as he crossed the goal line, and I was only a step or two behind Forrest, and I suddenly felt the greatest desire to put both my cleats right on Andrie's spinal cord and break it. We had been victimized by these stupid plays—scooped-up fumbles, deflected passes, blocked kicks, high-school tricks—so many times during the season that I felt murderous. I'd never in my career deliberately stepped on a guy, but I was so tempted to destroy Andrie, to take everything out on him, that I almost did it. A bunch of thoughts raced through my mind—I'd met Andrie off the field a few times, and I kind of liked him—and at the last moment I let up and stepped over him.

We couldn't do a thing when we got the ball—Jethro caught Bart for a loss one time, but I thought I'd checked him long enough; I thought Bart held the ball too long—and they took over again and added a field goal, and so, at the half, instead of leading 17–0 or 21–0 or something like that, we were barely in front 14–10.

Ray Wietecha chewed us out pretty good between the halves. "One guy's giving the quarterback all the trouble," he told us. "One guy. C'mon. Don't let up out there. There's a lot of money riding. Get tough, damn it, get tough." Ray didn't mention any names, but we all knew that Ski was having a lot of trouble with Andrie, that Andrie was doing most of the damage.

We just couldn't get unwound in the third quarter. I still felt I had Jethro under control, but he caught Bart two more times, not back deep but out of the pocket, after Bart had had enough time to throw if he could have found anyone open. The ends were having trouble cutting. On the first play of the last quarter they used the halfback option—an old favorite play of ours—and Dan Reeves passed 50 yards for a touchdown. We were losing 17–14, and the wind was whipping us, too.

Five minutes later my roommate was wide with an attempted field goal, and when the ball sailed by to the left, I had a little sinking feeling, a little fear that the clock might run out on us. I thought maybe the time had come for us to lose. Dallas controlled the ball for about ten plays, staying on the ground as much as they could, eating up the clock, and all the time my frustration built up, my eagerness to get back on the field, to have another chance to score.

With five minutes to go we got the ball on our own 32-yard line, and right away Bart threw a little pass out to Anderson, and Andy picked up five, six yards. The linebackers were laying back; they were having trouble with their footing, trouble cutting. Chuck Mercein ran for the first down, and then Bart hit Dowler for another first down, and we were inside Dallas territory. I began to feel we were going to make it, we were going to go for a touchdown. At the worst I figured we'd go down swinging.

On first down Willie Townes got through and caught Andy for a big loss, and we had second and about 20. But Bart capitalized on the Dallas linebackers' difficulties getting traction. Twice, with the ends still having problems with their footing, he threw safety-valve passes to Anderson, and twice Andy went for about ten yards, and we had a first down on the Dallas 30, and I could feel the excitement building in the huddle. But we had only a minute and a half to play. Bart passed out to Mercein on the left, and Chuck carried the ball down to the Dallas 11. I walked back to the huddle, wondering what Bart was going to call, and he called a give 65, and I thought, "What a perfect call. We haven't used it all day. What a smart call."

It's a potentially dangerous play, a give 65. We block as though we're going through the "five" hole, outside me. Gilly pulls and comes over my way, and everything depends on the tackle in front of him, Bob Lilly, taking the fake and moving to his left. The play can't work against a slow, dumb tackle; it can only work against a quick, intelligent tackle like Lilly. We figured Lilly would key on Gilly and follow his move, but we didn't know for sure. Everybody blocks my way on this play, Anderson coming for the hole as though he's carrying the ball, and nobody blocks the actual target area, Lilly's area. If Lilly doesn't take the fake, if he ignores Gilly pulling, he kills the actual ball carrier, Mercein.

But Lilly followed Gillingham, and the hole opened up, and Chuck drove down to the three-yard line. With less than a minute to play, Anderson plunged for a first down on the one, and, with only two time-outs left, we huddled quickly. "Run over there," Gilly said in the huddle. "Run that 55 special. They can't stop that."

Bart called the 55, and I thought to myself, "Well, this is it, toad. They're putting it directly on your back, yours and Forrest's." I didn't make a very good block, and the five hole didn't open up, and Andy got stopped at the line of scrimmage. We called a time-out with 20 seconds to play. Then Bart called the same play again, and this time Andy slipped coming toward the hole—I don't know whether he could have gotten through—and slid to about the one-foot line, and we called time-out with 16 seconds to play, our last time-out, and everybody in the place was screaming.

We could have gone for the field goal right then, for a tie, hoping that we'd win in overtime. We decided to go for the victory. In the huddle Bart said, "Thirty-one wedge and I'll carry the ball." He was going to try a quarterback sneak. He wasn't going to take a chance on a handoff or on anybody slipping. He was going to go for the hole just inside me, just off my left shoulder. Kenny Bowman, who had finally worked his way back to the lineup, and I were supposed to move big Jethro out of the way. It might be the last play of the game, our last chance.

The ground was giving me trouble, the footing was bad down near the goal line, but I dug my cleats in, got a firm hold with my right foot, and we got down in position, and Bart called the "hut" signal. Jethro was on my inside shoulder, my left shoulder. I came off the ball as fast as I ever have in my life. I came off the ball as fast as anyone could. In fact, I wouldn't swear that I didn't beat the center's snap by a fraction of a second. I wouldn't swear that I wasn't actually offside on the play.

I slammed into Jethro hard. All he had time to do was raise his left arm. He didn't even get it up all the way, and I charged into him. His body was a little high, the way we'd noticed in the movies, and with Bowman's help I moved him outside. Willie Townes, next to Jethro, was down low, very low. He was supposed to come in low and close to the middle. He was low, but he didn't close. He might have filled the hole, but he didn't, and Bart churned into the opening and stretched and fell and landed over the goal line. It was the most beautiful sight in the world, seeing Bart lying next to me and seeing the referee in front of me, his arms over his head, signaling the touchdown. There were 13 seconds to play.

The fans poured on the field, engulfing the Cowboys, pummeling all of us. Chuck Howley, the Dallas linebacker, got knocked down three or four times accidentally, and he was furious. I had to fight my way through the crowd to the sidelines. Bart came off the field looking like he was crying, and he probably was. The Cowboys still had time to get off two plays, two incomplete passes, and the game was over. I tried to get to the dressing room quickly, but I got caught around the 30-yard line, trapped in a mass of people beating me on the back, grabbing at my chin strap, grabbing at my gloves, trying to get anything for a souvenir. I had a sudden moment of panic, wondering whether I was ever going to get out of that mess alive.

Finally I reached the dressing room, and I was immediately aware that the whole place was wired for sound. Cameramen and cameras were all around, and Coach Lombardi cussed the cameramen and ordered them, flatly, to get the hell out. When we were alone, just the team and the coaches, Vince told us how proud he was of us. "I can't talk anymore," he said. "I can't say any more." He held the tears back, and we all kneeled and said the Lord's Prayer, and then we exploded with shouts of joy and excitement, the marks of battle, the cuts, the bruises and the blood, all forgotten.

The TV people returned, and I was one of the first men led in front of the cameras. "There's a great deal of love for one another on this club," I said. "Perhaps we're living in Camelot." I was referring to the idea of one for all and all for one, the ideal of King Arthur's Round Table, and I meant it. And then I talked about Lombardi.

I'd been waiting for a chance to talk about Vince. A story had appeared in *Esquire* magazine a few weeks earlier making him look like a complete villain, like nothing but a cruel, vicious man. The story had hurt Vince; I heard that his mother had cried when she read the story. I thought the story gave a distorted picture of the man; it showed only one of his many sides. "Many things have been said about Coach," I said on TV, "and he is not always understood by those who quote him. The players understand. This is one beautiful man."

I loved Vince. Sure, I had hated him at times during training camp, and I had hated him at times during the season, but I knew how much he had done for us, and I knew how much he cared about us. He was a beautiful man, and the proof is that no one who ever played for him speaks of him afterward with anything but respect and admiration and affection. His whippings, his cussings and his driving all fade; his good qualities endure.

Over and over, perhaps 20 times, the television cameras reran Bart's touchdown and my block on Jethro Pugh. Again and again millions of people across the country saw the hole open up and saw Bart squeeze through. Millions of people who couldn't name a single offensive lineman if their lives depended on it heard my name repeated and repeated and repeated. All I could think was, "Thank God for instant replay."

Kenny Bowman came up to me smiling and said, "Don't take all the credit, Kramer. Don't take all the credit. I helped you with that block."

"Shut up, Bow," I said. "You've got ten more years to play. You've got plenty of time for glory. I ain't telling anybody anything. If they think I made that block alone, I'm gonna let them think it."

I was only kidding Bowman, of course. But I've got to admit that I didn't tell many people about Bowman's part in the block. I stayed around the locker room as long as I ever have, talking to all the reporters, answering all their questions, accepting all their kind words. I felt like a halfback. I stayed till the last dog was dead.

I drove home from the stadium in an icebox. The heating unit in my Lincoln was frozen, and so was I. For an hour or two I relaxed with a few friends and with my family, letting the circulation come back all over my body. I watched part of the American Football League title game, watched the Oakland Raiders kill the Houston Oilers, and then I went to my room and changed into my fancy black-striped walking suit, putting it on over a white turtleneck sweater. I put on my black cowboy hat and stuck a fat cigar in my mouth, and I felt like a riverboat gambler. And then we all took off for Appleton, about 30 miles away, for the Left Guard Steak House, owned by Fuzzy and Max, for a big, beautiful celebration.

It was 20 degrees below zero outside, and the heating broke down in the restaurant, but the cold didn't bother me at all. I drank toasts with Hornung and toasts with Jordan and toasts with Max, and somehow I managed to notice that Donny Anderson had for company a girl who had once been a Playmate of the Month. Donny had certainly earned a big night out; he'd played almost the entire game, while Travis shivered on the bench.

I had a great time. At least, everyone told me I had a great time. Fuzzy and I got carried away by the whiskey man, and we ended up the evening greeting the new year with toasts—toasts, naturally, to the two greatest guards in the history of the whole world.

January 1

When I woke up this morning, my first thought was that the game against Dallas and the block on Jethro Pugh were only dreams. I thought that we hadn't really played the Cowboys yet. Then I felt the soreness in my legs, in my body and in my head, and I realized that I hadn't been dreaming, that we had played the game, that we had defeated Dallas 21–17.

For the third straight year we had won the championship of the National Football League. Even the soreness felt great.

SEARCH FOR THE WHITE DEATH

By Peter Matthiessen

In June 1964 two men, Peter Matthiessen, a writer, and Peter Gimbel, scion of the department-store family, visited the sport-fishing docks at Montauk, Long Island, and saw there, for the first time, a great white shark—17½ feet long and 4000 pounds—that had been brought in by one of the local boats. Both men were awed by the enormity of this creature of the deep and visualized how this shark—called "the white death" by fishermen around the world—could swallow a seal, or a large part of a man, in a single dreadful gulp!

Gimbel, one of the most renowned scuba divers in the world and an underwater-film maker, decided then and there to scour the oceans to make a film about this beast. Matthiessen went along to write about it. What follows, then, is the climax of that search.

Saturday morning, January 24, and still no sign of shark. Gimbel is muttering about bad dreams. In one dream he and Peter Lake had mutilated their legs with knives, then swum in the water to attract sharks. Their effort was in vain, and afterward they sat on the deck and compared their legs, which would have to be amputated. "We realized we'd made a mistake," Gimbel said, still worried by the dream. He looked up in surprise when everybody laughed, then laughed himself. In this time of stress he is upset unduly by a cold sore at the corner of his mouth, which he chooses to see as an intimation of his own mortality.

The day is a good one, with light wind. The *Saori* will stay on here despite the absence of white sharks. But everyone is growing apprehensive. Even if sharks were numerous, it will be difficult to get good underwater film in the poor visibility of these cold, turbid waters, especially if the whites avoid the air bubbles of the scuba tanks and cages. Dangerous Reef is a place notorious for the white shark ("The abalone divers don't care for it," Bruce Farley says. "Took a quick look and decided they'd do better someplace else"); yet no one has seen a fin. If only two years ago Rodney saw seven here at once, where are they now?

Rodney says that the sharks might be following the salmon schools that are moving through the gulf, and possibly their movements and feeding patterns have been affected by the past month of bad weather, which kept the water temperature well below the seasonal norm. Though warmer than at Memory Cove, it is four degrees colder here than it was when Rodney came at this same time in 1968. In salt-water environments, a four-degree gradient makes a big difference—it can keep oysters from spawning, for example—and it has been noted with captive specimens as well as in shark-attack statistics that a shark's interest in food rises markedly with an increase in temperature. In winter captive sharks scarcely feed at all. The white shark is an exception to a general rule proposed by an Australian authority, V. M. Coppleson, that shark attacks around the world are rare in water colder than 72 degrees; nevertheless, its feeding may be inhibited by unseasonal cold water and unstable weather.

Or so we speculate. On the radio this morning one of the tuna captains with a white-shark charter party out of Port Lincoln had some disturbing news: In his last three trips to Dangerous Reef he had raised only one shy white shark, and it would not come near the boat. "Not like it used to be," the radio voice said. "They're being slowly killed out, I reckon, like everything else in the world." This man blamed the gill-netters for the disappearance of the sharks, and certainly commercial netting is a factor. Like other large predators of land and sea, the white shark will not survive long without the protection that it is unlikely to receive from man, and possibly the Australians are correct in the opinion generally held here that the species is nearing extinction. I am happy that our expedition has no plan to kill one except in self-defense.

There are recent reports of white sharks farther north in the gulf and to the west of Cape Catastrophe, and there is a feeling aboard that the *Saori* should pursue these sightings. Pursuit might relieve the strain of waiting and improve morale, but chasing works no better with fish than it does with anything else: better to pick one likely place and chum the hell out of it, day and night. By the time the slow *Saori* got the cages to the scene of any sighting, the shark might be 20 miles away, and even if a shark were present, there is no guarantee that water clarity would be adequate or that the shark would approach the cage. Possibly inshore sharks have a hunting circuit, moving from point to point as wolves do, but more likely they move at random, taking prey as chance presents, and congregating now and then at likely grounds such as Dangerous Reef. Instinctively I agree with Captain Arno, who is relieving Captain Ben over this weekend. Arno is a wonderful bent old salt with white broken bare feet that never sunburn. Offered grog, he smites the table, crying out fiercely, "I *will!*" Says Arno, "Sharks have a head and a tail, and they keep swimming. Nobody knows where the shark goes. I reckon they don't know where they are themselves."

Although these days are painful for Gimbel, they are almost as hard on Rodney Fox, who must choose the fishing grounds and baiting techniques that will bring the missing sharks. Rodney performs his duties with efficiency and style, but his casual air of cocky indifference is deceptive. If anything, he takes too much of the burden upon himself and tends to construe the discussion of alternatives as implied criticism. For those aboard with a long interest in the sea and sharks, such discussions are fun and ease the strain, but giving a hearing to amateur opinions is hard on Rodney's nerves in a nervous time. Rarely does he permit the strain to show, but sometimes, muttering, "Too many cooks . . . !" he lies face down on the deck feigning deep sleep, and one day he actually took refuge in the hold, refusing to come out to eat his lunch.

Nevertheless, Rodney says, he has never worked with a nicer group of people. I feel the same, and so does everyone else. Even Lipscomb and I, who often disagree, manage to disagree in a friendly manner. After a year and a half this film crew is truly a unit, and its strength is mutual affection and acceptance: Each man knows precisely what can be expected of the man beside him and demands no more, because those who fail in one respect have made it up over and over in others. As relationships have grown, the people have become more self-sufficient. Even the hearts game, a loud nightly event aboard our boat, the *Terrier*, has given way to books and chess and backgammon.

There are other changes, in the crew's youngest members especially. A new, confident Cody is so loose that he threatens to join the extroverts, while Lake has arrived at a new awareness in his dealings with others. One day on the deckhouse, watching for sharks, Peter said, "Remember when I wrote you that I didn't really care about this film? Well, that's all changed—I *do*."

By now everyone cares about the film, quite apart from his own investment in it, if only because everyone cares about Peter Gimbel, who has his life's work on the line. A great part of the suspense of waiting for "Big Whitey," as the near-mythical ruler of these silent seas has become known, is the knowledge that his failure to appear could be fatal to the film. Therefore, the ship is quiet. Against these stark horizons, even the throb of hard rock music has a thin, tinny ring.

More than once I went ashore and prowled the tide pools. I have spent hours of my life crouched beside tide pools watching the slow surge of simple organisms still close to the first pulse of life on earth. On Dangerous Reef are gaudy giant limpets and companies of blue, black and banded periwinkles and the green snail and a brown cone and a very beautiful cream volute with zigzag stripings, also rockfish and the great fire-colored rock crabs that grow enormous in the deeps and a heart-colored sea anemone and a garden of hydroids, barnacles and algae. In every tide pool the seal pups played, and others lay on the warm rocks in a sleep so sound that they could be petted without awakening. When at last one did come to, it would stare for seconds in bare disbelief, then bleat in dismay and flop away at speed over the rocks.

In the white surge along the shore the seals rolled endlessly, turning and twisting, whisking clean out of the water in swift chases or ranging along, the sleek, sunshined dark-eyed heads held high out of the sea. A small surge would lift them out onto the granite, where, groaning, they dozed on the hot rocks in rows. The old bulls, though graceful in the water, were less playful. They stationed themselves on underwater ledges like old, mighty sentinels and let the white foam wash around them. Onshore, competitors were driven off in heaving neck fights that were mostly shoving contests. The animals swayed their heavy heads and necks in the way of bears, to which, among land mammals, they are most closely related. Sea lions are agile on the land, and a golden-maned bull protecting a cow and a new pup drove me up onto high ground. One cow was raked drastically on her hind end and right hind flipper by the parallel black lines of an old shark bite, and it was noticeable that the young never left the shallows and that even the adults kept close to the reef edges when not off at sea.

At noon today the *Sea Raider* brought word that an 11-foot white of 1300 pounds had been hooked at Cape Donington, where the *Saori* had anchored two nights before. Psychologically this news was painful, but the water clarity at Cape Donington is awful, and we could not have worked there. And at least it was proof that the species was not extinct.

In a letter to a friend this morning Valerie wrote that no shark had been seen but that she expected a 12- or 13-footer to turn up at about two o'clock. At 2:20 Peter Lake and Ian McKechnie saw a fin in the slick some 50 yards behind the ship. The spell was broken. We dragged on diving suits and went on watch, but the fin had sunk from view in the still sea. A half hour passed and more. Then, perhaps ten feet down off the port beam, a fleeting brown shadow brought the sea to life.

Suspended from a buoy, a salmon was floated out behind the boat to lure the shark closer. Once it had fed at the side of the boat, it would be less cautious; then, perhaps, the engine could be started and the cages swung over the side without scaring it away. But an hour passed before the shark was seen again. This time a glinting rusty back parted the surface, tail and dorsal high out of the water as the shark made its turn into the bait. There was the great wavering blade exactly as Al Giddings had described it and the thrash of water as the shark took the salmon, two hours to the minute after the first sighting. Stan Waterman cried, "Holy sweet Jesus!"—a very strong epithet for this mild-spoken man. He was amazed by the mass of shark that had been raised clear of the water. Even the Australians were excited, try as they would to appear calm. "Makes other sharks look like little frisky pups, doesn't it?" cried Valerie with pride.

Then it was gone again. Along the reef, 100 yards away, the sea lions were playing tag, their sleek, heavy bodies squirting clean out of the water and parting the surface again without a splash, and a string of cormorants, oblivious, came beating in out of the northern blue.

Gimbel, annoyed that he had missed the shark, was running from the bow. He did not have long to wait. From the deckhouse roof I could see the shadow rising toward the bait. "There he is," I said, and Rodney yanked at the shred of salmon, trying to bring the shark in closer to the ship. Lipscomb, beside me, was already shooting when the great fish breached, spun the sea awash and lunged after the skipping salmon tail. We stared into its white, oncoming mouth. "My God!" Gimbel shouted, astounded by the sight of his first white shark. The conical snout and the terrible shearing teeth and the dark eye like a hole were all in sight, raised clear out of the water. Under the stern, with an audible *whush*, the shark took a last snap at the bait, then wheeled away. Sounding, it sent the skiff spinning with a terrific whack of its great tail, an ominous boom that could have been heard a half mile away.

For a split second there was silence, and then Lipscomb gave a mighty whoop of joy. "I *got* it!" he yelled. "Goddamn it, I *got* it!" There was a bedlam of relief, then another silence. "Might knock that cage about a bit," Rodney said finally, hauling in the shred of fish. He was thinking of the baits that would be suspended in the cage to bring the shark close to the cameras. Gimbel, still staring at the faceless water, only nodded.

Just after five o'clock the shark reappeared. The late sun glistened on its dorsal as it cut back and forth across the surface worrying a dead fish from the line. There was none of the sinuous effect of lesser sharks. The tail strokes were stiff and short like those of swordfish, giant tuna and other swift deep-sea swimmers. This creature was much bigger than the big oceanic sharks off Durban, but for a white shark it was not enormous. Estimates of its length varied from eleven feet, six inches ("Ron always plays it safe and underestimates," said Valerie) to fourteen feet (Peter Gimbel: "I saw it alongside that skiff, and I'm certain it was at *least* as long—I'm *certain* of it!"), but much more impressive than the length was the mass of it and the speed and power. "It doesn't matter *what* size the bastards are," Rodney said. "A white shark over six feet long is bloody dangerous."

The day was late. In the westering sun a hard light of late afternoon silvered the water rushing through the reef and, nearer, the blue facets of the sea sparkled in cascades of tiny stars. More out of frustration than good sense, the choice between trying to film the shark immediately and trying to lure it to the baits alongside, in the hope of keeping it nearby overnight, was resolved in favor of immediate action. The motor was started up and the cages swung over the side, and the cameramen disappeared beneath the surface. But the great shark had retreated and did not return.

By dark the wind exceeded 25 knots and went quickly to 30, 40 and, finally, toward one in the morning, to 50 or better—a whole gale. On deck I lay sleepless, rising every little while to check the position of the light on Dangerous Reef. The reef is too low to make a windbreak, and, even close under the lee, the *Saori* tossed and heaved under heavy strain. But Captain Ben, who knew exactly what his ship would do, slept soundly below. Toward three the wind moderated, backing around to the southeast, where it held till daybreak.

This morning the wind has died to a fair breeze. Waiting, we sit peacefully in the Sunday sun. The boat captains hand-line for Tommy rough, a delicious small silver relative of the Australian "salmon." Others tinker with equipment, play chess and backgammon, write letters and read. Peter Lake has put a rock tape on the sound machine, and on the roof of the pilothouse, overlooking the oil slick, I write these notes while listening to The Band. Onshore, for Jim Lipscomb's camera, Valerie, in lavender, is baby-talking with baby seals, and I hope that most if not all of this sequence will die on the cutting-room floor. Unless it points up the days of waiting, such material has no place in the climax of the film; it will soften the starkness of this remote reef as well as the suspense surrounding the imminence of the white shark. Stan and Valerie, with a background of lecture films and a taste for amateur theatrics, share Jim's appetite for "human-interest stuff," which might yet reduce this film to the first million-dollar home movie.

Toward dark another shark appeared, a smaller one, much

bolder. Relentlessly it circled the ship not ten feet from the hull. On one pass it took the buoyed tuna at a single gulp.

Since it passed alongside, the size of this shark could be closely estimated: All hands agreed that it was between nine feet and ten. But if this was accurate, the shark yesterday had been larger than was thought. Rodney now said that it was over 12, Valerie between 13 and 14, and Gimbel thought that it might have been 16 feet. "I thought so *yesterday*," he said, "but I felt foolish with everyone else saying twelve." I thought 13 feet seemed a conservative minimum. In any case it had twice the mass of tonight's shark, which was plenty big enough. As it slid along the hull, the thick lateral keel on its caudal peduncle was clearly visible. The merest twitch of that strong tail kept it in motion. Underwater lights were lit to see it better, but this may have been a mistake; it vanished and did not return the following day.

On January 26 the *Saori* returned to port for water and supplies. There it was learned that four boats, fishing all weekend, had landed between them the solitary shark that we had heard about on Saturday. The *Saori* could easily have hooked two, but what she was here for was going to be much more difficult. Meanwhile, a sighting of white sharks had been reported by divers working Fisheries Bay, west of Cape Catastrophe on the ocean coast, where three whites and a number of bronze whalers had been seen schooling behind the surf. The bronze whaler, which may be the ubiquitous bull shark *Carcharhinus leucas*, is the chief suspect in most shark attacks on Australia's east coast.

On the chance that the shark school was still present, we drove out to the coast across the parched hills of the sheep country. Over high, windburned fields a lovely parrakeet, the galah, pearl gray and rose, flew in weightless flocks out of the wheat; other parrakeets, turquoise and black and gold, crossed from a scrub of gum trees and melaleuca to a grove of she-oak, the local name for a form of casuarina. Along the way were strange birds and trees in an odd landscape of wind-worn hills that descended again to the sea-misted shore. From the sea cliffs four or five whalers were in sight, like brown ripples in the pale-green windy water, but the white sharks had gone.

At daybreak on Wednesday the *Saori* sailed for the Gambier Islands, on the Antarctic horizon south of the mouth of Spencer Gulf. A big ocean swell rose out of the southwest, from the far reaches of the roaring 40s, but there was a lee of sorts east of Wedge Island. The Gambiers are remote, and no gillnetting is done there, and white sharks had been seen often in the past. Occasionally the sharks would seize a horse when the animals raised here in other days were swum out to the ships. Now the old farm was a sheep station, visited infrequently by man. With Ron, Valerie and Stan, I went ashore exploring. Gaunt black machinery, stranded by disuse, looked out to sea from the dry golden hills, and the sheep, many of them dead, had brought a plague of flies. Only at the island's crest, in the southwest wind, could one be free of them.

Wedge Island is a beautiful, silent place, a great monument like a pyramid in the Southern Ocean. That night white-faced storm petrels fluttered like moths at the masthead light. Some fell to the deck, and I put them in a box. Once the deck lights were out, they flitted off toward the island. These hardy little birds come in off the windy wastes of sea just once a year to nest in burrows in the cliffs.

Overhead, shined by the wind, the austral sky was luminous. With the stem of his pipe Ben Ranford pointed at the universe. "Canis Major," he pronounced with satisfaction, "the brightest star in all the heavens." In World War Two Ben was captain of a destroyer in the Australian navy and is still the complete seaman, clumping here and there about his ship in white coveralls and big black shoes without one wasted motion. He could have stripped the *Saori* from stem to stern and reassembled her in the dark. No man could do his job better than he, and yet Ben knew that this ship might be his last.

At dawn the day was already hot and still, the baits untouched, the ocean empty. Only a solitary eagle, white head shimmering in the rising sun, flapped and sailed over the sea, bound for the outermost islands.

Two weeks had passed, and there was no underwater footage, and running from place to place was not the answer. A decision was made to increase the volume of bait and chum and concentrate it at Dangerous Reef. The two sharks raised there were the only two that had been seen, the resident sea lions were an asset, and the reef was only three hours from the abattoirs and fish companies at Port Lincoln. The ship sailed north again into Spencer Gulf, rounding the west end of the reef and anchoring off its northern shore at noon. A southwest blow was expected that afternoon, backing around to the southeast by evening.

White shark number three came after dark on January 27, seizing the floating bait with a heavy brush thrash that brought a bellow of excitement from Gimbel, working on deck. No sooner had a light been rigged than the fish reappeared, making a slow turn at the perimeter of green night water. Then it rifled straight and fast for a carcass hanging at the ship's side, which it gobbled at and shook apart, oblivious of the lights and shouting men. Though not enormous, this aggressive brute was the one we wanted. By the look of it, it would not be deterred by cages or anything else. Then it was gone, and a cuttlefish rippled in the eerie light, and the sea thickened with a bloom of red crustaceans.

All baits were hauled in but a small flayed sheep, left out to stay the shark until the morning. At dawn the unraveled bait line lay on deck. Taking the sheep, the shark had put such strain upon the line that, parting it, it had snapped back clean out of the water. But there was no sign of the shark, and it never returned.

That morning the *Sea Raider* came out from Port Lincoln with big drums full of butchered horse. The quarters hung from the stern of the *Saori*, which was reeking like a charnel house. Buckets of horse blood, whale oil and a foul chum of ground tuna guts made a broad slick that spread northeast toward Spilsby Island. The cages, cameras lashed to their floors, were already overboard, floating astern. The sky was somber, with high mackerel clouds and a bank of ocean grays creeping up out of the south and a hard wind. Petrels dipped and fluttered in the wake. The ship was silent.

Vodka in hand, Gimbel came and went, glaring astounded at the empty slick that spread majestically to the horizon. About 5:30 I forsook my post on the deckhouse roof and went below. Peter was lying in a berth, face tight. I said, "I'm taking a shower even though there's still light enough to shoot. There'll be a shark here before I'm finished." He laughed politely. I had just returned to the cabin, still half-dry, wrapped in a towel, when a voice yelled, "Shark!" down the companionway.

By the time we reached the deck, bound for the wet suits, the sun had parted the clouds. With luck there would be underwater light for 'at least an hour. Already a second shark had joined the first, and both were big. I went into the sea with Peter, and Stan and Ron soon joined us in the other cage. Almost immediately a great, pale shape took form in the blue mist.

The bolder of the sharks, perhaps 12 feet long, was a heavy male, identifiable by paired claspers at the vent. A second male, slightly smaller, stayed in the background. The first shark had vivid scars about the head and an oval scar under the dorsal, and in the molten water of late afternoon it was a creature very different from the one seen from the surface. The hard rust of its hide had dissolved in pale transparent tones that shimmered in the ocean light on its satin skin. From the dorsal fin an evanescent bronze shaded down to luminous dark metallic gray along the lateral line, a color as delicate as that bronze tint on a mushroom that points up the whiteness of the flesh beneath. From snout to keel the underside was a deathly white, all but the black undertips of the broad pectorals.

The shark passed slowly, first the slack jaw with the triangular splayed teeth, then the dark eye, impenetrable and empty as the eye of God, next the gill slits like knife slashes in paper, then the pale slab of the flank, aglow with silver ripplings of light, and finally the thick, short twitch of its hard tail. Its aspect was less savage than implacable, a silent thing of merciless serenity.

Only when the light had dimmed did the smaller shark drift in from the blue shadows, but never did it come to the hanging baits. The larger shark barged past the cages and banged against the hull to swipe and gulp at the chunks of meat. On the way out it repeatedly bit the propeller of the outboard, swallowing the whole shaft and shaking the motor. Then it would swing and glide straight in again, its broad pectorals, like a manta's wings, held in an upward curve. Gills rippling, it would swerve enough to miss the cage, and once the smiling head had passed, I could reach out and take hold of the rubber pectoral or trail my fingers down the length of cold, dead flank, as if stroking a corpse. The skin felt as smooth as the skin of a swordfish or tuna. Then the pale apparition sank under the copper-red hull of the *Saori* and vanished in the gloom, only to reappear from another angle, relentless, moving always at the same deceptive speed, mouth gasping as in thirst. This time it came straight to the cage and seized one of the flotation cylinders of the cage roof. There came a nasty screeching sound, like the grating of fingernails on slate, before the shark turned off, shaking its head.

The sharks off Durban had probed the cages and scraped past, but never once in hundreds of encounters did one attack the cages over and over. This first one arched its back, gills wrinkling, coming on mouth wide. Fortunately, it came at cruising speed and struck the least vulnerable part of the cage. The silver tanks, awash at the surface, may have resembled crippled fish, for they were hit far more often than anything else. When their teeth struck metal, the sharks usually turned away, but often the bite was hard enough to break the teeth out. Sometimes, as it approached the cage, one would flare its mouth wide, then close it again, in what looked very much like the threat display of higher animals.

To escape the rough chop at the surface, the cage descended to 15 feet, where Gimbel opened the roof hatch and climbed partway out to film. He was driven back each time. At one point, falling back in haste, Peter got his tank hung up on the hatch and was still partly exposed when the shark passed overhead, a black shade in the golden ether made by the sinking sun. From below the brute's girth was dramatically apparent; it blotted out the light.

The shark paid the cages such close attention that Gimbel burned up a ten-minute magazine in 15 minutes. When he went to the surface to reload, Valerie Taylor and Peter Lake took over the cage. "Listen!" Gimbel yelled at them, still excited. "Now, watch it! They're nothing like those Durban sharks; so don't take chances!" Then Stan came out of the second cage, and by the time he was reloaded, Ron was ready to come out. This gave me a chance to go down a second time.

For a while the atmosphere was quiet as both sharks kept their distance from the ship. They came and went like spirits in the mist. But emergencies are usually sudden, and now there came a series of near emergencies. First the bigger shark, mouth open, ran afoul of one of the lines. The length of rope slipped past the teeth and hung in the corners of its mouth, trailing back like reins. So many lines were criss-crossed in the water—skiff lines, bait lines, hydrophone cable and tethers to keep the cages near the bait—that at first one could not tell what was going to happen, and I felt a clutch of fear. Swimming away, the shark was shaking its head in irritation, and then I saw that the line was the tether of the other cage, where Gimbel had been joined by Peter Lake. The line was very nearly taut when the shark shook free. Lake was using a camera with a 180-degree "fisheye" lens and was getting remarkable shots, but the close call rattled him considerably. At the surface he yelled all the obscenities. "To hell with *that* shit," he concluded. "I'm going below to hide under my berth!" But Lake's trials were not over. A few days later, when the *Saori* returned to Dangerous Reef for continuity shots and supporting footage, a shark, tangled in a bait line, bent the whole cage with its slow thrashing. It actually *stretched* five of the bars, shaking the whole cage like a dice cup before Lake could get his leg knife out and cut it free. At the surface he had difficulty joking: "When I saw those bars starting to go, I felt like I had jumped at twelve thousand feet with my parachute eaten by rats."

Often the larger shark would appear from below, its ragged smile rising straight up past the cage. Already its head was scarred with streaks of red lead from the *Saori*'s hull. On one of these ascents it seized a piece of meat hung from the taffrail just as the current swung the cage in toward the ship, so that the whole expanse of its ghostly belly, racked by spasms of huge gulping, was perpendicular against the bars. I scratched the belly with a kind of morbid sympathy, but at that instant we were jarred by a thrash of the tail. The cage had pinned the shark upright against the rudder of the *Saori*. While Waterman filmed at point-blank range, it lashed the water white. "I wasn't really worried about you guys," Gimbel said later. "I just knew it would knock hell out of you." The cage was swiftly heaved aside, and the shark glided for the bottom with that ineffable silent calm, moving no more rapidly than before. Except for size, it is often difficult to estimate shark age, and, watching it go, it was easy to believe that this beast might swim for centuries.

I turned to congratulate Waterman on the greatest footage

of a feeding white shark ever taken, but bald eyes rolled in woe behind his mask, and he made a throat-slitting gesture with his finger and smote his rubber brow, then shook his fist at his camera, which had jammed. Gimbel got the sequence from the other cage, 30 feet away, and Lipscomb caught one angle of it from the surface, but Stan was inconsolable.

Gimbel was still trying to film from the roof hatch, and now he ducked down neatly at a shark's approach, only to find himself staring straight into its face. The main cage door had opened outward, and the shark was so near that he could not reach out to close it. Badly frightened, he feinted with his camera at the shark, which cruised on past, oblivious.

Between bites the sharks patrolled the cages, the *Saori* and the skiff, biting indiscriminately. There was no sense of viciousness or savagery in what they did, but something worse —an implacable need. They bit the skiff and they bit the cages, and one pushed past the meat to bite the propeller of the *Saori*. It was as if they smelled the food but could not distinguish it by sight and therefore attacked everything in the vicinity. Often they mouthed the cage metal with such violence that teeth went spinning from their jaws. One such tooth found on the bottom had its serrated edge scraped smooth. It seemed to me that here was the explanation for the reports of white-shark attacks on boats: They do not attack boats—they attack *anything*.

When I left the water, there was a slight delay in getting the skiff alongside, and Rodney warned me not to loiter on top of the cage. "They've been climbing all over it!" he called. At one point Valerie, having handed up her exhausted tank, had to retreat into the cage, holding her breath as a shark thrashed across its roof over and over.

We had entered the water about 6:00, and the last diver left it at 7:30, by which time every one of us was shaking hard with cold. In the skiff, transferring from the cages to the ship, people were shouting. The excitement far exceeded any I had seen in the footage of the greatest day off Durban. As Gimbel said, "Christ, man! These sharks are just a hell of a lot more exciting!"

The next morning, a sparkling wild day, the two sharks were still with us, and they had been joined by a third still larger. Even Ron estimated the new shark at 14 feet, and

Gimbel one or two feet more; it was the biggest man-eating shark that anyone aboard had ever seen. Surging out of the sea to fasten on a horse shank hung from a davit, it stood upright beside the ship, head and gills clear of the water, tail vibrating, the glistening triangles of its teeth red-rimmed with blood. In the effort of shearing, the black eye went white as the eyeball was rolled inward; then the whole horse quarter disappeared in a scarlet billow. "I've watched sharks all my life," Ben Ranford said, "but I've never seen anything as terrifying as that." Plainly, no shark victim with the misfortune to get hold of a raft or boat would ever survive the shaking of that head.

Last night in the galley Ron had suggested to Peter that swimming with one white might be possible, and Peter agreed. But this morning there were three, and the visibility was so limited that one could never tell where or when the other two might appear. The talk of swimming in the open water ended, and a good thing, too. In its seeming contempt for the great white shark, such a dangerous stunt could only make an anticlimax of the film's climax.

The cage will sink a foot or so beneath the surface under a man's weight—a situation to be avoided in the presence of white sharks—and the next morning, entering it, I performed with ease what I had heretofore done clumsily, flipping directly out of the skiff and down through the narrow roof hatch headfirst. Even before I straightened up, the largest of the sharks loomed alongside, filling the blue silence with its smile. I felt naked in my flimsy cell until Stan joined me. This shark was two or three feet longer than the next in size, but it looked half again as big, between 1800 pounds and a fat ton. In white sharks over ten feet long, the increase in girth and weight per foot of length is massive. The white shark that I saw dead at Montauk, only two or three feet longer than this one, had weighed at least twice as much.

The new shark was fearless, crashing past skiff and cage alike to reach the meat and often attacking both on the way out. Like its companions, who scooted aside when it came close, it attacked the flotation tanks over and over, refusing to learn that they were not edible. Even the smallest shark came in to sample the flotation tanks when the others were not around. I had seen one of its companions chase it; so probably its shyness had little to do with the *Saori*. Unlike the sharks in the Indian Ocean, the whites gave one another a wide berth. Occasionally one would go for the air tank in the corner, bumping the whole cage through the water with its snout, and once one struck the naked bars when I waved a dead salmon as it approached. Clumsily it missed the proffered fish, glancing off the bars as I yanked my arm back. Had the sharks attacked the bars, they would have splayed them. "He could bite that cage to bits if he wanted to," Valerie had said of yesterday's shark and got no argument. For the big shark today, the destruction of the cage would be the work of moments. From below we watched it wrestle free an enormous slab of horse, 200 pounds or more. As it gobbled and shook, its great pale body quaked, the tail shuddering with the effort of keeping its head high out of the water. Then, back arched, it dived with its prize toward the bottom, its mouth trailing bubbles from the air gulped down with its last bite. Only one pilot fish was ever seen at Dangerous Reef; we wondered if the white shark's relentless pace made it difficult for a small fish to keep up.

Numbers of fish had come to the debris exploded into the water by the feeding, and the windstorm of the night before had stirred pale algae from the bottom. Visibility was poor; yet the sharks worked so close to the cages that the morning's filming was even better than the day before, and the cameramen worked from 9:00 until 1:30. By then the ten months of suspense were over.

We were scarcely out of the water when the wind freshened, with the threat of rain. The cages were taken aboard and battened down while a party went ashore to film the *Saori* from the reef. Then, in a cold twilight, drinking rum in the galley fo'c'sle, we rolled downwind across Spencer Gulf, bound for Port Lincoln. Though the sea was rough, the fo'c'sle was warm and bright, filled with rock music. Valerie saw to it that the supper was cooked properly, and wine soon banished the slightest doubt that we all liked one another very much. "Is there anything more splendid," Waterman cried, "than the fellowship of good shipmates in the fo'c'sle after a bracing day before the mast?" After three weeks in the fo'c'sle Stan had embraced the 19th Century with all his heart.

Peter Gimbel, sweetly drunk, swung back and forth from fits of shouting to a kind of stunned, suffused relief and quiet happiness. He looked ten years younger. What was surely the most exciting film ever taken underwater had been obtained without serious injury to anybody. The triumph was a vindication of his own faith in himself, and because he had earned it the hard way and deserved it, it was a pleasure simply to sit and drink and watch the rare joy in his face.

THE RAID AT APALACHIN

By John M. Ross

Sergeant Edgar Croswell, of the New York State Police, was basically what you would call a small-town cop. His beat as an agent for the Bureau of Criminal Investigation rarely involved serious crime. Usually it was investigations of up-state New York domestic battles, gambling parties or motor-vehicle violations. But he was carrying on a quiet crusade of his own to nab one Joseph Barbara. Croswell suspected Barbara, wearing a cloak of respectability as the operator of a beer distributorship and soft-drink bottling plant, of being the chief mobster in the Binghamton area. Croswell also believed that Barbara was somehow tied in with the nation-wide Mafia—but he couldn't prove it. Then things began happening around Barbara's country estate at Apalachin. Strangers with swarthy faces and Italian-sounding names be-gan registering at local motels and hotels. Black limousines, some with out-of-state plates, began pulling up in Barbara's driveway. Croswell knew something very big was up—but what could he, one cop alone, do about it?

Sergeant Edgar Croswell, of the New York State Police, wheeled his unmarked police car into the driveway of a new motel on the outskirts of Apalachin, a tiny town in the placid countryside of south-central New York.

"What have we got here, Ed?" his partner, Trooper Vincent Vasisko, asked as they started for the motel office.

"Rubber-check complaint," Croswell replied matter-of-factly.

Croswell's beat was like that. He came up against very little serious crime. Mostly he investigated domestic battles, gambling parties or motor-vehicle violations and, more rarely, a stickup on payday. But otherwise it was nice and peace-ful. And this afternoon of November 13, 1957, seemed to

213

promise nothing out of the ordinary.

In the motel office the proprietor's wife dug out the bogus check and gave the details of the incident to the officers. Croswell listened sympathetically and made notes. A car turned into the driveway, and Croswell instinctively glanced out the window.

"In here, Vin," he said, nudging his partner and pointing to a sitting room just off the lobby. Quickly they ducked out of sight behind a door.

The driver of the car was Joseph Barbara, Jr., and Croswell had spotted him as quickly as a bird dog picking up a scent. The Barbara family had made life in the sticks a little more interesting for a restless and inquisitive sleuth like Croswell. From the very day in 1944 when Croswell was assigned to the substation at nearby Vestal, New York, Joseph Barbara, Sr., had been the sergeant's pet project. He was an extremely intriguing project, but a frustrating one, too.

Through relentless work over 13 years Croswell had succeeded in pinpointing Barbara as the chief mobster of the area. A suspect in three Pennsylvania murders in the early Thirties, Barbara wore a cloak of respectability as the operator of a beer-distributing and soft-drink bottling plant in nearby Endicott, New York. Croswell's close scrutiny of the operation, however, had established the suspicion that the large consignments of sugar, supposedly used for the manufacture of soft drinks at the Barbara plant, were being detoured into the production of bootleg whiskey.

In his work as a Bureau of Criminal Investigation agent for the area fanning out of Binghamton, Croswell also found Barbara's name bobbing up in almost every important case. It mattered not what crime was being investigated—gambling, extortion, murder—somewhere along the line Barbara would enter the picture. But linking him with a crime and being able to charge him with it were two different matters. Barbara was a skilled hand at protecting himself in the clinches, and he had outfoxed the law again and again.

Croswell, who is described by fellow officers as a "24-hour cop," never lost heart in his pursuit. Three times a week, often on his own time, he would drive up to the $100,000 Barbara mansion on an Apalachin hillside and look the place over. If there were strange cars on the property, the sergeant would jot down the license numbers and cross-check them with his list of Barbara's known associates. Sometimes he would pull into the driveway and take pictures of the house— simply to needle Barbara and his family.

Croswell also obtained a court order to place a wiretap on Barbara's residence and business telephones. The results of this operation proved rewarding, and several Barbara henchmen were taken into custody from time to time. Barbara, however, managed to stay in the clear, and Croswell was waiting patiently for him to slip.

Behind the motel door Croswell responded to Trooper Vasisko's inquisitive nudge. "Barbara's kid," Croswell whispered.

Young Joe Barbara announced to the motelkeeper that he wanted to reserve three double rooms for the nights of November 13 and 14 and that the bill should be charged to the Canada Dry Bottling Company of Endicott, his father's plant. The motel owner's wife asked him to register for his guests, but young Barbara refused, explaining that his father was having a meeting of some of his Canada Dry associates and it was impossible to say who would use the motel rooms. He picked up the three keys and left.

"Looks like Joe's having a little powwow," Croswell observed as he and Vasisko came out of hiding. "Maybe we'd better take a look at what's happening at the bottling plant."

Finishing up their business at the motel, Croswell and Vasisko headed for Barbara's plant in Endicott, across the Susquehanna River. It was after quitting time when they arrived, and all was quiet. They checked the parking area and found no suspicious-looking cars. After an hour of observation they decided the plant wasn't the place they were looking for.

"Let's try the house," Croswell suggested.

It was 7:00 P.M. when the lawmen completed the seven-mile trip back to Apalachin. Barbara's rambling fieldstone mansion sits off a lightly traveled dirt road on the highest hill in the area. It has no fence or shielding trees and no guards except two friendly boxers that roam the grounds and contribute some token barking when a stranger arrives.

In the wide driveway to the Barbara place the officers spotted four expensive and well-polished cars. Croswell recognized one as belonging to Patsy Turrigiano, a convicted still operator of Endicott. He wrote down the license-plate numbers of the other three cars and headed back to the station in Vestal to check out the identification. Replies to his tele-type queries indicated that one car was owned by Alfred Angelicola, of New Jersey; another by James LaDuca, of Lewiston, New York, near Niagara Falls; and the third by the Buckeye Cigarette Service, of Cleveland, Ohio. It was an interesting combination.

"With Turrigiano up there," Croswell pointed out, "this looks like it might be an alcohol deal. Guess we'd better let the ATU men know about it."

The sergeant called Agents Arthur Ruston and Kenneth Brown of the Alcohol and Tobacco Tax Unit of the U.S. Treasury Department, who had been working with Croswell on his investigation of Barbara. The agents said they would be over immediately.

In the meantime the sergeant returned to the motel to see what was happening there. The big car with the Ohio plates was parked out in front. The motel proprietor told Croswell that two men had arrived around 8:30 P.M. and had gone directly to their room.

"How about taking a couple of cards down to them so they can register?" Croswell asked. "It might be interesting to see what they put down."

A moment later the motel owner returned, fuming. The men had refused to register, claiming, "Joe will take care of it in the morning."

"I'm gonna throw those bums out," the innkeeper roared.

"You'll be doing us a favor if you let them stay," Croswell assured him. "We can keep an eye on them here."

Croswell now was joined by Ruston and Brown, and they paid another visit to the Barbara house. The same cars, with the exception of the Ohio car, were in the driveway. They went back and staked out the motel, and around 11:30 P.M. LaDuca's car arrived. The officers sat tight.

Their cautious vigil at the Barbara place and the motel continued until 2:00 A.M., when both points seemed to be buttoned up for the night. Croswell went back to his bachelor quarters at the Vestal station and studied the situation.

Barbara's meetings with top gangsters and racketeers were not new to Croswell. The country cop had hooked into an earlier conclave that not only underscored Barbara's power in the Binghamton area but also linked him with the hierarchy of the notorious Mafia, the terrorist syndicate of crime and corruption that milks Americans of more than two and a half billion dollars per year.

Croswell made his first breakthrough when a speeding motorist was picked up by a New York State trooper in Binghamton in October 1956. The driver, Carmine Galante, of Brooklyn, New York, a two-time graduate of Sing Sing and a prime suspect in the 1943 murder of Carlo Tresca, an anti-Fascist newspaper editor, didn't have a driver's license. In this embarrassing situation Galante tried to pass off the license of one Joseph DiPalermo. It might have worked except for one thing—Galante couldn't give the correct birth date on the license when the troopers questioned him. Galante was arrested.

The alert trooper, knowing of Croswell's painstaking study of Barbara's activities and associates, thought the sergeant might be interested in this prize quarry. He called the Vestal station, and Croswell came on the double.

Galante had two companions with him when he was arrested. One, who identified himself as Frank Garofalo, volunteered to accompany Carmine to the station. The other traveler wisely chose to take off like a large bird. Croswell's subsequent investigation turned up the reasons why. Garofalo had no criminal record, although he had long been suspected of trafficking in illegal alcohol. Croswell thought the unidentified companion very likely was Joe DiPalermo, the man whose license had been shown to the trooper. At one time associated with Charles (Lucky) Luciano, DiPalermo had been Galante's partner in many ventures.

Further checking by Croswell showed that all three men for many years had consorted with Joseph and Salvatore Profaci, who were identified by the Kefauver Committee in the 1951 hearings as "top leaders of the Mafia."

Hopeful of linking these top-ranking hoodlums with Barbara, Croswell covered all the hotels and motels in the area. At the Arlington Hotel in Binghamton he hit the jackpot. The hotel records showed that Barbara had made reservations for five guests and that he and Garofalo, along with Louis Volpe, John Bonaventre and Joe Bonanno, all known to the police, had signed the register. There was no indication how many others had attended the meeting in Barbara's two-room suite, but it was apparent that Galante, and possibly DiPalermo, also had been there.

Charged with three motor-vehicle law violations, Galante faced a jail term and a heavy fine. The fine didn't worry Galante's associates; that was only money. But poor Carmine sitting in the cooler—if only for 30 days—was something else. Machinery was put in motion immediately to keep Galante out of jail. Politicians, elected officials, lawyers and influential businessmen either visited or telephoned Broome County for the next few days trying to square the rap.

When this strategy failed, Captain Chris Gleitmann and Sergeant Peter Policastro, of the West New York, New Jersey, Police Department, visited Croswell. According to Croswell and Trooper Vasisko, Captain Gleitmann explained that Galante worked for a friend of the West New York police chief. The friend was "a fellow named Joe." And the chief wanted to keep Galante from going to jail. Gleitmann fenced nervously for a few moments and finally, according to the sworn testimony of Croswell and Vasisko, offered Croswell a bribe of $1000 if he would handle the necessary arrangements to turn Galante loose.

"If that's not enough, I can get more," the captain allegedly promised.

Gleitmann and Policastro were invited to leave.

Galante was fined $150 and served 30 days in the Broome County jail. Croswell and Vasisko filed a report on the bribe offer, which, after a delay of more than two years, resulted in the indictment of Gleitmann and Policastro, along with Ernest Modarelli, West New York director of public safety, and Police Chief Frederick Roos, on bribery charges. The latter two also were charged with ignoring the New York police report of the bribe offer.

At the time of the indictment it was revealed that a direct telephone line existed between Galante's Avco Vending Machine Company in West New York and the West New York police headquarters.

After the Galante episode Croswell had requested all hotels and motels in the area to advise him of any reservations or occupancies by Barbara or charges to Barbara's plant account. The sergeant never heard from any of the innkeepers, although he had reason to suspect that at least one other conclave was held thereafter.

On the morning of November 14, 1957, Sergeant Croswell wondered how many more pieces of his favorite jigsaw puzzle would fall into place as a result of Joe Barbara's latest convention. Would it move him any closer to the day he could take Barbara by the collar and haul him off to jail? Or would the well-camouflaged operations of Joe and his sinister associates simply add another tantalizing chapter to Croswell's diary of frustration?

Croswell had no way of knowing that U.S. Immigration officials had a 14-karat tip from an informer in Italy that a secret summit meeting of America's gangland empire was imminent—no way of knowing that he, a country cop on a peaceful hillside, would, before the day was out, be cast in the role of dealing the dreaded Mafia the most punishing blow it has suffered in almost a century of corrupt and bloody operation in the United States.

Croswell started the day by calling his boss, Inspector Robert E. Denman, at Sydney, New York, and telling him of the strange cars at the Barbara place.

"I don't know if it will lead us to anything," Croswell told the inspector, "but we'll continue to check it out."

Croswell, along with the ATU men, made the motel his first stop. LaDuca's car was gone, but the Ohio car was still where it had been parked the night before. Croswell asked the motel owner's wife to check the rooms. She returned with the information that the three rooms were empty, no luggage had been left behind, and that all six beds had been slept in.

The next stop was Barbara's plant in Endicott. They looked over the parked cars and cased the building. The trail was cold.

"Well, that means we have to go over to Apalachin," Croswell said.

At 12:40 P.M. Croswell turned into Barbara's big driveway. His eyes widened as he saw nine expensive cars parked in the wide area in front of the four-car garage. The sergeant coolly began to copy down the license-plate numbers of each, while a young dalmatian in the kennel run at the end of the garage barked continuously. Just as Croswell completed his notations, a group of ten men appeared from behind the garage. They stopped in their tracks and peered suspiciously at Croswell. The sergeant sized them up carefully.

In an instant they were joined by a few others. Then

someone pushed the panic button, and all of them began to yell excitedly. A few took off on the dead run toward the house. Croswell put his car in reverse, and as he slowly backed out, he became fully aware of the magnitude of Joe Barbara's picnic. Toward the rear of the huge house Croswell saw approximately 25 more cars—expensive Cadillacs, Imperials and Lincolns. Behind the garage a group of men were gathered around a big stone barbecue pit laden with sizzling steaks. More guests filled the elegant fieldstone summerhouse, which became a sheltered outdoor terrace when its many doors were folded into place. It had a bar, music, café tables and chairs and a well-stocked buffet.

"Wow, what a clambake!" Croswell said as he headed out of the driveway.

Followed by the ATU men in their car, Croswell drove down the narrow dirt road for about a mile, angled his car to block the road and then went into conference with the federal agents and Trooper Vasisko.

"Let's find out who Joe's got at his party," Croswell said.

The sergeant then quickly laid his plans for stopping each car that came down from Barbara's place. Croswell had studied the land around the Barbara estate many times. There was only one road out, since a couple of wooden bridges had fallen and blocked off other avenues of escape. Barbara's cronies had to either come down the dirt road by car or try to make it on foot through an extensive wooded area to the rear of the Barbara house.

Croswell put in a call on his short-wave radio to Sergeant Walter C. Kennedy at the Vestal station. Kennedy arrived within five minutes, was briefed on the situation and left to notify the zone commander at Horseheads, New York, of the need for all available uniformed personnel. Vasisko also was dispatched to the station to telephone news of the development to Inspector Denman, and Agent Brown rode along with him to pick up another car. This left Croswell and Agent Rustin to man the roadblock.

Shortly before 1:00 P.M. the first vehicle came down the road. It was a light truck operated by a local ex-convict, Bartolo Guccia. Croswell recognized him and let him pass. The truck went down the road a short way, turned around and came back up and returned to Barbara's. Obviously, this was a test run.

The spot Croswell had selected gave him a clear view of the open area around the Barbara house. As soon as Guccia arrived back at Barbara's, apparently with the unhappy news of the police roadblock, Croswell saw several of Barbara's guests take off like frightened deer across the open fields, headed for the woods.

Almost immediately the first car, a 1957 Imperial, came down. Croswell stopped it and told the five occupants to get out. He and Agent Rustin searched the car and each individual and then asked the five to identify themselves. The first one to step up was Russell Bufalino, of Kingston, Pennsylvania. He showed licenses indicating that he was the owner and operator of the car. Croswell recognized the name immediately; the police dossier on Bufalino pegged him as the boss of eastern-Pennsylvania gambling operations.

"That's a big one to start with," the sergeant told himself. The next one was more impressive, however.

"Vito Genovese," the pasty-faced, bespectacled man announced.

Croswell gave him a long second look. Every cop knows this name. Lawmen point to him as perhaps the most powerful man in the underworld—boss of the northeastern area and heir apparent to the declining kingpin, Frank Costello.

The others identified themselves as Gerardo Catena, Dominick Oliveto and Joe Ida, all lesser lights.

"What are you fellows doing up here?" Croswell asked.

There was silence for a moment. Finally Genovese responded. "Do we *have* to answer your questions?" he asked politely.

Technically he did not have to do anything more than identify himself. Croswell, of course, realized this. Reluctantly he had to tell them that they were not required by law to answer.

Genovese gave him a weak, crooked smile as the hoodlums were permitted to return to the car and continue.

Three more cars came down the road. These were owned and operated by local thugs. Croswell knew them. He searched them, checked out the cars, jotted down their names and told them to move on.

"This is too big a job to do out here in the road," Croswell told Rustin. "I think we'd better take the rest of these fellows over to the station."

It took a little while for Croswell to get the assistance he needed for this large-scale operation. Troopers had to hurry from scattered points like Horseheads (45 miles), Whitney Point (25 miles), Waverly (25 miles) and Binghamton (13 miles). Under normal conditions only six or seven men are on duty at the nearby Vestal station. By the time all available personnel had reported, Croswell had 21 men to work with—17 uniformed troopers, two Bureau of Criminal Investigation men and the two ATU agents. A modest force for the job at hand.

When the first reinforcements arrived from Vestal, Croswell turned the roadblock over to a pair of troopers and then got on his short-wave radio to direct the roundup of the shy guests who were attempting to escape through the woods.

The cars continued to roll down the dirt road, but now the occupants were escorted by troopers to the tiny station at Vestal. Within a couple of hours the station was bulging with the greatest assortment of murderers, extortionists, dope peddlers, vice lords and racketeers ever assembled under one police roof in the history of U.S. crime.

At first they were herded into two small offices. But as more fell into the trap, a larger recreation room and, finally, one of the bedrooms of the troopers' sleeping quarters had to be opened to accommodate the unwilling guests.

"We didn't worry about their comfort," Croswell recalls. "In some of the rooms they were jammed in like it was rush hour on the New York subway, and there was hardly enough room to sit on the floor. No one complained, though."

When Croswell arrived at the station, he set up the procedure for processing the convention delegates. One at a time they were brought into the sergeant's office and directed to take off their shoes and empty the contents of their pockets on a desk. They were told to count their money and return it to their pockets. If they had personal papers, they were examined by Croswell. They were interrogated, and a personal-history sheet—including details like age, height, weight—was filled out for each.

As each man finished the questioning, his history sheet was turned over to an officer who checked the information via teletype and tried to determine if the individual was wanted by his local police. In some cases where the teletype replies were inconclusive, direct long-distance telephone calls were placed to law-enforcement agencies.

It was an enormous undertaking, since the delegates to this convention represented 11 states and came from such scattered points as California and Florida, as well as Puerto Rico. Of the 60 rounded up, only nine did not have criminal records. The others had an aggregate of more than 100 convictions and 275 arrests. However, none of the 60 were on a police "wanted" list.

The frisking of the individual hoods indicated that even the Mafia sometimes benefits from past mistakes. In the only other raid of a crime convention on record, in Cleveland in 1928, 13 of the 21 delegates were armed. This time not a single weapon was found. Three of the Apalachin confreres —Genovese, Joe Profaci and Joe Magliocco—had also been at the Cleveland clambake.

"These fellows were pretty well rehearsed for the occasion," Croswell points out. "Most of them carried no personal papers or cards. Few had wallets. They simply had their driver's licenses in their shirt pockets and a roll of bills in their trousers.

"Their feeble attempts to explain their presence at Barbara's also followed a pattern. They had dropped in to see Joe, they said, because they heard that Joe had been sick. It was just a coincidence, they claimed, that they all happened to get there at the same time. And, of course, they told us this with straight faces, too."

It was true that Barbara had been ill. Earlier in the year he had undergone a serious heart operation. But the claim of "coincidence" in the mass sick call was shot full of holes a few days after the convention, when Croswell dug up an interesting tidbit. Barbara's houseman had placed a $431 meat order with Armour's in Binghamton a week before the convention, calling for 200 pounds of steak, 20 pounds of veal cutlets, a whole boiled ham and a can of luncheon meat. The cut of steak specified was so choice that it was not immediately available in Binghamton, a city of 80,000 population, and the order had to be rushed to a packing-house in Chicago. Barbara, apparently was not taken unawares by the coincidence of 60-odd friends dropping by at the same time.

Croswell's investigation also uncovered the significant fact that 19 of the visitors had arrived in a body at Broome County Airport on the morning of November 14, after a TWA flight from Newark, New Jersey. In checking the plane's manifest Croswell discovered that all 19 had used fictitious names—in most cases the names of unsuspecting neighbors back home.

Croswell had to call on his last shred of patience as he endured the frustration of netting only evasive answers, or utter silence, over more than 12 hours of interrogation. Occasionally an unusually fanciful tale by a hoodlum would provide some comic relief.

For instance, when Simone Scozzari, of San Gabriel, California, was asked for his occupation, he proudly replied, "Unemployed for twenty years." When he emptied his pockets, he produced $9000 in cash.

"Boy, you must have had some sock when you quit work," one of the troopers commented sarcastically.

Most of the thugs carried large sums of cash in $50 and $100 bills.

The best examples of creative thinking were turned in by the delegates who were apprehended after trying to escape through the woods. Two thugs picked up by the troopers near the wooded area behind the Barbara estate swore they had journeyed up from New Jersey on the Pennsylvania Railroad to look at some real estate. When the troopers pointed out that the Pennsy didn't operate within 70 miles of Apalachin, one simply shrugged his shoulder and complained, "I don't know why you fellows don't believe us."

James LaDuca, whose car had been spotted by Croswell at both the Barbara home and the motel the night before, was picked up by troopers near the Binghamton city line, about four hours after the trap was sprung. He was riding with three other hoods in the Ohio car Croswell had checked out the night before. The shoes of the four were dirty and muddy, and their clothes were disheveled, apparently from the rough overland hike. Nevertheless, they insisted that they were just passing through Binghamton on their way from Buffalo.

Croswell told LaDuca he had previously seen him and his car at the motel. LaDuca said that was impossible. Croswell searched LaDuca and found a package of matches bearing the motel's name, but LaDuca stuck to his story.

LaDuca's car was located later in Barbara's garage. Croswell theorizes that LaDuca and the other three men worked their way through the woods and back to the motel without being detected. There they picked up the Ohio car and had almost succeeded in escaping the area when they were nabbed.

The task of rounding up the dismounted gangsters wasn't as difficult as it might seem.

"Actually, these fellows were easy to spot," Croswell says. "They were dressed just about like Hollywood gangsters— dark coats, wide-brimmed hats, white-on-white shirts, pointed shoes and dark suits hand-tailored from imported cloth. They couldn't be mistaken for farmers or picnickers.

"A few of them managed to get through the woods and reach a nearby house. They rang the doorbell and told the lady of the house that their car had broken down and they were stranded. They asked her to call a cab for them. The lady agreed but told them to remain on the steps. A pair of our cruising troopers came along while she was telephoning, and they spotted the men immediately. When the lady returned, she saw her callers being hauled off by the troopers."

Only four slipped through the net. Croswell believes two managed to hire a taxicab, since he has a report of a hack being in the area at that time. The other pair probably got a lift from a motorist to the railroad station. The names of all four, however, have been learned.

One of the prize packages snatched from the woods was former city councilman John C. Montana, of Buffalo. Montana had done such a fine job of window dressing his operation as a respectable liquor dealer that he had been chosen Buffalo's Man of the Year in 1956. Upstate New York police, however, long had suspected him of underworld ties.

When Montana was finally corralled, he asked if he might speak privately to Sergeant Croswell. He told the sergeant a heart-tugging story, according to Croswell. All this was so embarrassing for a man of his position, Montana pointed out. He had dropped in to see his friend Barbara not knowing who was going to be there. When he saw who the other visitors were, he immediately tried to leave. That was when he encountered the troopers, he said.

When he realized his story wasn't getting through to Croswell, he reached for the patent device of the criminal, according to the sergeant. He said he knew many important people in Buffalo, Croswell says, and that some of these friends could be very helpful to the sergeant.

Croswell walked away from him in disgust and later made a special report on Montana's proposal.

Most of the delegates were 50 to 65 years old. Of the 60 men rounded up, 34 were foreign-born, and all were of Italian birth or descent, though none had any difficulty speaking or understanding English. In the weeks that followed it was odd how many of those who were ordered to appear in court or before investigating bodies clammed up by saying they couldn't handle the language.

Croswell encountered good manners from his panic-stricken guests with only two exceptions. They were John DeMarco, of Shaker Heights, Ohio, and John Scalish, of Cleveland, Ohio. Both were surly and completely uncooperative. DeMarco had a record that included murder, blackmail and bombing and a stretch in the Ohio State Penitentiary. Scalish's past-performance chart showed three counts of robbery, parole violation and two terms in the same prison. As a special reward Croswell saw to it that they were the last to leave the Vestal station.

When Croswell first realized the importance of the mammoth conclave he had uncovered, his impulse was to lock up all the participants overnight so that a more penetrating study could be made of each. He huddled with Lieutenants K. E. Weidenborner and J. A. Murphy on legal procedure. They took lawbooks from the shelf and searched them like men reaching for a straw. Finally they had to admit sadly that there was no way the hoodlums could be detained, not even for something like disorderly conduct.

The New York State Penal Law, Section 722, clearly states the grounds for charging an individual with disorderly conduct. It deals with persons of evil reputation consorting for an unlawful purpose. The *mafiosi* fitted that category perfectly. However, the law further states that this must be carried on in a public place. Furthermore, Croswell and his aides couldn't prove the delegates were consorting for an unlawful purpose, nor were the officials in a position to immediately prove the delegates were persons of evil reputation.

There was no legal basis for holding them on a conspiracy charge, and vagrancy had to be ruled out because Tioga County, which had jurisdiction over the meeting, doesn't have such a law on its books. Under New York law Croswell was obliged either to place charges against them and arraign them before a judge "without unreasonable delay" or turn them loose.

At 1:30 A.M., almost 13 hours after the net had fallen on the underworld executive session, the last of the hoods was released. Most of them had been held for seven or eight hours.

"It almost broke our hearts to have to toss all those big ones back," Sergeant Croswell says. "I'm only a country cop, not a legal expert, but it seems obvious to me that there aren't enough teeth in our laws when we have to release a band of men who have dedicated their lives to lawlessness before we've had time enough to give them a thorough sifting.

"We did everything we could within the legal bounds. We made sure we had no fugitives from justice. We checked them for weapons or incriminating evidence. And we tried to squeeze from them every pertinent bit of information they and the law would allow. If nothing else, we were able to get them out in the open where anyone could take a legal shot at them."

This is a modest appraisal, indeed, of the results of the raid at Apalachin. In tearing away a large piece of the veil of secrecy that has shielded the Mafia these many years, Croswell put more heat on the big operators of organized crime than they had felt in many a year.

The roster compiled in the tiny police office at Vestal has given America's law-enforcement agencies a broad and authentic picture of the "syndicate" for the first time. It conclusively established the ties between Murder Incorporated in New York, the Purple Gang in Detroit, Al Capone's old mobsters in Chicago and other terrorist mobs in Florida, New Orleans, Cleveland and California. And it signaled the launching of investigations in almost every area of the country into the activities of the delegates to Joe Barbara's elegant soiree.

Most of the convention delegates hid behind the protection of the Constitution's Fifth Amendment, claiming their testimony would be self-incriminating. The few who elected to testify made a mockery of the proceedings by spinning fanciful, and often hilarious, tales of the purpose of the outing at Apalachin.

John Montana, for instance, said he was on his way to Pittston, Pennsylvania, on the day of the Apalachin raid, when his three-month-old Cadillac developed brake trouble. It just happened that he was near the home of his old friend Joe Barbara, and Montana was sure Joe would have a mechanic sitting around the premises who could repair the brakes.

Joe Profaci, the "Olive Oil King," said he got to Apalachin by mistake. He took a wrong turn while driving from New York to Scranton, Pennsylvania, and, lo and behold, where did he wind up? Near Apalachin, of course. And with friend Barbara recovering from an illness, wasn't it perfectly natural for Profaci to drop by to see him?

Anthony Guarnieri, who identified himself as a seller of women's dresses and men's shirts, happened to be in Endicott on November 14, 1957, where he met Patsy Turrigiano. The latter said he was going over to see Joe Barbara. Guarnieri claims this was an amazing coincidence, since he had three shirts he had made up for Barbara sitting on the rear seat of his car awaiting delivery.

"I might as well go with you," Guarnieri says he told Patsy. It was as innocent as that.

Bartolo Guccia, the Endicott ex-convict who drove the truck on the test run of Croswell's roadblock, told investigators that he was simply picking up a weekly fish order at the Barbara home. Asked why he had returned to the mansion once he had successfully passed through the roadblock, Guccia informed them that he had forgotten the fish order and went back to double-check.

"By the way," one of the interrogators asked, "what was the order?"

"Three porgies and a mackerel," Guccia snapped.

At first the mobsters seemed to fare quite well in the weeks that followed the tabulation of the roster at Apalachin. There was embarrassment for many members of the underworld hall of fame, of course. A few slaps on the wrist, too. Some of the hoodlums lost their beer and alcohol licenses, notary-public commissions and pistol permits. One ex-convict was returned to jail for violation of parole, and Barbara, the host with the most, was pressured into selling his lucrative bottling plant.

It took the authorities a few months to develop the information Sergeant Croswell and his men had compiled at Apalachin. By the spring of 1958 there was enough ammunition accumulated to launch a broadside attack against the very roots of organized crime.

The call to action was sounded by the U.S. Justice Department, when it announced its all-out drive to put the "100 top hoodlums" behind bars or out of the country. It called for the pooling of all available information on the mobsters by various other federal agencies, including the FBI, the Immigration Service, the Internal Revenue Service, the Bureau of Narcotics and the Treasury Department. And it announced its intention of invoking antitrust laws to trap labor racketeers and others who manipulated sinister operations from behind respectable fronts.

The Council of State Governments and the National Association of State Attorneys General pitched in with pledges of assistance and cooperation. Milton Wessel, 35, was named by the attorney general to lead the attack, placing him at the head of the newly formed Special Group on Organized Crime. And the battle was on.

Almost immediately the Immigration Service began to move against the foreign-born Apalachin confreres, charging them with "illegal entry" in some cases or classifying others as "undesirable aliens." The ax fell first on Russell Bufalino, the alleged Mafia chieftain in the eastern-Pennsylvania area. He was ordered deported. Joe Profaci was next. Ten others waited in the wings.

The Bureau of Narcotics cemented its case against kingpin Genovese and three other Apalachin delegates, and after a four-month trial they were found guilty of conspiring to import and sell narcotics.

Thus, in two swift strokes, three of the Mafia's most powerful leaders were being readied for the skids. But more was to come.

The New York Commission of Investigation, a thorn in the sides of the *mafiosi* from the outset, stepped in to deal the mobsters the most severe blow of the post-Apalachin period. After a long line of gangsters had succeeded in hiding behind the Fifth Amendment at [the August 1958] hearings and investigations, the commission granted immunity to seven Apalachin participants when they attempted to follow suit. The seven—Carmine Lombardozzi, Rosario Mancuso, Costenze Valenti, Frank Valenti, Joe Riccobono, Paul Castellano and Michael Miranda—still refused to talk. The commission then ordered the men tossed into jail.

The thugs cried, "Foul!" and sent their high-priced lawyers scurrying for an appeal. In the first test the appellate court upheld the order. The mob's attorneys took it a step higher. By the time the New York Court of Appeals handed down its decision on March 13, 1959, the seven Apalachin delegates had spent more than seven months in the cooler. The court said they must remain there until they decided to loosen their tongues. It was a crushing blow.

The brothers Valenti, reaching for what they hopefully thought was a legal loophole, announced they would talk. Interpreting the court decision somewhat loosely, the Valentis figured all they had to do was furnish answers—any answers —to the questions about Apalachin and they would be set free. So, when they appeared before the commission, they sang the old tune about "sitting up with a sick friend."

The court ruled that the Valentis had not complied with the order, since they did not furnish "bona fide" answers.

Costenze Valenti was in a rage when attendants carted him back to his cell. Thumbing an angry finger in the direction of the judge, he bellowed, "Who does this guy think he is—God?"

The New York Commission set out to round up more Apalachinites and send them through the same talk-or-jail routine. But now the hoodlums made themselves scarce. Some were so scarce that police began to speculate on the possibility that the Mafia was permanently silencing some of its members.

The legal net did trap two of the most elusive fish—Joe Barbara and his 23-year-old son, Joe, Jr. Some 17 months after the Apalachin picnic, the law succeeded in indicting Joe, Sr., on income-tax charges.

Barbara did not give in easily. In December 1958, New York police had taped a subpoena on the door of his mansion, directing him to appear before the Investigation Commission in New York City. The envelope also contained $16 to pay his round-trip railroad fare—a legal requirement. Barbara ignored the subpoena. The police made him keenly aware of the invitation on his door by barking through bullhorns that could be heard a quarter of a mile away.

"Come out, come out," the horn blasted, "there's a subpoena on your door."

Barbara didn't touch it, and his lawyers claimed in court that he had not been legally served. They were overruled. Now the Barbara barristers cited the $16 check for carfare and said this was not enough to pay Big Joe's way to New York. The round trip, they claimed, was 206 miles between Apalachin and New York, and figured at the legal rate of eight cents per mile, this was 48 cents short. Again they were squelched by the court.

On March 13 Big Joe was indicted, and lawmen pointed out that it probably cost Barbara more than $500 in legal fees to debate the issue of 48 cents.

Two weeks earlier Joe, Jr., was routed from his bed in the middle of the night and taken in his pajamas to New York City, where he was booked on perjury charges.

Looking at the scoreboard approximately 18 months after Apalachin, the law showed some impressive figures. Ten of the Apalachin 66 were in jail, six more were indicted, three faced prompt deportation, three were found guilty of narcotics charges, one had died, and the remainder were either under warrant or subpoena—but, mostly, were missing, meaning in hiding.

None of the investigations or official hearings have succeeded in finding the reason or reasons for the gangland convention. Speculation has ranged far and wide concerning the convention's agenda. Some claim it tied in with the murder of Albert Anastasia and the distribution of some of the spoils of his former crime empire. Others say it concerned Havana gambling interests of the Mafia. And still others list such items as narcotics, labor racketeering, the jukebox industry and other assorted forms of shakedown on the program.

Lieutenant James S. Mooney, of the New York City Police, told the McClellan Committee that the Apalachin meeting had been called for the purpose of "trying" *mafioso* Carmine Lombardozzi, who had stepped out of line with the syndicate. Mooney says his informants reported that Lombardozzi had been sentenced to death, but the convention commuted it to a $10,000 fine. Many students of Mafia operations, however, were unwilling to go along with Mooney's theory, which sounded like a movie plot.

"From what we know of their activities, we're inclined to believe that they had very little time to discuss anything before the party was broken up," Sergeant Croswell says. "Most of them had just arrived on the morning of November 14, and the early part of the program seemed to be devoted to eating and drinking and renewing old acquaintance. Then we arrived on the scene.

"It should be remembered that the motel and hotel reservations were for two nights, which means they weren't rushing their program. Undoubtedly they planned to do a lot of business that night and the next day. But I guess we spoiled that."

Hailed by the Society of Professional Investigators as its Man of the Year in 1958 and cited by many other law-enforcement agencies for his extraordinary police work, Sergeant Croswell has been strangely brushed aside by his own New York State Police. He has received no promotion, no increase in pay, no citation on his record.

Some of this undoubtedly can be traced to the attempts of one big-city newspaper to miscast Croswell in the role of "goat" in the Apalachin raid. This campaign developed shortly after the last of the hoodlums was released, and newspaper, radio and television men from the four corners of New York swarmed over the tiny police station for details of Croswell's fantastic roundup. The sergeant stayed up all night to answer the questions of the newsmen, but this wasn't enough. More reporters showed up the next day.

Croswell took the time to fill in a come-lately reporter from a New York City newspaper. When the sergeant suddenly was called from the office, the overzealous reporter pounced on the opportunity to inspect some of the official papers on Croswell's desk. He found one confidential report about the raid particularly interesting, pocketed it and headed for a newspaper office in Endicott to have it photostated.

Tipped off by a friend on the Endicott paper's staff, Croswell placed the New York reporter under arrest when the latter made the mistake of trying to return the document to the sergeant's desk. Later Croswell relented, stripped the reporter of whatever notes he had gathered on the raid and chased him out of the station.

The next day the reporter's paper lashed out in a page-one blast at Croswell, stating that he had botched the opportunity of holding the crime lords in jail. The paper demanded an investigation of Croswell's work at Apalachin, and the governor and the state police complied almost immediately.

Croswell came through the two investigations with flying colors. The New York Joint Legislative Committee on Government Operations, in its final report, stated that the convention probably would have passed unnoticed and become "no more than another rumor in law-enforcement circles" but for the "superior" work of Croswell. Arthur L. Reuter, acting commissioner of investigation, praised Croswell's performance and reported that there was "insufficient legal basis" for holding the mobsters after interrogation. He pointed out that there was a "complete absence of competent proof beyond a reasonable doubt that any were presently living as thieves or criminals," as would be required to invoke an anticonsorting law.

But with or without medals, and with or without a boost in rank or pay, Sergeant Croswell has become a legend among New York lawmen. Troopers refer to him as "Apalachin Ed" —the country cop who trapped the Mafia.

THE MAN WHO
FLEW LIKE A BAT

By Martin Caidin

*Red Grant is a little man in stature—but a big man in the
courage department. He learned parachuting with the 507th
Parachute Infantry in World War Two and then got into it
for profit sort of by accident. He began to jump for various
air shows in the U.S. and Canada and had many narrow
brushes with death. Red did all the air-circus tricks you've
heard about. He carried sacks of flour under his arms and
released the flour behind him in huge contrails in a swooping
pattern before popping open his chute, he rode the top wing
of a biplane as it looped and rolled over the horrified crowds,
and he stood up in a racing convertible and climbed a flimsy
rope ladder up to a low-flying plane. But his one goal was to
someday fly the bat wings. The bat wings are a 180-pound
assemblage of nylon and wire that transforms the wearer into
a human airplane. There are wings and webbing between the
legs. A man can control his flight and perform spectacular
free-fall maneuvers—but it's the most dangerous of all parachute techniques. Red learned to use the bat wings and became fairly proficient with them. Then he decided to try to
pull off a real stunt: He would try to make the first international batwing flight, from the U.S. into Canada. The occasion was to be an air circus in Houlton, Maine. He figured
it would be simple—just bail out with enough altitude to allow him to glide across the Canadian border, then parachute
down. He made it easy. But the next jump, this time in Kentucky, was a different story. As he propelled himself out of
the plane, he was brought up with a terrific jolt. Somehow
his gear had gotten fouled up on the way out, and now he
found himself hanging precariously from the bottom of the
plane, with the ground 10,000 feet below. How could he
free himself? Was the pilot aware that he was still with
him? . . .*

In all the history of barnstorming, air shows and special air circuses, there have been only 76 *batmen*—and R. W. "Red" Grant, diminutive in stature but a giant in courage and skill, is the last of the breed. The batman is perhaps the most unusual of all the men who leap through the air. He tumbles out of an airplane three miles up and quickly becomes a human projectile that swoops, darts, turns, spirals, dives and glides—until his arms almost begin to pop out of their sockets from the hammering pressure of the air against his special bat wings.

Clem Sohn, one of the veteran barnstormers in business before World War Two, started the dangerous stunt back in 1935. Sohn was already famous for his long-delay drops from airplanes, and when he rigged up a set of home-built wings and sails to attach to his body, hurtling through the air like a huge bat or an aerial manta ray, he proved to be an immediate crowd sensation. The proof was in the gate; dollar income soared wherever he appeared. In 1937 he took his wings to France. Parachuting in Europe before World War Two was already a sport of great enthusiasm, and the Continentals had the habit of looking down their noses at parachuting in the United States. But the batwinged Sohn proved an immediate smash hit. In a way he reached the peak of his career in France.

He bailed out one afternoon before a packed crowd of several thousand Frenchmen. They went through the appropriate gasps and clutching of breasts in fright as Sohn started his batwinged glide toward the earth. Sohn jerked the ripcord of his main chute, and the crowd sat up straight and started rising to their feet when the silk streamered instead of cracking open into the full canopy. They were all on their feet and screaming when he deployed his reserve pack and that one streamered, also. Both chutes fluttering behind him like two useless rags, Clem Sohn smashed into the ground at 90 miles per hour. The first spectators to run to the scene found a red pulp instead of a man. Sohn was very dead.

It was ten years later that Red Grant had occasion to think clearly of Clem Sohn. At that moment Grant, who said the vision of Sohn came to him like a flash, was plummeting toward the earth. And, like Sohn, he also had trailing behind him two long, whistling and very useless ribbons of silk. With some frantic maneuvering and handling of the shroud lines,

Grant managed to get a canopy open just before he would have plunged into the earth to his death. Muses Red Grant:

It's a miracle I'm still alive. Only a damn fool would have gotten into this business in the first place—a business I got into by accident.

As most of you remember, the fall of 1945 was a crazy, mixed-up period. What was left of my outfit, the 507th Parachute Infantry, came back from the ETO to get paid off. I changed into civvies after seven years in the regular army and immediately got into trouble.

I went up to Denver to see a chick I had been more or less engaged to during the war. Killing time, I went into a typical soldier trap to have a beer. There was an argument going on at the bar. Some services-of-supply soldier was mouthing off at a B-girl; then he hit her. All five-feet-seven of me got up from the table, and I went over and clipped that bird twice. He slumped out of sight. A low growl came from behind me—I had committed the cardinal sin of hitting a *soldier*. Some more rear-echelon commandos came from nowhere, and I hightailed it out of there and went flying up the street. I caromed off three guys who grabbed me and yelled, "Whoa there, little man!" I looked up at three bruisers wearing the patch of the 82nd Airborne on their shoulders. I knew them all; so we went back and cleaned out the bar. Afterward we went up to my hotel room and toasted Fightin' Slim Jim Gavin with three fifths of Old Joyful.

Next day I cleaned up and went to see my fiancée. She was downright cool, and I didn't get the drift until I saw her flicking her eyes back and forth from me to the picture on the mantel. It was taken in London, and I looked like a Mexican general: white silk scarf, fruit salad down to there, the *fourragère*—the works. When she told me she couldn't possibly introduce me to her friends until I put on my uniform, boots and ribbons, I walked out the door and haven't seen her since.

I had no job, no fiancée, no prospects. Soldiering was all I knew. I was used to living under pressure, never knowing from one day to the next whether I would get killed or be doing the killing. Most of the guys who came out of the greatest adventure of them all settled down; a few of us weren't ready to face the same desk day after day. For me there was always that next hill to climb. . . .

It was the end of the First World War all over again. Then Red Grant, through dating another chick, ended up at a meeting of the Civil Air Patrol in Denver. He fidgeted while the meeting went on; the CAP was getting together an air show. Grant's ears perked up a bit when he heard the words *parachute jumper*, and the next moment everyone heard from his date that Red Grant *was* a jumper. He agreed to their request to make a jump at the air show. Red's girl would provide the transportation herself; she would fly a beat-up old PT-23 trainer. With something interesting happening for the first time since he came back stateside, he went out and rented a full jumper's rig.

"It wasn't until I was alone in my hotel room that night," admits Red, "that I realized I didn't know a damn thing about free fall; all my combat jumps had been static-line drops from C-47s. I worried about it all night.

"There was nothing to it. Alice got the PT-23 up to three thousand feet, and I stepped out on the narrow wing and went off into space, keeping my left hand over my head to act as a rudder. The landing strip rushed up to meet me, I pulled the D ring, my bones were wrenched by the shock of the chute opening, then I landed on the runway standing up. The crowd roared—and I had just made fifty bucks."

Red jumped again that afternoon; this time, however, he pulled the D ring just a bit too late, missed his target and almost plowed into the grandstand. He was gathering up the folds of the parachute when a woman approached him.

"How many free falls have you made?" she asked.

"You just saw the first two," Red admitted candidly.

"Well, you stupid so-and-so," she said easily, "if you live a year jumping like that, you'll be lucky. But if you do live, you'll be one of the best."

Red stared openmouthed at her. That was his introduction to Fay Cox, whom he calls "America's greatest female parachutist."

At the end of the day Red Grant had made $100 and decided he had just started on a new career. He began to jump for different air shows throughout the United States

and Canada. He went through one minor disaster after
another but always avoided major injury. He stresses with
candor:

I knew cold fear. In Valley City, North Dakota, on
Labor Day of 1948, I went out of a Super Cub at
8000 feet in a freshening wind. I fell through space
until I could smell the earth; then I pulled the rip-cord
handle. Nothing happened. I pulled with both hands,
and the handle came off, leaving the rip cord still in the
housing. It can't happen, but it did, and I was hurtling
toward the earth with a useless rip-cord handle in my
hand and a stupid look on my face.

I went for the reserve chute and frantically threw
handfuls of silk away from me. I was on my back when
the chute popped, and it felt like I had kicked myself in
the back of my head with my heels. I looked up and saw
to my horror that I had a double Mae West—four small
puffs of silk instead of one big one—and that three
panels had blown. I tried to work the fouled lines off
the tops of the reserve canopy, but they stayed fast and
the silk began ripping to shreds. I was still struggling
with the lines when the earth rushed up and slammed into me. The air was smashed from my lungs, and then
somebody turned out the lights.

I woke up ten minutes later in a field covered with
boulders the size of my head. Ripped silk was all over
the place. That little angel sitting on my shoulder had
saved my life. No bones were broken, but by late that
night I had turned a sickly shade of yellow-green from
my neck to my ankles. When I heard the taped playback
of the radio announcer's hysterical description of my
fall and probable death, the reaction hit me and my legs
gave way—it was the nearest I ever came to fainting.

Undaunted by his brushes with death, Red Grant added
new gimmicks to his act. He was a natural crowd pleaser,
the kind of man who forms one of the major elements of
any circus. He leaped from airplanes—or, rather, just fell
out of them—with open bags of flour beneath each arm. It
is an extremely difficult way to sustain a long free fall, since
the jumper has no opportunity and lacks the means of stabi-

lizing his plunge. Notwithstanding the kind of problem that would give a sky diver the screaming horrors, Red plunged from on high with the flour streaming from the two sacks, with his "twin flour contrails" weaving a pattern through the sky. By changing body position and the angle of his legs, he actually achieved a controlled descent. Finally he tossed aside the bags, which fluttered behind him like falling moths, and jerked open his chute.

Red was much more than a stunt jumper. Like other stunt men, he rode the top wing of a powerful Stearman, especially rigged for air-show work, secured to "that bucking bronco only by straps on my feet and thin cables kept taut by locking my knees together." Like Frank Clarke, Tommy Walker and many of the great barnstormers, he stood up in a convertible and leaped aboard a rope ladder dangling from an airplane that passed overhead. Despite the variety of gimmicks he added to his routine, he kept inching toward what he wanted most of all—jumping the bat wings.

It was in Jackson, Mississippi, that the crowd—the "pack of jackals"—finally drank its blood, and Red Grant got his bat wings. As he recalls the day:

I went on early in the show, jumped and free-fell a long way while three ships weaved around my flight path, wrapping me in great white swaths of smoke. I touched down gently and sat on the grass to watch Billy Fisher wring out his little Ross Parakeet. . . . Billy taxied out, swung into the wind and shoved the throttle forward. The burst of power shot the Parakeet into the air like a rocket. He rolled, half-rolled and snap-rolled just off the deck. Then Billy pushed the nose up and got up to 1200 feet and leveled off. The nose dropped straight down, and the shriek of his engine tore apart the sky. At 800 feet the sound of the engine changed key, and a puff of smoke erupted from the cowling. The nose came up sharply in a high g-load maneuver, and the engine ripped loose from the mounts and hurtled backward through the cabane struts. Parts of the upper left wing tore off and fluttered away in the slipstream. I was on my feet yelling to Billy to get out. I saw him stand up in the cockpit, then settle back in the bucket. The plane did a crazy kind of flat turn and skidded drunkenly away from the thousands of people in the stands below. The Parakeet half-rolled and went in inverted. Fisher was killed instantly.

The m.c. stayed on the mike and kept the crowd from smashing through the barriers to get at the wreckage and a few bloody souvenirs. Then he asked me to ride the top wing of the Stearman to get the crowd's mind off the tragedy. I secured the cables, the pilot revved up the engine, and we took off. It was the most horrible moment of my life when we climbed out over the wreckage of Billy's plane. I looked down past my feet at the pilot and saw unashamed tears streaming under the rubber rims of his goggles.

After four years of working air shows I finally got my bat wings. Our regular batman came up to me and said, "Red, I've had it. The equipment is all yours." Then he walked away. I stood there wondering if that was the way I would wind up—defeated by too many women and too much booze before I was 35.

I looked at the equipment I had inherited with two feelings: pride and fear. There was a lot of tradition behind those wings, and there was a lot of built-in danger.

You get in the wings like pulling on a pair of pants, except the pants are like webbing, stretched between the legs. The wings start at the ankle and go out at an angle almost to shoulder height. The wings are supported at the top by heavy round wooden poles, which are gripped with each hand halfway down the length so you can control the flight attitude. The whole rig is permanently attached and can't be ditched in flight if something goes haywire. The wings go on over the regular jump suit, along with the main chute and the reserve, which hangs halfway down in front. An altimeter is attached to the reserve pack.

Including the boots and buffet hat and oversize goggles, the whole rig weighs 180 pounds. Bear in mind that I'm a little guy, tipping the scales at 140. Once I'm clear of the ship, I am a human airfoil, prey to the laws of flight. But there is no engine for power, and only sheer endurance keeps the wings taut and at the proper attitude.

Red made his first batwing jump in August of 1949. He was scheduled to go into his act immediately after the comedy routine performed by Gloria Lynch. Gloria, at 24 years of age, was only four feet, six inches tall, as pert and cute as a new button. She dressed in a pinafore and wore her hair in pigtails and looked exactly like a little girl—instead of one of the best female pilots in the flying business. Her act called for her to skip up to the announcer and beg for a ride in an airplane. Finally, with a carefully worked-out routine, she won the sympathy of the crowd and the announcer "gave in." He summoned a pilot, and Gloria went out to a biplane, where she was strapped into the front seat. As the pilot started to the rear seat, Gloria slapped home the throttle. She staggered into the air with a chorus of shrieks and horrified screams from the audience, who were convinced that they were about to see the little girl killed. On his first day as a batman, Red was circling high over the field, waiting for Gloria Lynch to finish her act before he jumped.

He watched the little biplane far below him, dragging the field and roller-coasting in its mock landing attempts. Then something went wrong. An updraft snatched at the airplane, whisked away its lift and left it helpless in the air. The ship plunged into the field. Red's pilot sideslipped out of the sky like a bomb as he banged down to a landing. The two men ran from their ship to the crumpled wreckage just as rescuers were pulling Gloria from the cockpit.

She was a lot shorter now. Both feet had been torn off at the ankles.

Red's debut was postponed; the tragedy to Gloria overshadowed any "show must go on" routine. Nobody wanted to fly anymore that day.

Finally he jumped the wings. Wisely he paid strict attention to everything that happened and swiftly gained great skill with his bat gear. "Then," he explains, as confidence began to override natural caution, "I became confident enough to think I could pull off one of the biggest damn-fool stunts ever dreamed up in aerial show business. Nobody had ever made an international batwing flight, and I elected myself to be the first man to try."

Red planned to make the big attempt when the circus made its showing in Houlton, Maine. The idea was for him to bail out with enough altitude to cross the border into

Canada, glide to a safe landing area, crack his chute and land. He picked his possible touchdown sites carefully, the newspapers played it up big, and the gate grew in leaps and bounds. The promoters were delighted.

The day before the jump Red decided to rest easy and went off to Presque Isle to loaf. He missed two boys who had hustled to the field to get the batman's autograph. The kids asked Rod Joclyn, one of the circus pilots, where the batman could be found. Rod told them that Grant had flown off but would be back later. He told the kids to wait by the corner of the hangar.

"Now, he'll be flying high and fast when he comes," Rod explained carefully, "so you'll have to listen close to hear the birdlike noises he makes in flight." The kids waited till sundown gazing up into the sky with their hands cupped by their ears.

Despite the hullabaloo raised about Red Grant's international bat flight, show business demanded a lot of work before he would go into his climax. First he did his long free fall, with two smoke planes writhing earthward about him. What happened on his next act nearly canceled out the ballyhooed stunt. He was to go through the bit of standing on the wing while the pilot jostled the airplane about. Red explained:

> We were going to do this one in an Argo, a biplane built in late 1918. They had wisely manufactured no more than 19 of these beasts. I climbed up on the top wing, secured the thin cables and got ready for the takeoff. The pilot was feeling frisky as hell and turned that old biplane every way but loose. It's cold, windy and lonesome up there on the wing, and when the pilot starts violent aerobatics, the world goes insane: Sky, earth and horizon whirl crazily, blending together in a mash of colors. The blast of wind from the prop wash threatens to tear me loose from my slender moorings and fling me backward into space.
>
> The pilot decided to give us all a little extra thrill: He stalled out at the top of a loop, and the plane fell off into a vicious spin. We did about five turns before he leveled off and dragged the field. My knees were weak when we landed, and when one of the cables holding

me to the wing snapped, I fell straight back and wedged my butt in the windscreen. I was stuck fast, my legs dangling on either side of the fuselage. Somebody came out with tools and cut the windscreen apart so I could get free. Somehow I had lost all confidence in that pilot. . . .

Fifteen minutes later Red was bundled and strapped into his cumbersome gear, jammed into the seat beside the pilot of a Piper Tri-Pacer and climbing steeply for his X in the sky where he would shove himself out of the airplane and begin his long glide to Canada. But first there was that climb to altitude, and of all the things a jumper dislikes the most, it's waiting while the airplane sticks its nose into the sky and drags itself away from the earth. The jumper has nothing to do but sit. And when you're bundled into your gear and jammed into an airplane, that sitting means thinking, and a swift train of thoughts rumbles through your mind. It's not clear thinking; the man with the chutes on his back sweats out the climb by trying hard to concentrate on his procedure for the bailout. There are mental pictures of falling away from the airplane, of body movements, then a swift scan of the landing area, not seen in static position but expanding steadily and rapidly. On his way to altitude Red offered himself silent congratulations on not having eaten before taking off.

"I figure that if I get clobbered," he explains, "the time the docs save in pumping out my stomach can be put to better use saving my neck."

By the time the Tri-Pacer leveled off, Red noticed:

My hands are getting cold. In a few minutes they are like lumps of ice. I look at the altimeter. We are at 14,600 feet and I am not wearing gloves. It's easier to feel the rip cord with my bare hands, but nearly three miles up it's freezing cold. Then I see the signal far below—a car circling slowly on the runway. It's time to go.

I look down and pick out the clump of trees I have selected as my jump point. The right wheel blocks the trees from sight, and I reach over and hit the pilot on the shoulder and scream, "Chop it!" The pilot cuts back the throttle, and I place my hands on either side of the door and propel myself backward clearing the struts. The Tri-Pacer shoots forward away from me, the sound of its engine is quickly lost in the rush of air past my head. I am on my back, staring up at the sky, my wings extended. My arms quiver with the strain, and I am chilled clear through.

Snap! I half-roll out automatically with a sharp wrench and am now flat and stable—a true winged projectile hurtling steeply and swiftly through the sky. There is no sound except the whistling of the wind and the popping of loose fabric on my jump suit. My eyes search the earth, seeking the swath cut through the woods that marks the border. I see it a little to the left and raise my right arm slightly to bank in that direction. I cross the border at 8000 feet and—for the benefit of the crowd behind me at the airport—bank steeply and execute a 360-degree turn to let them know I made it.

I am down to 5000 feet, peering ahead to spot the cleared areas chosen the day before. I see one, then another and another. But 5000 is too high to pull, and I keep going. My arms are beginning to feel the strain of the long glide. Approaching the next cleared area, I realize I can't hold out much longer and start a series of ever-steepening spirals that will get me down quickly. A thousand feet over the deck I pull the rip cord. My body is wrenched violently, and I see champagne bubbles rising up before my eyes. Thank God there is no crosswind, for I am too exhausted to fool around with the shroud lines. The ground rushes up, and I land with a bone-jarring thump.

Too beat to rise, I lie on the ground letting the cool breeze wash over my eyes. I stay flat on my back for ten minutes, waiting for the recovery team. Then I hear a jeep coming through the woods in low-low gear.

Newsmen inveigled the customs officials of Canada and the United States to grab Red from the Canadian and the American sides of his anatomy, his legs straddling the border, and pretend to be fighting over him. Red went along with the publicity tug-of-war over his body and made the front pages throughout the entire area. Back at the airport 25,000 people gave him a standing ovation.

Later, pilots estimated that Red Grant had flown the wings over a ground distance of four miles, while dropping less than three miles—a new record for the world.

Red was immensely pleased with his jump from the United States into Canada, but a short time later he was reminded once again—in the most ominous fashion possible—that every jump is a new leap straight into the jagged maw of unpredictable danger. He went out of a Cessna L-19 flown by a Kentucky Air National Guard pilot. Red always faced the problem of never knowing from what type of plane he would bail out, and the L-19 chilled him to the quick. Its door was narrow and confined, and it seemed nothing but trouble in respect to making an exit with all his gear in a high wind. But the show was on, no other planes were available, and Red clambered into his seat. Then the pilot, a young lieutenant, strapped himself into the front seat and secured his body with a new type of shoulder harness. The harness was secured with a cable that ran inside the cockpit from the belly of the ship and was linked to an inertial system that provided limited freedom of movement. The L-19 dashed down the runway into the wind for no more than 70 feet and leaped into the air, hanging on its prop and scrabbling for the sky. At 10,000 feet the lieutenant leveled off and eased back on the throttle. Then Red got ready:

They signaled from the ground to *go!* and I unbuckled the seat belt and strained to heave myself up in a semiupright position so I could get out of the door. I felt like a Labrador retriever trying to get out of a sardine can. I couldn't make it facing the door; so I worked myself around so my back could go out first. I gave the pilot the signal to chop the throttle, then heaved myself out into the blast of the slipstream.

I was brought up short with a wrenching jolt. Oh, my God! *I had fouled my gear on something!* I dangled underneath the belly of the airplane, unable to move. My first thought was, Can the pilot keep the airplane stable? He *had* to—my job was to free myself from whatever it was that locked me to the airplane.

I looked up and saw that the handgrip on my right wing was caught on the cable that ran underneath the belly of the ship. The lieutenant had told me the cable was stressed for 2500 pounds; so breaking the cable was out of the question.

I reached for the cable but missed it by inches; the terrific buffeting from the wind was bouncing me around like a wet rag. I tried for the landing gear, but the wind pressure blew me backward. I flapped there under the belly of the ship, completely helpless.

It was getting harder to draw air into my lungs, and I remembered that a trooper at Fort Bragg the year before had got hung up like I was and had died before they could untangle his harness. I beat on the belly of the plane to let the pilot know I was still there. Then, to my horror, I began to oscillate back and forth under the landing gear. I saw that each swing brought me closer to the wheels. I made countless frantic grabs for the wheels, missing each time. With each miss I felt panic rising inside me. I fought it down. After an eternity I managed to grab one of the rubber tires and hung on, fighting the blast from the prop.

I heaved myself up a few inches and looked straight into the anxious face of the pilot. He cut back the throttle and yelled, "Can you pull yourself back into the plane?"

"Negative! Negative!"

The pilot unbuckled his harness and reached across the right-hand seat, stretching his right arm outward while keeping his left hand on the control column. That scared me as much as anything. I could just see him grabbing my hand and me pulling him out there with me —a great act, with both of us hanging from the landing gear, but what would we do for an encore?

"It won't work!" I screamed. "Try to pull me up there!" But he couldn't hear me. I groped upward, trying to reach the door, but the hurricane of wind whipped me back. I felt real despair and was sure we were both going to die.

What was he doing now? A strap whipped out from the door and almost hit me in the face. I reached for it and missed. I tried again. Failure. Once more and I had it. I pulled myself painfully upward and shifted my weight, hoping to lessen the pressure that locked me to the cable. Up, up, up.

Suddenly I was free.

I fell away from the plane and fought down an instinct to pull the rip cord. I kept falling through space until I caught a flash of sunlight glinting from a pond. The thought passed through my mind: *If I don't pull, I'm going to get wet!* I yanked the rip cord.

The shock of the opening jerked me upright in the harness, and the sight of that orange-and-white canopy billowing above my head was the most beautiful thing I had ever seen.

I owe my life to the coolness of that pilot. He could have panicked and gone over the side with his chute, leaving me to my fate in the sky. But he didn't; he stuck it out, and I was allowed to live.

Red Grant didn't learn until later just how much he really did owe to that young lieutenant in the front seat. When Red's weight snagged on the cable, the officer was slammed back in his seat and immobilized. He zipped open his flight suit and shrugged it off his shoulders.

Red stared at two deep, bleeding grooves where the cables had sawed back and forth through the pilot's flesh when Grant had started to oscillate. The lieutenant, who was in agony during Red's own torment, would carry those scars the rest of his life.

STRAIGHT FROM THE LION'S MOUTH

By Ben East

John Kingsley-Heath was ranked as one of the top white hunters in Africa. He was a real pro and a much-sought-after guide by American sportsmen. Until 1961 he had been attacked only once by a wild animal. On that occasion he got too close to an elephant he was stalking, and the bull grabbed him up in its trunk and flung him into a swamp. But now, ten years later, it didn't look as though he was going to be that lucky. A quarter ton of raging, wounded lion hit him full force in the chest and knocked him down. Now he was on the ground with the lion on top of him, its front paws wrapped around his shoulders, its claws raking his back, its great mouth preparing to open to bite him through the head. That would be it—instant death. . . .

The leopard bait was an impala that had been shot and hung in an acacia tree on the edge of a dry riverbed. It had ripened in the hot sun for three days, long enough so that John Kingsley-Heath and Bud Lindus were sure that if there were leopards in the country, they could not resist it. The hunting party had hung a number of baits—zebra, gazelle, impala— but, for some reason, both the white hunter and the client felt that this was the one that would get them what they hoped for.

The time was August of 1961. Kingsley-Heath was on safari with the Lindus family—Bud, his wife, Pamela, and their 14-year-old, Roger—along the Ruaha River in the semiarid desert country of central Tanganyika.

Operating out of Nairobi and conducting hunts in Kenya and Tanganyika at the time, John Kingsley-Heath was rated among the top white hunters of Africa. He had held a professional hunter's license since 1951, barring a brief interruption during the Mau Mau emergency, and was known by name and reputation to many sportsmen in the United States.

Lindus was a retired oil salesman from Honolulu, and he and his wife were old clients of John's. Bud rated African hunting very high, and Pam and the boy shared his enthusiasm for it.

The main object of the hunt this time was a really good trophy lion. Two years earlier Lindus and Kingsley-Heath had been led up the garden path by a big-maned male in the Kajiado district of Kenya. That one seemed to have the uncanny ability of disappearing at exactly the crucial minute, whether they approached him on foot or by car. He hid in the day, ate their baits at night. Try as he would, Bud never got his sights on him.

He had come back to Africa now determined to do better. Buffalo and kudu also were on his list, he wanted a good leopard for his wife, and if they came across an elephant with satisfactory ivory, they didn't mean to turn it down.

They had sharpened their hunting sense on buffalo in the thick bush country of northern Tanganyika before moving down to the Ruaha. Two bulls had gotten within a yard of them before going down permanently. After that they felt they were ready to take on most anything, including the biggest lion in Tanganyika, if they could find him.

Camp had been made on the bank of the Ruaha, under large acacia trees that spread overhead like huge green umbrellas. Thousands of sand grouse watered in front of the tents every morning. The wing shooting was wonderful, and they were soon out of shotgun shells and sending back to Nairobi for more.

Alvin Adams, a friend of Bud's from the States, had come out to join them for a fortnight, wanting a big leopard, and was hunting with Kevin Torrens, the second white hunter on the safari. The numerous leopard baits had been hung partly in the hope of helping Al get his wish.

Bud and John hunted lions, elephants and kudu for days with no success. Tracks and signs were plentiful, but they couldn't seem to come across anything of the sort they were looking for. Leopards refused to touch their baits, and they began to wonder whether their luck was in or out. But when they hung the impala in the tree at the edge of the river two or three miles from camp, Kingsley-Heath had a hunch they were going to get action.

Bud, Pam, Roger and he came into camp for a late lunch the afternoon of the third day after that, and when they finished their sandwiches and tea, John suggested they go have a look at the bait. It was time for things to be happening if they were going to.

They drove out in the hunting car, through dry scrubthorn country, taking along two gunbearers and trackers, Kiebe and Ndaka. Halfway to the leopard bait, however, John sent them off to follow up some elephant tracks, with instructions to rejoin him near the bait tree.

They drove the hunting car to within 600 yards of the tree, left it and walked carefully the rest of the way. One peep around a large bush told them that a leopard had taken his fill. It was late afternoon now, almost time for him to return for his evening meal. There was not a minute to waste. They'd sit for him at once.

It was quickly decided that Pam should have this first chance. Bud and Roger went back to the car to wait, Pam and John stole carefully up behind a thick bush and secreted themselves in the bottom of it, first making a little hole for their guns.

Pam was carrying a rifle of European make, as light as the Tanganyika game laws permitted, for the sake of minimum recoil, mounted with a 4X scope. Kingsley-Heath's gun was a Winchester Model 70 in .300 Magnum caliber, with a 6X Kollmorgen scope. Neither of the rifles was right for what was going to happen, but there were good reasons for choosing them.

Sitting up for a leopard can be on the sticky side, especially if you are not used to it, since you know that if you fail to make a clean kill, you have one of the most dangerous animals in Africa to deal with. Pam had made no secret of the fact that she was nervous. Unless the cat fell dead at her shot, she had asked John to back her by putting another into it immediately.

That was why the white hunter had brought the scope-sighted Winchester. A six-power scope may seem unusual for a job of that kind, but it has its advantages. To begin with, it enables the hunter to increase his distance from the bait, and often he can select a better hide by moving off a bit. Too, a leopard almost invariably comes on a bait late, when the light is failing fast, and the more powerful the scope, the better its light-gathering ability.

Had the two gunbearers not been off following the elephant tracks, Kingsley-Heath would have had one of them in the hide with him carrying his .470 Westley-Richards double, but he couldn't very well handle two guns by himself.

He and Pam made themselves comfortable, with their rifles trained on the spot where they expected the leopard to appear. For 20 minutes nothing happened. The silence of late afternoon was setting over the bush. Puffs of wind blew through the acacias, stirring up little dust devils, but the breeze was from the bait tree; so they had no worry on that score. Now and then a bird twittered, and the shrunken river whispered around its sandbars. Save for those small sounds, nothing broke the stillness.

It was an uneasy quiet, and as the minutes dragged on, John began to be suspicious. Something wasn't quite right. Was the leopard approaching from behind? Had he scented them and slunk away? They tried to keep a sharp watch all around, but there was no movement in the brush or grass. The time ticked off, and John's uneasiness grew. Then, suddenly aware of movement or noise behind his right shoulder, he turned his head ever so slowly and was looking a huge-maned lion in the face, just 20 feet away.

The whole situation was clear to him in a flash. The leopard had not come to the bait because the lion had kept him away. The lion couldn't reach the impala himself, and now, hungry, disappointed and angry, he had spotted the two people in their thick bush, had not seen or smelled enough of them to know what they were and was stalking them for a kill. And he was close enough for that final, lightning-fast rush with which a lion takes his prey at the last second, too.

When Kingsley-Heath turned his head and they stared into each other's eyes, the big cat recognized him for a man, but it was too late for that to make any difference. John saw his expression change from the intent look of a stalking lion to one of rage. His face wrinkled in a snarl, and he bunched his feet under him for the spring.

It all happened a great deal quicker than it can be told. One second John was staring at the leopard bait; the next he was looking the lion in the face, the animal was gathering for its leap, and the hunter was swiveling his rifle around from the hip.

"The eyes of the big cats, I think more than those of any

other animal, mirror what is going on behind them," Kingsley-Heath told me long afterward. "At the instant of attack, those of a lion seem to be on fire. The burning yellow orbs of this big male fairly blazed into mine, and there was no misreading their message."

John did not wait to bring the rifle to his shoulder. He was sitting on his hunkers, as he described it, and he whipped the gun across his knees and pulled off at the lion, all in a split second, trying for the thickness of the shoulder. The shot struck a little too far back, but the animal reacted to the 180-grain softnose as most lions do to a hit, whipping his great head around and biting savagely at the wound.

Pam and John were not conscious, then or afterward, of running through the six-foot bush where they were hidden, but they did it and never got scratched. They got clear and raced for the car. In the thicket behind them Simba was growling and roaring and thrashing in pain and anger. They ran until they were far enough away to be safe, then stopped to get their breath and congratulate themselves on a very narrow escape.

"We have to get this chap," John told Bud when they finished panting out their story. "You and I will have a lion war."

The two gunbearers were not yet back from their elephant scout. Pam and Roger were left in the car, and Lindus and Kingsley-Heath took their heavy rifles and hurried off. John's was the .470, Bud's a .450/400 double made by Manton and Company, a London firm. Both were good lion guns, but because they had not expected to encounter a lion and had thought they might get a chance at an elephant that afternoon instead, they had only solid ammunition along instead of the softnose loads they would have preferred.

The lion had left the place where he was shot in a hurry, and it was plain from the blood that he was reasonably well hit. The blood spoor led down to the bottom of the dry riverbed. There, although he was bleeding heavily, it had dried in the sand and lost its color, making it difficult to follow in the evening light.

He ran along for a way under the riverbank, climbed up a small gully and went into a thicket of mswaki bush, an evergreen that grows like a very thick weeping willow, with the outer branches draping right down to the ground, leaving a cavelike opening underneath. This thicket was leafy, the lion had left little sign on the hard-baked sand, and the two men went down on their hands and knees to track him through gaps between the bushes.

They didn't crawl far before Kingsley-Heath pulled up short. "This is no good," he told Bud. "If we go ahead with our eyes on the ground, we'll walk right down his throat. Kiebe and Ndaka should be back at the car by now. We'll get them and let them do the tracking while we watch over their heads."

Kiebe was a particularly good man to have along in a situation of that kind. A Kamba by tribe, he had hunted for 25 years, eight of them with John and before that with Miles Turner, one of the most famous of East African white hunters. John had saved Kiebe's life a time or two, and the tracker had saved his. Tracking down a wounded lion was nothing new to Kiebe, and he was absolutely without fear. Kingsley-Heath knew he could count on him no matter what happened. The second tracker, Ndaka, was a stand-in but willing and brave.

The two of them were at the car, and the four hurried back to the place where John and Lindus had left the lion track. It was lucky they had quit when they did, for 15 yards ahead they found the bloodstained bed where he had been lying.

He had moved about 30 yards into another thicket while they were gone, still bleeding. They tracked him foot by foot, with Kiebe in the lead. It was not a job any of them liked, but they had no choice. Once a hunter starts an affair of that kind, it's up to him to finish it, no matter how sticky it gets.

Kiebe wiped warm blood off the leaves and held up a hand to warn his bwana that they were getting close. Then the lion announced his presence with an angry growl from the mswaki just ahead, and they saw him race across a narrow opening into the next bush.

It was almost dark now, and in a very few minutes they'd have to give up. They left the track and circled, hoping to push him into the open, but nothing stirred and no sound came from the thicket. They wasted precious time, the light got worse, and at last John whispered to Kiebe in Swahili, "This is for tomorrow. We'll let him stiffen up and beat him out in the morning."

The tracker's reply was a finger jabbed sharply to the left. There, under a low bush 50 feet away, the lion lay broadside, breathing heavily, watching them. John could barely make out the shape of his heavy body in the dusk.

The range was close enough, but they were shooting with open sights in very bad light and had to be absolutely certain of a hit. Kingsley-Heath took Lindus by the arm without saying a word, and they shortened the distance to 40 feet, moving warily to the nearest tree, where a leaning branch would give them a rest for the rifles.

The shot belonged to the client, and since Bud was a first-class rifleman, John did not expect there'd be any need for him to fire. But he made one serious mistake: He overlooked the fact that in the half-darkness the flash of Bud's rifle would blind him for that critical fraction of a second when the lion might come for them in case Bud failed to kill it where it lay.

Bud's 400-grain solid took the cat in the shoulder a bit high, but because the bullet was not a softnose, it went all the way through without opening up, doing only slight damage to the lungs. And in the instant when John should have hammered another in, he could see neither lion, thicket nor anything else.

In all the years he had been a professional hunter and all the hunting he had done on his own, Kingsley-Heath had been attacked by an animal only once. That had happened in the very beginning, when he was training under an old hunter. He approached too close to an elephant he was stalking, and the bull knew he was there. It waited until he was within reach, grabbed him up in its trunk and sent him flying into a swamp tangle. By good fortune he escaped unhurt except for a slight stiffness in the right shoulder. This time he wasn't going to be that lucky.

The lion came in a rush the first few feet, then covered the rest of the distance in two great bounds. John had time only to yell at Bud to dodge behind him, when a huge ball of snarling fury landed at his feet.

He slammed a 500-grain solid into the great cat's head between the eyes, point-blank, and but for a fluke, that would have ended the affair. But because the lion was badly wounded, when he hit the ground in front of John, his head jerked forward and down, like a man who has jumped off a stool. The heavy bullet struck him square between the eyes, as the hole in the skull showed later, but instead of going through his brain and leaving him deader than mutton, it passed down between his lower jawbones and out at the side of his throat, hardly more than blinding him with the rifle flash.

He leaped past John within a foot and landed between the two men, headed for Bud. John saw that Bud's rifle was tangled in branches and he couldn't get it down. The quarters were too close for a second shot without endangering him. Kingsley-Heath took one step and clubbed the lion on the head with the barrels of his .470 as hard as he could. The cat grunted, shook his head and wheeled around, and before John had time to pull the second barrel, he pounced.

A quarter ton of growling, raging cat hit Kingsley-Heath full length, and he went down as if he had been electrocuted. "It felt about like that, too," he said afterward. There was no pain and he was not stunned, but the shock of the blow as the lion crashed into him, with its forepaws over his shoulders and its huge body bearing him to the ground, was beyond description. His gun went flying out of his hands, and then he was lying on his back with the lion on top of him, its front legs wrapped around him and its paws under his shoulder blades.

A lion, even wounded, often pauses for a second after his initial leap has knocked his victim down, and this one did just that. That tiny pause saved John Kingsley-Heath's life. He knew that within a second or two the lion would bite him through the head, and he smashed his right fist into its nose with every ounce of strength he had. He broke the bones of the hand, but the lion opened its mouth at the punch, maybe to growl, and John followed through. He rammed his fist down its throat, and its teeth closed on his arm halfway to the elbow.

John heard the bones crunch but in a strange, detached way, not as a sound from outside but as if he were hearing the arm break from inside his own body.

So long as he kept his fist down its gullet, the lion could not get at his head or throat. He could feel its claws under him, ripping his sheepskin hunting jacket to shreds and his back with it. He knew that if it got its hind feet in his belly, it would tear his guts out with one rake. He twisted on his left side, drew his legs up to protect himself and concentrated on trying to keep his broken arm in its mouth.

The statement has been made more than once that a man attacked by one of the big carnivores is overcome with a merciful numbness, so that he feels little or no pain or fright at the time, perhaps because the shock overwhelms his nervous system. Kingsley-Heath thinks the part about being benumbed is true, but for a different reason. The victim of such an attack is fighting for his life and knows it, and he believes that a man in that situation has little sense of feeling. In his own case he felt very little pain through the whole mauling. When it was all over, his back looked as if he had been flogged with a cat-o'-nine-tails, but it hadn't hurt while it was happening.

Nor did he smell the lion's breath or have any sensation of feeling its mane against his face, although he knew it was there. He did have a bad bit of nightmare in the hospital later, when he felt lion saliva all over his fingers and woke up in a cold sweat trying to get his mangled arm out of the cat's jaws.

Actually, the lion took care of that for him. It shook him as a terrier shakes a rat, rolling him back and forth, and freed itself of his fist and arm about the way a big fish gets rid of a bait.

It takes far longer to describe such an experience than to live through it. Everything was happening at once. "Get my gun!" John yelled at Kiebe in Swahili. *"Kamata bunduki yangu! Piga the bloody thing!" Piga* means hit, but in this case he meant shoot, and the tracker knew it.

Then he saw Bud come into sight over the lion's rear quarters, and the .450 bellowed twice. But because John was lying under the cat, Bud could only shoot far back. They learned later that he broke a hind leg, but the lion paid no attention, neither flinching nor turning its head. It just went on growling and mauling its victim and took no notice of Bud, Kiebe or Ndaka. That is typical lion behavior. Once Simba gets his victim down, he stays with it. A wounded leopard will rush from one member of a party to another, biting at the first man he can reach, then striking instantly at a fresh victim, only to leave that one and run for the next. A lion takes time to finish what he begins.

Kiebe grabbed up Kingsley-Heath's gun now, checked swiftly to see which barrel was loaded, ran in and shoved the muzzle against the lion's shoulder, heedless of his own danger. But from where John lay beneath the brute, he saw that the bullet, whatever it might do to the cat, would also smash through his knees, and he screamed at Kiebe, "For God's sake, don't shoot there!"

The tracker backed away a step and blasted the one round remaining in the .470 into the lion's back just behind the shoulders. That put Kiebe out of the fight, for the rest of John's ammunition was in his pocket under the lion. But the shot was strong medicine and well placed. It broke the spine, and the beast twisted off him. A wounded lion doesn't quit as long as he is breathing, however, and this one wasn't finished yet. Back it came on its front legs, with its back end dragging, and quick as John moved, he wasn't quick enough to get to his feet before it was on him again.

It would have taken him through the left side of the chest with its huge canine teeth, and one bite there meant certain death, but he threw up his left arm to fend it off. He had no time to jam the arm down its throat, as he had done with the right. He simply shoved it into the lion's face. It grabbed and crushed the arm just above the wrist, and once more John heard his own bones break like matchsticks, not as he would have heard another man's but as a noise coming from inside him.

At this point Ndaka did a very brave thing. He threw himself on the lion and stabbed it again and again in the ribs and throat with a six-inch knife. Then Lindus, who had been stuffing fresh shells into the breech of his double while Kiebe got in his shot, stepped close and sent two more solids crashing into the lion. The great body jerked and sagged and rolled off Kingsley-Heath.

As he struggled to his knees, half-helpless from two broken arms, he jabbed his left foot into its face to kick himself away. That was the wrong thing to do, even with a lion breathing its last. Its jaws closed on John's shoe, and it bit down, and for the third time he heard the crunch of breaking bones, in his foot and ankle now. And that time, he remembered, it hurt like hell! He wrenched his foot free, but the lion died with his shoe in its mouth.

They left the cat where he lay. They'd have to run the risk of hyenas tearing him up before morning. Bud and the natives carried John to the car and wrapped him in the rain curtains to keep him warm. Then they set off in the darkness for camp. There was no moon, and they couldn't follow their tire tracks; so rather than get lost, they stopped and made a fire and let off a shot every ten minutes. It's a rule on safari that if anyone fails to return to camp by an hour after dark, the search-and-rescue operation gets under way at once. They knew that by now Kevin Torrens, the other white hunter, was out looking for them.

Kingsley-Heath's wounds had clotted well, and he was bleeding only a little, but he drank water like a mad thing. Kiebe and Ndaka left to try to find the way to camp, and shortly after that the injured hunter and his clients heard the hum of a motor, and then the lights of Kevin's Landrover appeared.

It was two in the morning by the time they found their way back through the scrubthorn to camp. Torrens cleaned up John's wounds, poured disinfectant into them and had him swallow three times the normal dose of antibiotic tablets, washing them down with hot tea. Next, John got down two cups of soup and began to feel quite comfortable. But about that time he went into shock, started to tremble violently from head to foot and kept it up for hours.

They had a radiotelephone in camp, but by now it was Sunday morning (the lion attack had occurred on Saturday evening) and the government radio in Nairobi was closed down; so Torrens left for the nearest phone at Dodoma, 120 miles away, 30 of it rough track through the bush, to call for a plane. They had scratched out a small airstrip near camp earlier.

Kevin got through to Peter Whitehead, manager of a leading Nairobi safari firm, at 6:15 on Sunday morning, and 45 minutes later Dr. Brian McShane, Kingsley-Heath's physician and good friend, was airborne and on the way with a supply of blood and the other things he needed to fix the injured man up temporarily. Bill Ryan, another professional hunter from Nairobi and also an old friend of John's, came along to take over the safari. It was a two-and-a-half-hour flight. They touched down at the camp at 9:30 that morning.

By that time John had sent the safari boys out, and they had brought the lion to camp. The hyenas had not molested it after all. It was a magnificent brute, the biggest Kingsley-Heath had ever had a hand in killing—ten and a half feet long and weighing out at 497 pounds. It must have weighed a bit above 500 alive, before it lost blood. There in the Dodoma district the lions live mostly on buffalo, and the full-grown males are among the finest trophies in all of Africa. This one was paler than average, but not quite a blond, with a very heavy mane. As his friends remarked later, at least John had been savaged by a decent lion, not one with just a ruff around its neck. Bud got the pelt, and it's a safe bet he will never take a trophy that will give him a more exciting time. John kept a tooth and claw and had them mounted as paperweights.

Dr. McShane poured blood into him and set about patching him up for the flight back to Nairobi. He had two broken arms, a broken hand, a foot chewed and badly crushed, a horribly lacerated back and a few deep holes in various parts of his body. As he was being carried into his tent after the attack, he had heard Kiebe tell the other safari boys, *"Bwana ameliwa na simba,"* which is Swahili for "The bwana was eaten by a lion." Maybe Kiebe exaggerated a little, but he was close enough to the truth that the bwana didn't feel like contradicting him.

Kingsley-Heath entered the Princess Elizabeth Hospital in Nairobi that afternoon, August 13, and stayed until October 2. He was on the dangerous list for a few days, but the surgeons repaired his broken bones, and by great fortune he escaped infection, which is very likely to follow an attack by one of the big cats because of their habit of feeding on putrid meat. The fact that he had been able to get down a massive dose of antibiotics a few hours after the accident probably accounted for his luck on that score. He did not think that the lion was cleaner than average.

The mauling proved far worse than the aftermath, and most of his stay in the hospital was not a bad ordeal. Bud and Pam finished their hunt as they had planned, with Bill Ryan's help. They took a couple of fine kudu, and by the time they got back to Nairobi two weeks later, John was able to sit up and drink champagne with them, by way of celebrating his escape. He was well enough to leave on an easy safari the day he got out of the hospital.

For the courage he had shown, Kiebe received the Queen's Commendation for Brave Conduct a few months later. Asked what his thoughts were at the time, he replied matter-of-factly, "Do you suppose I am going to do nothing when a lion is about to kill my bwana? What would we do without him? We would have no safaris." And the only reward he wanted was corrugated iron to roof his house.

The following February, Kingsley-Heath had the satisfaction of helping to whack another good lion in Kenya. "I'm all for a lion war anytime now, and I suppose I shall be the rest of my life," he told me.

There was an interesting sequel to the story. On August 12, 1962, a year to the day from the time the lion mauled him, he sat up for a leopard at that same tree and at the same hour. He had a lady client again, and they sat in the same bush where Pam and he had waited. The leopard put in an appearance as the light was starting to fade, the client fired, and the cat tumbled, hit hard but not dead. In the twinkling of an eye John found himself in exactly the same predicament he had faced on the fateful evening a year earlier, except that this time he was dealing with a leopard rather than a lion. Not that that is much to be preferred.

It was too dark for tracking; so they went back to camp and returned the next morning. The blood spoor led into a bush nearby, and to the white hunter's great relief, the leopard lay dead there. So if there was any jinx connected with that tree, it had been laid to rest. But in all of Africa there is not another tree that John Kingsley-Heath will remember so vividly and long as that acacia on the edge of the dry riverbed. He says so himself.

"HEAVE TO OR I WILL FIRE!"

By Commander Lloyd M. Bucher, USN
with Mark Rascovich

> 30 Infiltrators from North Korea kill policeman and 5 others in Seoul—3 South Korean army divisions and elements of US 2nd Inf. Division participate in search operation.
> —*New York Times, January 22, 1968*

> Remember you are not out there to start a war!
> —*Rear Admiral Frank L. Johnson's parting advice to Commander Bucher January 9, 1968*

The capture of the U.S.S. Pueblo *electronic spy ship on the high seas by North Korea in 1968 sent shock waves of anger and indignation throughout all America. Never had the United States been so abjectly humiliated—and the U.S. public wanted to know why. First came the jumbled rhetoric in the halls of Congress, then the navy's confused explanations and then the aborted official inquiry of the* Pueblo *commander and crew after their return from Communist captivity. The true story lies somewhere between a great mishmash of bureaucratic mismanagement and a panoply of inspiring personal courage. The pivotal figure, though, remains Commander Lloyd M. Bucher. Surrounded by fully armed North Korean sub chasers and torpedo boats and already wounded himself by flying shrapnel, he had to decide whether to fight back against overwhelming odds or surrender the practically defenseless ship. Would any of us have done it any differently under the circumstances? Decide for yourself after reading about his fateful seven-hour brush with extinction.*

I rolled out of my bunk shortly before 0700 hours of the morning of January 23 feeling stiff and unrested after having stayed up for most of the night checking contacts and waiting for my radioman to establish communications with Japan to report our inquisitive visitors of the previous day.

My awakening cup of coffee in the wardroom tasted bitter, like the one I had drunk just a few hours earlier. I noticed a humid, sour smell permeating the interior of the ship and decided that if the warming fair weather held, we would hang out our bedding for a good airing when lying to while the CTs checked the ether outside Wonsan. Going to the bridge, I was struck by a cold that seemed a comparatively mild 20 degrees, noticed the light four-knot wind out of the north-west, the sea heaving with gentle swells, and a high, thin overcast reflecting the first pale light of dawn. The rugged Korean coast was still hidden in darkness through which a few faint lights glimmered on higher ridges. They were just clear enough to establish our position and confirm it as 25 miles offshore by checking the bottom contour with our depth-sounder. I ordered the OOD, Gene Lacy, to close that distance to 15 miles and put us on station within effective range for monitoring any electronic traffic in the Wonsan area, then returned to the wardroom for breakfast, feeling this was going to be a routine day with relief from the usual bitter weather of the Sea of Japan.

The watch changed at 0745, but Gene Lacy had relieved an hour early as OOD. The sun burned through the patches of stratus clouds, and details of the coastline began to emerge out of its dark sawtooth silhouettes, enabling us to take accurate bearings on prominent features shown on our charts. By 1000 hours we could clearly make out and identify the craggy headland of Hado Pando and its pendant islands of Yo Do and Ung Do lying across the northern entrance to Yong Hung Bay. These landfalls gave reliable fixes, but as had become my habit since his fiasco off Sasebo, I double-checked Murphy's navigation before ringing up all-stop and going dead in the water exactly 15.5 miles away from the nearest North Korean soil. There was no other shipping in sight as Friar Tuck manned the hydrographic winch for a Nansen cast and Harry Iredale ambled back to the fantail to take a BT reading. A work party went on deck to clear the night's small accumulation of snow and ice. From the fo'c'sle came the slurping clatter of our washing machine being fed its first load of laundry, the noisiest equipment aboard since the main engines were shut down. Below decks the CTs sat before their consoles in chairs that rocked rather than wrenched as they concentrated on their intelligence watch. Steve Harris reported to the bridge that their sensors were picking up the emissions of two distant search radars conducting normal sweeps and that, for an interesting change, there was some "chatter" on nearby Korean voice-communication frequencies.

"Anything indicating an interest in us?" I asked him over the phone.

"Not that we can read, Captain. Probably routine traffic, but we're recording and will go back over the tapes."

Going back over the tapes and extracting coherent translation might take anything up to four or five hours, and I wished that Sergeant Hammond and Sergeant Chicca had come to me with more than a long-past 16-week course in the Korean language, enabling them to pick up the gist of radio conversations without time-consuming playbacks and references to a dictionary. But I knew they were doing the best they could with the training they had been given for this assignment and in the meanwhile reassured myself by carefully searching the empty sea and deserted coastline with my binoculars. We might as well have been adrift in a virtually uninhabited part of the world. The only faint suggestion of activity was a barely visible smudge of smoke hanging over what I knew to be the location of Wonsan; the town and harbor itself were hidden behind spits and islets of its deeply indented bay. There was absolutely nothing to suggest we were some 15 miles off the entrance to North Korea's principal east-coast commercial and naval port, not a single patrol craft, coastwise tramp, nor even a lowly fish boat. I was in a way disappointed, deciding that yesterday's flurry of excitement had been a passing thing. They had come out to let us know they knew of our presence and, having decided we were irritating but harmless capitalists conducting oceanographic research in the Sea of Japan, were now ignoring us and had withdrawn into their hermetic Communist isolation. It moved me to make up another SITREP to supplement the one we had been trying to send all night, the meat of this message being:

. . . No significant ELINT. . . . No longer under surveillance. . . . Intentions remain in area. . . . This is last SITREP this incident. UNODIR reverting to EMCON.

This was meant to convey to higher commands in Japan that the situation had cooled off since my last message, I was peacefully proceeding with our mission and reverting to our status of radio silence. Radioman Hayes, red-eyed and weary from his efforts to establish a workable frequency with headquarters throughout the night, roused himself with equal dedication to overcome the difficulties in finding a suitable frequency for this less critical, but necessary, reassuring signal of the morning. The noon watch change was reporting to the bridge when these messages were finally receipted for by our headquarters in Japan. Hayes staggered down to the mess deck for a hot lunch, anticipating to digest it through a long afternoon nap in his bunk.

Quartermaster Law relieved Gene Lacy as OOD, taking over *Pueblo,* which was still lazily rolling within a few hundred yards of the spot where she had stopped two hours earlier, the slight southeast current butting against the northwest breeze to hold her position, which, nevertheless, Law carefully checked with bearings on Hado Pando and Ung Do. Gene made his prescribed tour of the ship upon leaving the bridge, inspecting the decks and interior spaces, including his own main engine room, where he found Chief Goldman and Engineman First Class Blansett keeping themselves busy with maintenance and sprucing up of their diesels, and the auxiliary engine room, where Engineman First Class Scarborough was watching over humming banks of generators that were never relieved from the demands of electrical power from the SOD hut. The crew's mess was into its second sitting, with 25 men hungrily digging into ample portions of meat loaf, succotash, potatoes and gravy. In the galley our cook, Harry Lewis, and his assistants were making certain that they would have second helpings, plus double portions, for the third sitting, due in 20 minutes. The quality of food and service was amazing when considering it all originated out of a space measuring eight-by-thirteen feet. In the wardroom Gene squeezed himself into our table, where we were receiving the identical fare as the enlisted people, with the slight refinement of having it served on a tablecloth by a steward. Anemic rays of sunlight focused through the double portholes, throwing wandering spotlights on stains of soup, coffee and catsup that our wheezing laundry machine had been unable to deal with since the last violent seas.

"Everything OK on your watch, Gene?" I asked him.

"Yes, sir," he answered with his cheerful smile, "and we're catching up with some housekeeping in this nice weather."

"Yeah. Almost like the balmy winters on Newfoundland's Grand Banks," Skip quipped. "Like the man said at briefing —a real milk run."

"At this time of the year the Grand Banks average fourteen point five degrees warmer than the Sea of Japan," Steve Harris answered. "Gulf Stream, you know."

Our luncheon chatter was interrupted by a call from the bridge, Quartermaster Law reporting that a vessel had been sighted about eight miles to the south of us and appeared to be approaching. I told him to keep her under observation and let me know if and when she closed to within five miles. Eating and conversation resumed. The sighting was routine and worried nobody.

But I had just started my second portion of meat loaf when the telephone buzzed again and Law reported the ship was now five miles away and rapidly closing. It had covered three miles in four minutes, indicating a speed of better than 40 knots. It was no longer a routine sighting. I excused myself and hurried up to the bridge. As I departed the wardroom, I heard Gene make a last casual crack:

"Maybe this won't be another dull day after all!"

Topside I found the weather unchanged except that the bite of the air suggested the temperature was suddenly reversing itself and sliding back down into a hard freeze. The sun glowed without warmth through wintry clouds, and the visibility was still good enough for me to spot from the pilothouse the distant dark shape bobbing toward us through flashes of white—the foam of a powerful bow wave. I climbed on up to the flying bridge, where I trained the "big eyes" on the approaching vessel, which showed me enough details for a tentative identification: a submarine chaser flying the North Korean ensign, bearing down on us at flank speed.

I was not alarmed, only slightly annoyed that he would show up at lunchtime. I told Quartermaster Law to call Lieutenants Harris and Schumacher to the flying bridge with their identification book and Photographer Mack with his cameras. When the sub chaser kept coming on without change of speed or course, I decided to make sure we looked in every respect what we wanted to appear to be—an oceanographic-research vessel operating on the high seas. The international day signals indicating such activity were hoisted, and I called my oceanographers from their meal to put on an extra Nansen cast for the benefit of our visitors. Then I scrambled down the ladder to the pilothouse and checked our position to make sure we *really* were in international waters. Our cross-bearing fixes on the coast were still clearly visible, but Law had confirmed them with radar when he first sighted the sub chaser. *Pueblo* was now a tenth less than 16 miles off the island of Ung Do, still lying dead in the water with a slight southeasterly drift. There was no doubt in my mind that we were completely legal and that all I had to do was match my orders to any situation that might develop. I was joined by Steve Harris, who climbed back to the flying bridge with me, took a long, careful look at the much closer sub chaser, flipped through his identification book, then announced his conclusions:

"She's a Russian-built, modified SO-1-class submarine chaser. One hundred thirty feet overall by twenty-one feet beam. Speeds up to forty-eight knots through seastate two. Normally armed with depth charges and automatic cannons, but other configurations, including missiles, may be encountered. Normal complement is three officers and sixteen crewmen."

"That's what I make her out to be, Steve," I agreed with him. "Now, get below and find out if your CTs can eavesdrop on any talk with her base. It might be fun to know her impressions of us."

"We'll do our best, Captain. Our circuits are still open to report her presence."

"OK, but don't get everybody in an uproar. Remember that another one like her just peacefully steamed past us the other evening," I reminded him.

"Yes, sir. I'll keep you informed," he answered.

Word had spread through *Pueblo* that something more interesting than a routine contact was afoot, and a number of off-duty people were drifting out on deck to take a look. Bearing in mind that we should not show more crew than the normal 30-odd carried by a legitimate oceanographic-research vessel, I had the order passed over the ship's IMC that everybody was to remain below and out of sight unless engaged in official topside business. Those remaining visible were the oceanographic people on the foredeck and personnel assigned to the bridge, all dressed in the conglomerate non-regulation cold-weather clothing that I permitted on this distant independent mission. I was myself wearing a heavy leather flight jacket and a woolen ski cap crowned by a fuzzy red tassel.

The SO-1 closed to 1000 yards, and I was able to see through my binoculars that her bridge was not only crowded with men scrutinizing us through their own, but that her twin automatic cannon was fully manned and aimed at us. She was charging us in a state of general quarters—battle stations! But that did not signify to me that battle was imminent. Only the same kind of harassment that *Banner* had endured many times and that I had been briefed to expect for my own ship.

I did not want an enlisted man in charge of the deck during a potentially sensitive situation; so I called for Gene Lacy to relieve Quartermaster Law as OOD. Then I ordered the engine room to start up our diesels and be ready to answer bells.

As the SO-1 began cutting a wide but tightening circle around us, she broke out an international-signal flag hoist that read, WHAT NATIONALITY? and to which I immediately answered by having my signalmen raise our American flag. I noticed that this caused a flurry of activity on the Korean bridge and decks, bringing me through my binoculars a silent pantomime picture of surprise and momentary confusion. However, this in no way changed their belligerent show of challenging us at battle stations.

By now Skip Schumacher and Ensign Tim Harris had joined me on the bridge, looking over the situation with an eager, youthful curiosity that neither could hide beneath attempts at acting unperturbed. To both of them the sight at close quarters of a Communist naval vessel swarming with genuine Commie crew was still a novelty. But I reminded them that they were participants, not just spectators, in the confrontation. To Skip I ordered, "Get going on the message form for a JOPREP PINNACLE report. Contact is a KORCOM, modified SO-1 sub chaser challenging and receiving confirmation of our nationality." To Tim I ordered, "Make yourself at home in my bridge chair and start keeping a running narrative log on whatever show they decide to put on."

At this moment Gene Lacy suddenly sang out, "Three high-speed torpedo boats, bearing one sixty, range short ten thousand yards with zero angle on the bow!"

Grateful that he had had the foresight to keep a sharp

lookout beyond the diversion within our immediate vicinity, I aimed my binoculars toward the sighting, which was in the general direction of Wonsan, confirmed it and called after Skip, "Add that to the JOPREP PINNACLE! Ask them to keep the circuits open for more."

I meant by that, a full-fledged harassment operation appeared to be imminent, as opposed to the surveillance by a single unit of the North Korean navy I had initially anticipated. But no additional tension became evident on *Pueblo*'s bridge. Our sister ship *Banner* had on several occasions been surrounded by several intimidating Red Chinese or Russian vessels, and apparently we were about to be given the same treatment by the KORCOMS. It flashed through my mind that here was the unexpected opportunity to really test, according to our orders, their reaction to our presence near their territorial waters. *Near*—not inside them. Of this I had to keep myself absolutely certain and ordered Murphy, who was in the pilothouse beneath me, to again check our position with radar fixes, then sent Quartermaster Law down to double-check his results. Still 15.8 miles off the nearest land.

The SO-1 was making its second circle around us and had closed to within 500 yards; so we could clearly see her crew wearing their peculiar foot-soldier uniforms. They now raised a second hoist of signals, which read, HEAVE TO OR I WILL FIRE!

"What the hell does he mean by that?" I wondered aloud. "We are already lying dead in the water!"

"Maybe he can't think of anything else nasty to say to us," Tim suggested as he recorded the development in his narrative.

It was true that *Banner* had received the same unfriendly greeting on previous missions, but I called down the voice tube to Murphy and asked him to look up the signal in the "dictionary" and make certain there was no other meaning. There wasn't. Then I hurriedly dropped down the ladder to the pilothouse, where I personally checked the radar for range and bearing to nearest land: *15.8 miles*—3.8 beyond North Korean claimed territorial waters. It was impossible that *all* of us were making a mistake. This was pure intimidation of the Communist kind. So I confidently climbed back up to the flying bridge and ordered my signalmen to make the international flag hoist: I AM IN INTERNATIONAL WATERS.

Three torpedo boats were now within a mile and still approaching at full speed to join the larger SO-1 sub chaser, who continued circling with her signal fluttering from her yardarm, her cannons training directly at us with gun crews ready. Photographer Mack, busy snapping pictures through his telephoto lens, found himself looking right down their barrels. But if the atmosphere aboard *Pueblo* had changed, it was one of bracing for a test of nerves, not battle. And there was a perverse element of luck developing out of our previous communication difficulties with Japan. Because of delays in transmitting our last SITREP, the channels had not been secured when this incident started and were being kept open as it developed. Steve Harris, secluded in the SOD hut with his CTs, was visually blind and trying without enlightening results to interpret excited Korean jabberings that were filling their voice-communication channels. I had him instructed to keep his teletype going with casual "chitchat" to Japan, revealing we had unwelcome company and to keep the circuits open for further messages. Skip then urgently asked me if we should upgrade the priority of our JOPREP PINNACLE message from FLASH to CRITIC. CRITIC was a new priority that had been devised to flag important messages that were to go through immediately to all echelons of higher command, including the White House. As this was a brand-new system, only just promulgated to the fleet, it had never been used by anyone, to my knowledge; so I asked Skip for a quick review of the purpose of the use of CRITIC. He gave me a quick rundown, and I immediately decided to go with CRITIC and ordered him to make it so. CRITIC would indicate a possible international incident was impending, and it would be passed all the way up the chain of command to the White House, in Washington. It was by no means a matter of pushing the panic button—only alerting high-level authorities to a situation where serious trouble might, if it deteriorated, require their immediate attention. I fully intended, even at this stage, to remain in the area and stated so in the JOPREP.

However, it was at this time that a certain uneasiness began to bother me, at least subconsciously, over my old worries about an inadequate destruct system that would require a couple of hours to dispose of all our classified publications and equipment. As the four torpedo boats closed in, broke their loose formation and deployed themselves to cover us from all sides, near enough for me to see with the naked eye that they had fully manned machine-gun mounts aimed at us, I became aware of how rapidly things were happening. It had only been a little over 20 minutes since the SO-1 was first sighted. Another disquieting thought intruded upon my mind, one quite contrary to my previous concern about *Pueblo*'s poor reserve buoyancy in case she was accidentally holed in a collision during wild harassing maneuvers by Communists. I expressed it by suddenly asking Gene Lacy:

"Could we scuttle the ship quickly if we had to?"

He gave me a searching glance that was more thoughtful than startled, then calmly answered, "Not quickly, sir—about two hours to flood the main engine room after unbolting and disconnecting the saltwater cooling intakes. Then she would not sink without breaching the bulkhead to the auxiliary engine room—another tough, long job."

"And in the meantime we'd wallow without power for maneuvering or communications."

"That's right, sir."

I surprised myself by pursuing the matter further and calling down the voice tube for soundings by our depth recorder. "Thirty fathoms, sir!" came the immediate reply. That drove all scuttling considerations out of my mind: too shallow a depth to justify an extreme destruct action that would take too long and too easily canceled out by Korean divers who would eventually recover the ship's contents. Besides, I told myself, the situation was not that critical and was unlikely to become so. Instead I reminded myself of a recent special order from chief of naval operations to the effect that no U.S. ships operating on the high seas were to permit themselves to be intimidated by the actions of Communist-bloc ships. I had to henceforth rely on my briefings and sweat out an unfamiliar predicament without betraying the slightest personal doubts to my officers and men. They were beginning to show some nervousness (I noticed Tim smoking a cigarette, which was unusual for him), and I could only steady them by keeping under control any of my own. Calling down the voice tube again, I ordered the navigator to get together a plotting team to record all hostile movements of the harassment "for future study by the desk jockeys at Staff!"

We were now completely covered by four North Korean warships. The three torpedo boats were circling us within 50 yards with their machine guns aimed at our bridge and their decks filled with what looked like soldiers or marines armed with Russian-type automatic carbines. I could clearly see their oriental features scowling under the brims of their fur caps. The SO-1 was jogging a little farther off our port quarter, its 57-millimeter cannons ready to fire at point-blank range and her threatening signal of HEAVE TO OR I WILL FIRE still fluttering from her yardarm. Presuming she was the flagship of the pack, I added to my answer of AM IN INTERNATIONAL WATERS the international signal for INTEND TO REMAIN IN THE AREA. Noticing that my signalman was a little shaky as he tied in the flag hoist, possibly as much from the intense cold as from the mounting tension, I breezily exclaimed for the benefit of all the personnel on the flying bridge:

"We're not going to let these sons o' bitches bullshit us!"

No sooner had I spoken that encouraging defiance than I heard the sudden sibilant swoosh of jets overhead and, looking up, saw the unmistakable shapes of a pair of Russian-built MIGs flashing by on a low pass over my ship. Then I spotted a fourth torpedo boat appearing out of nowhere and bearing down on us from a distance of less than a mile. And to further complicate things there was another small but swelling shape cutting a white wake over the leaden seas outside Yong Hung Bay—another KORCOM sub chaser coming out to join in the fun!

Gene Lacy showed his mounting concern by asking me, "Should we think about going to general quarters, Captain?"

While I am not known to back away from a fight when challenged, my instructions to not act provocatively, together with Admiral Johnson's parting admonition specifying that I was not here to start a war, had to remain a primary influence on all of my actions. "I don't want to go to general quarters," I answered him, "because that would give these bastards the impression we're here to conduct hostile operations—all they'd need to turn a harassment into a full-fledged international incident."

Gene accepted my decision without question but with worry still clouding his handsome face.

Skip Schumacher returned to the flying bridge after taking

my first JOPREP PINNACLE down to the cryptographic room for transmission, and there came a sobering look of consternation when he found that during his short absence below, *Pueblo* had become boxed in by a total of six Korean naval units with two MIGs providing air cover. "I guess there is no doubt we've been detected," he exclaimed with a gulp.

"So they are honoring us with special attention," I told him. "Did you get off that JOPREP?" He nodded, still staring with some shock at all the activity around us. "OK! Then get set to plug in number two!" I ordered and started rattling off the bare facts of the developments over the past ten minutes to supplement our first report. But even as I did this, things were happening too fast for me to keep up with the message content.

One of the torpedo boats drew close alongside their SO-1 flagship, communicating first by semaphore, then by megaphones, which amplified their gibberish loudly enough for us to hear it echoing across the 300 yards of slow swells. They drew close together, bumped for a moment while a dozen armed, stocky figures jumped across from the larger vessel; then the smaller one started backing down toward us with the obvious intention of putting a reinforced boarding party aboard *Pueblo*. I shouted at Skip to include this unexpected action in the message, then swore:

"I'll be goddamned if they are going to get away with it!"

The sight of this brazen attempt had me more furious than worried, but I instantly realized the time had come to remove ourselves from a harassment situation that went beyond my briefings and seemed on the brink of getting out of control. *Banner* had never experienced a serious threat of seizure on the high seas, but these KORCOMS seemed crazy enough to try it. I did not want to test them that far and lost no time in calling down the voice tube, "All ahead one-third! Navigator! Give the best course to open from land!"

"Zero eight zero, sir!" came Murphy's reply, sounding a bit thin.

"Steer zero eight zero," I confirmed. "Build up speed to two-thirds, then full. We are making a dignified withdrawal, not a run for it." I happened to glance through the Lucite windscreen down at the well deck, where poor Friar Tuck was looking quite perplexed while standing by his hydrographic winch, which had some 30 fathoms of Nansen cast paid out over the side. "Delay all oceanographic activity!" I shouted down at him. "Haul in those damned bottles on the double!"

Gene Lacy left the flying bridge to conduct his duties as OOD from the pilothouse, and Tim followed him to continue his narrative down there, both grateful to get out of the biting cold.

A series of catarrhal coughs erupted out of our stack as the engine room answered the bells by throwing the idling diesels into gear and advancing the throttles. The rumbling and belching of smoke was out of proportion to the very slow reaction to overcome *Pueblo*'s inertia and get her moving. For a moment it looked like the torpedo boat foaming full astern with fenders rigged and decks crowded with armed men was going to touch our sides. She actually came within a few yards of doing so, and the boarding party was braced to jump over our railings, when we at last began gathering speed and the gap between us widened again. *Pueblo* moved ahead in a wide-turning circle toward the open sea, leaving behind the torpedo boat with its boarding party looking somewhat foolish, but then her sister ships began cutting back and forth across my bow in the old game of "chicken." I still hoped to get clear, but I had to consider now the eventuality that I would not. I ordered the word passed over the ship's IMC to prepare for destruction of all classified material, then had a long signal hoisted that I hoped would cause a stall while they broke it down: THANK YOU FOR YOUR CONSIDERATION—AM DEPARTING THE AREA.

There followed a slight—very slight—relief of the pressure against us. Just enough to sustain my hope that we could yet get out of this mess without further complications. The SO-1 hauled down her signal of HEAVE TO OR I WILL FIRE and appeared to jog along indecisively in our wake, dropping behind more than 2000 yards. But the torpedo boats still kept up their unwanted company. Two of them stuck close to our stern; the other two porpoised around our bows, zig-zagging as close as ten yards, with the obvious purpose of blocking our withdrawal. And I noticed that the second SO-1 sub chaser had caught up and was joining the fray, making *six* hostile vessels confronting us! Ironically, the good weather, for which we had been so grateful earlier in the day, was now playing into the enemy's hands, because the calm seas allowed them full use of vastly superior speed and maximum stability for their otherwise tipsy gun platforms. They were having no trouble at all in keeping up with *Pueblo*'s plodding 12 knots, nor in training their weapons on an easy target. But we kept stubbornly pressing along a course of escape, and for a few moments it looked like we might bluff our way through.

Lieutenant Murphy's voice rattled out of the tube with a less than confident tone: "Captain, shall I try to raise Kamiseya on the HIGHCOM circuit and let them know about this?"

The emergency had reached the point where the use of the HIGHCOM voice communication with Japan was justified. "Affirmative—go ahead and get them on the line," I agreed.

The first SO-1 began speeding up and rapidly regaining the distance she had lost during her brief hesitation. A now-familiar hoist of signal flags shot back up her yardarm: HEAVE TO OR I WILL FIRE! I ignored that beyond an instinctive reaction to present as small a target as possible, just in case her intentions were serious, and shouted down the voice tube to our helmsman, "Come right ten degrees!"

The SO-1 easily countered this maneuver by pouring on more speed and turning outside of me to give her gunners a broadside shot.

"Come right ten more degrees!"

Again the SO-1 adjusted herself to the evasion, and during the next few seconds, while I was considering that any more right rudder on our part would inevitably bring our heading back toward North Korea, she suddenly opened fire with a long-sustained burst from her automatic 57-millimeter cannon.

I heard the shells screaming overhead, exploding with peculiar crackling sounds against the radar mast, the whine of splinters drilling through the Lucite windscreen of the flying bridge. Even as I threw myself down on the deck to dodge the lethal hail of shattered steel and plastic, I felt pieces slashing into my legs and buttocks. A sliver of shrapnel seared squarely up my rectum with a red-hot shock of pain. For an instant the agony and humiliation almost overcame me, but then the adrenaline of rage took over, dulling all physical pain while sharpening every other sense of awareness. The muzzle blast of the SO-1's cannon came as a delayed series of dull, popping concussions that were intermingled with a rattle of machine-gun bullets hammering against the metal of our stack and superstructure, telling me that the torpedo boats had also opened fire on us. The salvo lasted for perhaps five or six seconds, blasting to shambles not only my bridge—but also all the high-level briefings that had been my guidelines for this mission. At that moment, if Admiral Johnson had been present, I might well have cursed him as roundly as I found myself cursing these Communists! But when the din of their opening attack ceased, I had to belay my temper even against them and keep acting as rationally as possible in the face of a situation that had literally blown up in my face.

"Commence emergency destruction of all classified pubs and gear! Be sure the word is passed on down to Lieutenant Harris in the SOD hut!" Then I looked around the flying bridge and shouted the next most important thing on my mind: "Anybody hurt up here?"

Gene and Tim had gone to the pilothouse a few moments before the shooting, and only Leach, my signalman, and Robin, manning the telephone, were with me. They had also hit the deck and were lying among the shards of the windscreen but scrambled to their feet with stunned expressions a couple of seconds after I did. They shook their heads in answer to my question, but I saw that both had been hit by shrapnel. Robin was bleeding from a neck wound and Leach had splinters in a leg. Quartermaster Law came bounding up the ladder exclaiming, "Is everybody OK here, sir?"

"A few nicks we can survive without the corpsman. How about below?"

"No casualties reported yet, sir," he answered, then cut loose a stream of profanities at the Communist vessels.

My own feelings were of an almost overwhelming need to retaliate by shooting back, to bring my ship to general quarters and battle stations. This command was on the tip of my tongue, but I choked it down. There were in fact no battle stations on *Pueblo*, and general quarters really meant nothing more than manning damage control. Our 50-caliber machine guns were no match for 57-millimeter automatic cannons, could only be reached by crossing exposed decks that would be raked by many machine guns from 30-yard range concentrating from both sides against our mounts while our gunners unlashed frozen tarpaulin covers, opened ammunition lockers and attempted to bring into action their totally exposed weapons. It was certain death to even try to shoot back. So I shouted down the voice tube:

"Set a *modified* general quarters! Nobody to expose themselves topside! I have the deck as well as the conn. Left full rudder, all ahead full!" Even if I could not fight back, I was damned if I would give up. As futile a gesture as it might seem, I ordered Leach to haul a protest flag to our yardarm and pressed my ship on toward the open sea.

There was a roar overhead as the MIGs made another threatening pass at *Pueblo,* and as I glanced up at them, I saw the lead plane fire a rocket. Whether the pilot intended it as a warning shot or had accidentally triggered his missile, I could not tell; it streaked high and far ahead of the ship, exploding in the sea a good eight miles away. But it was obvious the KORCOMS' air cover was fully armed and ready to support their surface action. I remained more concerned with their sub chasers and torpedo boats.

Perhaps 40 seconds had gone by since the first salvo, and now came the second. A stream of shells yowled through the rigging, some of them bursting against the masts and scattering another shower of shrapnel downward; others could be heard slamming through the stack and superstructure. And the torpedo boats cut loose with their machine guns at the same time, stitching through the pilothouse from both sides. All four of us flattened ourselves on the deck, and as soon as the cannon fire let up, I shouted, "Clear the flying bridge!" When I raised myself to scramble for the ladder, I noticed a large hole in the deck where my chin had just been and wondered how the hell I had escaped having the piece of shrapnel go through my head.

Machine guns from two of the torpedo boats were still shooting long bursts at us, propelling Law, Robin and Leach to jump for the lower bridge, where they landed, unhurt, in a heap. My own attempt to make a more dignified retreat via the ladder was given a precipitous impetus by bullets that missed me by inches. Even as I dropped down, I had a glance at the torpedo boat firing at me and saw that it had also unmasked its port torpedo tube and was training it outboard for a shot that could hardly miss blowing *Pueblo* sky-high.

Inside the flimsy protection of the pilothouse I found the entire bridge watch lying prone on the deck, with the wheel tended from that awkward position. I had to cringe, myself, while ricocheting bullets and bits of window glass flew around as I entered, but when the machine guns stopped firing, I yelled, "Everybody on your feet!"

Berens, the helmsman, was the first one up, muttering angrily to himself as he grabbed the wheel and steadied *Pueblo* on her course. Tim, who had hurled himself out of the captain's chair, picked up his pencil and narrative log, sat down again and resumed a furious scribbling. Everybody got back on his feet—ten or twelve people rising after having fallen all over each other in a fourteen-by-eight-foot space crammed with conning and navigation equipment—except my executive officer, Lieutenant Murphy, who remained prone on the deck, his spectacles askew on his nose as he whined at me:

"But, sir . . . they are still shooting at us! . . ."

"No kidding, Ed! So get off your ass and start acting like my XO!" When he did not instantly react, I gave him a kick that brought him more or less upright. He fumbled for the microphone of the HIGHCOM receiver, which he had dropped when diving for the deck and complained, "I've been trying to raise Japan, sir, and they said to shift frequency, but. . . ."

Now that some order had been restored to the bridge, it came uppermost in my mind to make sure the emergency destruction of the especially sensitive material kept in the cryptographic room and SOD hut be accomplished with all possible speed. But I suppose that I was becoming rattled myself, not from my wounds, which I hardly felt at all beyond the soggy trickling of blood, but from the first tangible evidence that some of my key people, myself included, might buckle under the stress of this confrontation. I picked up the wrong receiver while ringing the right telephone of the two located next to each other. Thirty seconds were lost while I kept ringing the wrong circuit and a distraught CT tried to answer me on the right one. When I finally realized my mistake and switched receivers, I was somewhat relieved by Steve Harris's report:

"Emergency destruct is in progress, Captain, and our communications are open with Kamiseya."

"Good! Keep up the destruct, but don't destroy today's crypto codes until I give the orders. I'll have another CRITIC message to go soon."

"Yes, sir." His tone was a little shaken, yet sounded as if he understood what had to be done and was prepared to do it.

Temporarily reassured that matters were being taken care of in the SOD hut, I returned my full attention to the bridge, checking our course (still angling out to sea at 135 degrees) and our speed (all ahead full) and our soundings (still 30 to 35 fathoms, which was too shallow according to accepted standards for effective dumping over the side of classified material in weighted bags). A quick glance through starburst holes of the pilothouse windows confirmed that all the KORCOM aggressors were staying with us and threatening further violence with complete impunity. Our radiomen, Hayes and Crandall, were initiating their destruction bill by carrying out files from their cubicle and rushing them to the incinerator located behind the stack; swirls of smoke smelling of burning paper told me that primitive destruct equipment was functioning. Quartermaster Law, Signalman Leach and CT Robin, together with the now-useless lookouts and photographer, were helping them pass out an amazing amount of classified matériel and documents from our cramped spaces, all of them aware of the importance of keeping these from falling into Communist hands. "Watch yourselves out there, and take cover behind the whaleboat if the shooting gets hot," I warned them. "But keep that stuff burning . . . burning . . . burning to ashes!"

"Sir, the HIGHCOM has gone dead!" Murphy screeched at me, waving the mike as if he could shake a response out of it.

Radioman Hayes overheard him while passing by with his arms full of pubs and paused a second to say, "I've rechecked the frequency shift, sir, and the output of the HIGHCOM. Maybe the antenna has been shot out."

"Well, never mind the goddamned HIGHCOM," I said to Murphy. "What about the plot of this action that I ordered a while back?"

Gene Lacy was returning to the bridge after checking in

with his general-quarters station at Central Damage Control. His face was ashen, but his voice steady enough as he reported to me, "No damage below, sir, except minor hits above the waterline."

"OK, Gene. We're still afloat and under way. We'll keep trying to bull our way through." I picked up some papers off the chart table and shoved them into the arms of Crandall as he rushed another load toward the incinerator.

Then the KORCOMS opened up another salvo that was accurately aimed directly at *Pueblo*'s bridge.

The 57-millimeter shells came ahead of the sound of their thumping muzzle blasts, and one of them passed through the pilothouse, drilling through the remaining glass of one window and out through the next, passing within inches of Gene's head and scorching Tim's left ear before zinging into the sea 100 yards beyond the ship. If it had exploded, we would all have been killed then and there. But we hit the deck completely alive and unhurt, listening for the following pizzicato of machine-gun bursts to let up before returning upright. I was stunned by Gene Lacy's wild-eyed look as he dragged himself back to his feet and suddenly yelled at me:

"Are you going to stop this son of a bitch or not?"

There was only a fraction of hesitation before he reached out himself and yanked the handles of the annunciator to ALL STOP. The blindly alert engineers isolated three decks down instantly rang the answering bells. There followed an abrupt break in the wheezing exhaust throb of our perforated stack, then a rapid deceleration downward of our 12-knot speed. I kept staring at Gene in utter disbelief for another 15 seconds—15 seconds that brought the stark realization that my most experienced officer, my most trusted friend aboard this ill-starred little ship, had robbed me of the last vestige of support in my efforts to save the mission, leaving me alone with an executive officer who had proven to be unreliable and two very young and inexperienced junior officers on my bridge. Suddenly the complete uselessness of further resistance flooded my brain. It would only result in our being shot to pieces and a lot of good men killed to no avail, because the North Koreans would in the end get most of our secret documents. Instead of lunging for the annunciator and racking it back to ALL AHEAD FULL, I turned my back on it and Gene and walked out on the starboard wing of the bridge.

The shooting had stopped. From 40 yards off our starboard quarter the KORCOM torpedo boat was bobbing along, its machine gunners staring back at me with grimly impassive oriental faces over the sights of their weapons. Farther behind them their SO-1 sub chaser dropped apace as we coasted to a stop, its smoking cannon still aimed at our vitals and a new signal rising to her yardarm:

FOLLOW ME——HAVE PILOT ABOARD.

RUMBLE IN HAIGHT-ASHBURY

By L. H. Whittemore

The American big-city policeman's world allows him little time for working out conclusions about his work. If he is lucky enough to return home unharmed at the end of the day, he still must repair his emotional equipment to be able to go through the black-to-white transition to family life and then face the ordeal of another day in the streets. In the topsy-turvy social turbulence of our time the cop is often labeled the villain or victim of individual events. But, in truth, policemen are usually ordinary, sometimes confused individuals trying to grapple firsthand with the ills of society while the rest of us simply theorize about prevention and cure. The incident that follows, a few brief, trying moments in the career of San Francisco patrolman Colin Barker, is typical of the problems policemen are facing every day and night on our cities' streets. And his courage in handling it is typical of normal police reaction. Unfortunately, the Barker-type solution seldom receives any publicity, and the more sensational cases that show policemen in a bad light are spread across the headlines.

"You'd better get out of here or they'll kill you."

The young patrolman heard the warning from a sad-eyed, black-haired hippie girl who attempted to smile. Fear and the expectation of violence had permeated Haight-Ashbury by the late summer of 1968. The flower children's "free, hang-loose community" was a shambles of pain, boredom and suffering. The Summer of Love, the year before, now seemed a century away. A nightmare of frustration, anger, disillusionment, despair, racial conflict and disease swirled about Haight Street, turning it into a tension-filled area simmering with hostility. Fights, holdups, muggings and rapes were common. Clamorous, raunchy mobs milled about on the sidewalks. Youngsters, many barely out of their teens, emaciated and wild-eyed, stood or sat in doorways alongside sleeping derelicts. Without enthusiasm they whispered their offers of sale to passersby: "Acid" (LSD) . . . "Speed" (methamphetamine) . . . "Smack" (heroin) . . . "Pot" (marijuana). Violence-prone white hoodlums on motorcycles declared they would beat up any black men they saw with white women. Meanwhile, young Negroes stood on the sidewalk and taunted passing white girls. A scarcity of marijuana had led to an increased use of hard drugs. The "home of the flower children and refuge of youth" had become a magnet for hate.

I followed Patrolman Colin Barker as he moved down the street, becoming at once part of the scene and distinctly outside it. Whatever it was that had brought all these disheveled young people together, whatever they were rebelling against, individually or collectively, now was symbolized by Colin's blue uniform; and they acknowledged the cop as the biggest nonconformist in Haight-Ashbury, a freak show with silver buttons, nightstick, flashlight, walkie-talkie, blue hat, gun. The youthful foot patrolman saw it in their eyes and consoled himself with the thought that their bitterness was too disjointed, too diffused, to gather into a unified rebellion over the sight of one nervous cop.

So he continued on his way into the crowd. To the tune of "Here Comes the Bride," someone sang, "Here comes the pig, here comes the pig, da da da daaaaa, da da daaaaa, da daaaaa. . . ."

Two young bearded hippies leaned against a store window and mockingly saluted at the cop as he moved forward slowly, one step after the other. A barefoot girl, her blonde hair swung to one side, cocked her head and formed the word *pig* with her lips. Throughout the insulting gesture she tried to keep her face radiant with charm. Another engaged the patrolman in a staring contest—and she won.

"Up against the wall!" shouted a young man acting as a police officer. For Colin Barker's benefit, he and his friend staged a mock frisk. The crowd chanted, "Down with cops!" Others who watched the patrolman coming gave more subtle greetings: a cold, ugly facial expression, a fist, a finger, a defiant yawn.

"Hey, he looks younger than me."

"Gestapo!"

"He's cute."

"I could be his mother."

"You should have had an abortion."

Patrolman Barker, who wore a crew cut beneath his police hat, indeed looked much younger than his 23 years. His face had no lines or blemishes, and he had a tendency to flush. His blue eyes reflected apprehension but idealism. His uniform appeared a bit stiff, especially where the walkie-talkie hung over his shoulder and rested awkwardly on his chest. Out of self-consciousness he adjusted it from time to time, and occasionally he felt his gun as if to make sure it was still there.

Amid the almost stifling surge of attention directed at him, the young cop seized an opportunity to go on the offensive. To several young men lounging on the hood of a green convertible, he yelled, "Is this your car?"

"No."

"THEN, GET OFF IT."

His own sudden authority, plus the chorus of hisses that followed, brought fresh color to Colin's face. There was no way out of the uniform that entrapped him, no method of disassociating himself from the dark-blue costume; so he assumed the role it signified. Moreover, the crowd seemed determined to make of him what it wished. The young people, strangely grim in their attempts at festivity, would force the cop to shoulder the case for the opposition. Simply by treating him as the enemy, they would force him to become it, in manner as well as in appearance.

"Hi, Officer," said a pretty young girl. "Want to buy a necklace?"

"No . . . no, thanks."

"Awwwww."

Another young girl stepped in front of him, making a fancy bow. "Good evening, Officer," she said. "Have a fine night."

"There's a pig in our midst!"

"Want a piece of bread, Officer?"

"No, no. No, thank you."

"It's good bread."

The patrolman paused before a doorway where three unkempt young men were sprawled out. "This isn't your doorway, is it?"

"Nope."

"Then, get on your feet."

As they picked themselves up, a wine bottle sheathed in a paper bag rolled off the top step and bounced to the sidewalk. Colin picked it up and went to the curb. He poured out the wine between two parked cars to a chorus of boos and hisses.

"Hey, he does that real groovy, like he ought to be promoted."

To a young man selling underground newspapers to passing cars, Colin said, "Come on, off the street." Then, looking over his shoulder, he called to the same three young men, "Don't block that doorway!"

"I have a dream," shouted a heckler in the crowd, lost from sight in the chaotic shuffling of bodies, "and I see a picture of a pig with a badge on him."

"Oink, oink! Oink, oink!"

"Officer, do I threaten the security of the United States if I don't take a bath?"

"I don't think so. I don't think what you do matters one way or another."

"Thank you, Officer. You're OK."

Colin paused again, this time next to a group of disheveled teen-agers with knapsacks sitting on the sidewalk.

"Come on, get up."

"We're tired."

"Get up!"

"All we're doing is sitting."

"Up!"

A young girl with long pigtails stood up and swung her leg over a motorcycle along the curb. On her blouse was an orange button with the words TICKLE MY FANCY. Her breasts were clearly defined beneath a bulging T-shirt.

"All of you—off the cars. Get off the motorcycle, please."

In the window of a store that Colin now paused at, a huge cartoon showed a caricature of Lyndon Baines Johnson urinating on the world.

"Officer, you got any spare change?"

"That's the wrong question to ask a policeman, young lady."

"Gee, Officer . . . just a dime?"

"Look——" Colin Barker clenched his fist and walked

past her. For some reason he could not put into words, being asked for money by a middle-class hippie girl, perhaps an ex-college senior, made him furious.

A girl selling beads in the street to tourists was Colin's next objective. "Hey, get off that street, will you?" She jumped back to the curb. Business was poor, anyhow; the tourists drove by with doors locked and windows up. From inside their cars they must have heard no sound as they tried to catch glimpses of the frantic scene. Colin looked backward for a moment. Youngsters were already in the street again, panhandling, lounging on the cars, "grooving on the scene," doing their thing.

"Hello, dear," said a new hippie girl, flashing her eyes seductively, challenging the patrolman's veneer of aloofness.

"Hi."

"Hey, Officer, are you for real?" asked a bold young man in the crowd.

"You got something to say to me?"

"I mean, dig—are you a *real* police officer?"

"No, it's Halloween."

On the sidewalk ahead, several boys and girls were kneeling over a lovely design in multicolored chalk. A huge set of flowers had been drawn in pink, purple, blue and white, and a message was printed below the flowers: "I, YOU, WE, ARE GOD." The design, which probably had taken at least an hour to sketch on the damp sidewalk, was about two feet in width and twice that in length.

"All right," said Colin, "get some water and scrub this off."

"Do we have to?"

"No, I'm just telling you for my goddamn health."

"Aw, come on. We worked hard on this. Is it really against the law?"

"You're blocking the entrance to this man's establishment," said Colin looking in the window of the laundromat. The middle-aged storekeeper shrugged from behind the glass. A crowd gathered and watched as the youngsters, supplied with buckets of water and heavy brushes from the laundromat, scrubbed the chalk design off the sidewalk. The colors ran together in a blotch before disappearing. Seeing the buildup of the crowd, Colin turned and continued his slow, deliberate stroll through hippieville.

Again a girl with bare feet jumped in front of him. Apparently emboldened by her friends, she held a flower to his face and danced backward as he approached. "Have a flower, Officer."

"No, thanks, but thanks."

"It's a *nice* flower, sir."

"I can't take it, really."

"Go on—take it."

"No, really——"

"PLEASE?"

Colin stopped, shaking his head. The girl stared up at him defiantly and shouted, "TAKE THE FLOWER!" Suddenly the patrolman's hand shot out and batted the flower out of her hand. The sound of his hand smacking hers seemed too loud. Red-faced, he turned on his heel and began walking back through the same block. "That wasn't very nice," called the girl. Now the patrolman was walking faster, more rigidly; now he was ready to spring out of his cloak of passivity. His hand gripped the nightstick, and his eyes, clear and intense, challenged everything in their field of vision. The images of the young people came into sharper focus. What he saw now was specific. In the beginning he had seen only a large mass of untidy teen-agers and young people; now they were each individuals, and he, as an individual, could no longer see the crowd as a whole.

As he walked, he heard someone following him, whistling for his benefit. The faces he passed were smiling, expectant, and the whistling came closer to his ear. Still he refused to turn around. He walked through the bodies, sometimes pausing deliberately to wait for someone to move out of his way rather than go around. The whistling grew louder at the back of his head. Colin stopped. The person behind him continued the harsh, metallic whistling on one long high note, and then there was a strange silence. Colin heard the person breathing behind him, but still he refused to turn around. Everyone was watching his reaction, waiting.

"ATTENTION!"

The sound made Colin Barker's ears pulsate with pain. Turning abruptly, he faced a tall, thin young man with flowing blond hair, dirty face and frazzled clothing.

Colin whispered, "What did you say?"

"I said, 'Fuck you, cop!' That's what I said."

In one furious gesture Colin threw the young man against the wall. He pushed aside a hippie girl and flayed at the young man with his fists. Within seconds the crowd built up and surrounded the fight. From a distance came the sound of a rock smashing through the window of a moving car. The young man screamed and kicked. Colin tried to grab his shirt, but the young man reached up and tore the patrolman's badge off, ripping the uniform. The crowd cheered, and Colin smashed his nightstick down, once, twice, a third time. The mob surged in, united, but Colin already was calling for help through his walkie-talkie. He stood back, holding the nightstick over his victim, and waited. Members of the crowd continued to heckle, but the brief show of unified anger seemed to disperse. The young man on the sidewalk, very much aware of his role in the chaos, shouted, "Revolution now! Kill him!" Colin folded his arms and said nothing.

"I hope," screamed the young man who groveled about like an animal, "that somebody jumps on *you* someday."

"Cool off, fella."

"Hey, you son of a bitch fascist pig! Go ahead, kill me!"

"Shut up, will ya? You make me sick."

"Then puke, you pig! Beat me! Get this pig off my back!" As the young man tried to get up, Colin pushed him back to the ground. "I won't be a slave to you! Hey, somebody shoot this pig!"

"Shut your mouth!" Colin demanded.

"Next time you see me, brother, you'll be behind my gunsight. You pig! You can't face up to a nigger, 'cause he'll put a twenty-two in your head!"

At last the paddy wagon rolled up, and two patrolmen jumped out. They helped Colin drag the screaming young man into the back of the truck.

"What's the trouble, Colin?"

"I think he's on LSD or something. He's out of his head."

Behind the paddy wagon, in an unmarked car, sat four members of the San Francisco tactical patrol. The four husky, uniformed cops stared at the crowd with contempt. One of them jumped from the car and stood, legs apart, challenging anyone to provoke him. Most of the crowd seemed to fear him, because the heckling abruptly stopped. Colin hopped into the cab of the paddy wagon as it rolled off down the fog-engulfed street to the station house in Golden Gate Park.

KING OF THE MOUNTAINS

By Maurice Herzog

In 1950 Maurice Herzog led a French team up the slopes of Annapurna, in the Himalayas. They were attempting to become the first climbers in history to reach an 8000-meter peak (26,493 feet). This is the story of that final assault.

Why had they given up? We could not understand it. Lachenal, who was moving at a fair pace and appeared to be going much more easily than during the last few days, was the first up the avalanche cone and across the couloir. It was the third time I had been over this route, and I knew it well by now, but again, as I went to meet them, I found it both difficult and dangerous. On the little platform beneath the ice wall where we had left a fixed rope, we came upon Terray and Rébuffat.

"What's happened?" I asked Terray.

He seemed disheartened. "We'd have been crazy to go on. What with the wind and this hellish snow, it took us more than seven hours yesterday to get from camp three to camp four."

"Did you find the tent?"

"Sure, but we had to straighten the poles, which had been bent over by the avalanche. We got the other tent up in a tearing wind. Rébuffat felt his feet beginning to freeze."

"I thought I'd had it," put in Gaston. "Fortunately, Lionel rubbed me and flogged me with an end of rope and at last got the blood circulating again."

"This morning," Terray went on, "the cold was worse than in Canada and the wind even stronger. I figured it out like this: If yesterday, when we were quite fit, we only covered just over a thousand feet in seven hours, we wouldn't have a hope of climbing the last four thousand feet under present conditions. I know we must do all we can, up to the limit, but I'm beginning to have doubts about our success."

Although Lachenal and I protested vigorously, the other two did not seem to be affected by our enthusiasm. Terray, for all his strength, had only just managed to cope with the snow (which covered the tracks afresh every day) and the slopes, which had to be mastered yard by yard and with the deterioration of mind and body brought on by altitude. But he did not care to dwell on all these obstacles—he had no wish to undermine our solid morale.

"We're going up," I said without the least hesitation. "When we come down, it'll mean the top's been reached—it's all or nothing."

And I felt that Lachenal was as determined as myself. The other two wished us good luck, but I read doubt in their faces. Now it was up to us.

We set to on the slope; Sarki, Ang-Tharkey, Lachenal and I took it in turns to go ahead to improve the tracks fortunately left by Terray and Rébuffat on their way down. The going wasn't too bad, but all the same, Ang-Tharkey was amazed at the difficulty of the ground.

Pansy had already told him that neither on Kanchenjunga nor on Everest had they ever struggled with such difficult terrain. It was the first time these Sherpa had done any climbing on ice and been obliged to get up vertical walls. But all went well; we pushed on steadily and found the going much easier than the previous times, which showed just how vital acclimatization is on Himalayan expeditions. It was now burningly hot, and by the time we reached camp three, we were sweating. What a truly magnificent camp this was, lost in the very heart of the mountains in a tiny snow-blocked crevasse! How snug and comfortable it appeared!

We had to conserve our strength; there would be no going farther today. Most of the time we just lay in our sacks, and the Sherpa handed us our meals through the entrance of the other tent. The weather was fine. This time everything was in our favor, and we would get to the top.

It took the Sherpa a long time to make tea because of the decreased heating power of the stoves at this height. A few cigarettes, followed by the ration of pills, which both sahibs and Sherpa obediently swallowed, and before dark everybody at camp three was already asleep.

In the morning we waited placidly for the sun, since the

day's program consisted of going only as far as camp four, which would take us barely four hours. But we should also have to move that camp again and repitch it right on the Sickle glacier. We each set about getting our things ready, and I took a few movie shots. Down below, the plateau on which camp two was pitched appeared to have become a regular village. Big valley tents and high-altitude tents stood side by side, and it looked altogether like an advanced base camp.

"Lionel and Gaston must be resting now," said Lachenal.

We decided to move off, taking advantage of the relatively good state of snow, and we reached the site of camp four more rapidly than we had expected. On the way I took more movie shots, in particular of the bergschrund by the plateau on which the camp was situated. The weather was still very fine. Ang-Tharkey and Sarki had gone splendidly, one of them on Lachenal's rope, the other on mine. It was still early, and we should therefore be able to move camp four right up on the Sickle glacier. We were pleased about this, for beyond this camp there would be no further technical difficulties to keep us back. We quickly took down one tent, which we ourselves would be carrying, as well as food and equipment.

"In less than an hour we ought to be up the big ice slope leading to the edge of the Sickle," I said to Lachenal. "It's not all that long." Ang-Tharkey and Sarki would come back to the present camp, where we were leaving the other tent. The following morning they would have to dismantle it and carry it up to the new camp four. From there we would start out for the next one—camp five.

Laden like donkeys, we sank up to our waists in new snow on the first few yards of the great ice slope. But shortly there was far less snow, and very soon only a thin layer of loose snow lying on ice. The angle was comparable with that of the steepest Alpine slopes. Now and again we cut a few steps, but most of the time we just went straight up on our crampons—though cramponing at this height was not exactly restful, and we puffed away like steam engines.

The Sherpa were not at all happy. They were not expert on this sort of ground, but as they were afraid of getting left behind, they made all possible speed. After a couple hundred yards of this exhausting work, we came to the edge of the

Sickle. Lachenal, who was leading, had a look around up there, and I did the same down below. Our choice fell upon an inviting site at the base of a serac just where we had emerged from the ice slope. It was an ideal place, protected from the wind both by the serac itself and by a little ice ridge that formed a natural screen. Lachenal was delighted:

"Once we've fixed things up, we'll be as snug as in my own little chalet at Chamonix."

We set to work at once, and the tent was soon in position. As it was already late afternoon, I packed Ang-Tharkey and Sarki off to the lower camp, none too happy at the prospect of going down such a difficult slope. But I knew that Ang-Tharkey would not hesitate to cut extra steps and, if necessary, to make a staircase the whole way.

"Good night, sir!"

We shook hands warmly, and our two Sherpa disappeared down the slope. Meanwhile, we arranged our shelter. Mist closed around us, and an icy wind got up, stinging our faces with blown snow. Neither of us had much appetite, but we forced ourselves to eat, and when the tea was ready, I set out in a row the collection of pills that Oudot had strictly ordered us to swallow. For all Lachenal's assertions, we were only relatively comfortable. We put our boots into our sleeping bags to prevent them from freezing and settled ourselves in for an excellent night.

When dawn came, I poked my head anxiously through the opening of the tent. The sun was rising, and it was fine and cold. It looked as if the monsoon would not arrive that day, and I felt much relieved, for the latest news had worried me. We were embarked upon a race against time. As soon as Ang-Tharkey and Sarki arrived, we shared out the loads and made up our sacks. We were shivering and could not leave our serac quick enough. Leaving one tent where it was, we set out; the other was for camp five.

A traverse to the left across the Sickle glacier enabled us to avoid an area of broken-up seracs. In this way we reached the base of a wide valley of large, steep snowfields with few obstacles in the way. Nobody said anything—every one of us was tense with effort, and the loads weighed us down. We thought of what lay ahead. For me the main question was the monsoon. It was now June 2, and we could not reasonably hope for more than four days of fine weather.

That would just give us time, but there was not a moment to lose. Now that we had only this great snowfield before us, we held the advantage: There were no technical obstacles —or at least hardly any. Not for a single moment did either Lachenal or I entertain the slightest doubt about our victory.

We stopped frequently and ate a bit of candy or nougat, for which we always had a great craving. Looking back down the mountain, the sight was enough to make one dizzy. The plateau of camp two was a mere pocket handkerchief, and the great Annapurna glacier, which took an hour to cross, was reduced to a small tongue of ice. In the distance, over the top of the Great Barrier, we could distinctly see Tibet; on the extreme left Dhaulagiri was partially hidden by the great rock wall of Annapurna. Our zigzagging upward tracks were visible the whole way.

The jagged ice ridge at the summit produced a curious effect—a snow-laden wind blew through it as if through the teeth of a comb. Mist straggled right across the sky over our heads. One of the buttresses of Annapurna towered above us in rose-red rock—it was the shape of a bird's beak and looked like the Bec d'Oiseau on the Grepon in the Mont Blanc massif. A thin rib of rock in the shape of a spearhead ran up to it.

"We're pretty sure," I told Lachenal, "to be able to find a place somewhere on that rib big enough for our 'coffin.' "

Lachenal agreed. "We'll use as many pitons as necessary, and, anyhow, we shall be on dry ground."

With dogged perseverance he and I took turns in making the trail. The two Sherpa got terribly winded, and we kept stopping to regain our breath. Two or three times we made long traverses to avoid the seracs and one particularly long crevasse. Often we sank in the snow, and each step seemed an eternity. Although we progressed upward, the rib always appeared to remain just as far off.

"Enough to take the heart out of you," complained Lachenal.

Gradually the difficulties lessened, the snow became firmer, and we did not sink so far. We had the feeling that we were climbing on an enormous roof. The slope was constant, and though it was at an angle of about 40 degrees, we were able to crampon up it. Every ten yards we halted, in cold so intense that our feet grew numb. But we could not afford any unnecessary delay. "On to camp five!" became for us a kind of refrain. The going became terribly exhausting, for the surface crust of the snow broke through beneath our crampons, and again we sank in at each step.

With a final spurt of energy we gained the rib of rock.

"Hell!"

What a disappointment! Those fine, clear-colored rocks were plastered with ice—there were no ledges, no holds. We should have to pitch camp right on the slope.

The Sherpa joined us. We were at 24,600 feet, and the height laid them out completely. They couldn't speak a word and made signs that their heads were hurting. But we all had to set to work. With our axes we made a level space. In order to accomplish this on such a steep slope, we had to move great quantities of snow. Every 30 seconds I had to rest; I felt as though I were suffocating, my breathing was out of control, and my heart pounding away. Yet the Sherpa, who were not in such good shape as we were, managed to carry on for five minutes without a break. An hour later the shelf was ready. It was close to the rib, and we were able to anchor the tent to the two pitons that Lachenal drove into cracks in the rock.

I had a brief conversation with Ang-Tharkey in pidgin English.

"Tomorrow morning Lachenal-sahib and Bara-sahib go to the summit of Annapurna."

"Yes, sir."

"You are the sirdar and the most experienced of all the Sherpa. I should be very glad if you will come with us."

"Thank you, sir."

"We must have the victory *together*. Will you come?"

At that moment I felt it my duty to take into consideration the Sherpa's very understandable feelings. After a pause Ang-Tharkey replied. He was grateful for the choice of action I had given him, but he held back.

"Thank you very much, Bara-sahib, but my feet are beginning to freeze——"

"I see."

"—and I prefer to go down to camp four."

"Of course, Ang-Tharkey, it's as you like. In that case, go down at once, as it is late."

"Thank you, sir."

In a second their sacks were packed, and just as they were setting off, they turned around, and I could guess their anxiety at leaving us alone.

"Salaam, sir. Good luck!"

"Salaam—and be careful!"

A few minutes later two black dots were on their way down the slope we had just come up. How strangely their minds worked. Here were these men, proverbial for their trustworthiness and devotion, who quite certainly enjoyed going high on the mountains, and yet, when on the point of reaping the victory from their labors, they prudently held back. But I don't doubt that our attitude struck them as even more strange.

Not a word did Lachenal and I speak. Our silence had something heavy and obsessive about it. This time we would not turn back.

It would be a grim night. The site was dangerous and the ground unstable. Under the action of the wind, the snow slid down the length of the slope and piled up above our shelter. We hoped it would not weigh too much on the tent. The pitons driven into the limestone, the axes driven right into the snow, gave us only moral support, and we had no illusions. We said nothing, but we both feared that the edge of the platform would collapse and carry the tent away.

Our minds worked slowly during this last night before the final assault. I had great difficulty in concentrating, and I couldn't get up an interest in anything. Conversation languished. With great effort, and only because we urged each other on, we managed to make some tea on the stove and swallow our pills with military discipline. It was impossible to swallow any food at all.

A fierce wind sprang up, and the nylon fabric of the tent flapped noisily. Several times we feared that the wind would blow the tent away, and at each gust we clung to the poles as a drowning man clings to a plank. It began to snow; the storm howled and moaned around us. The air was fraught with terror, and in the end we became terrified, too.

Every moment demanded a tremendous effort of will. There was no question of undressing. Pushing our boots to the bottom of our wonderful sleeping bags, we tucked ourselves in. Good old Pierre Allain! How we blessed him that night! And away flew our thoughts to the friend who had designed our marvelous equipment.

Lachenal settled himself on the outer side of the tent, while I curled up against the slope. It wasn't pleasant for either of us. Lachenal, on the edge of the precarious platform, felt as though he were slipping off into space, while I was threatened with suffocation under the snow that slid down and piled up persistently on the roof of the tent.

"It's made of nylon, and it's elastic," I tried to reassure Lachenal, "otherwise, the fabric would give way. Hell! I've forgotten to put my camera inside my sleeping bag."

I stretched out a hand for the precious object and slid it down beside me to the bottom of my sack, which was already cluttered up with my boots.

What a night! Lachenal slid farther and farther toward the edge, and I felt more and more suffocated. We looked at the time repeatedly. The situation was beginning to be alarming. I could no longer breathe. The weight of the snow was literally crushing me. Like a boxer on guard, I held both arms to my chest and so made a small space that allowed me to expand my lungs. The noise of the wind was ear-splitting, and every onslaught was accompanied by a high-pitched whistling. The tent poles bent over dangerously, while with the strength of desperation we tried to hold them in place. Why the tent was not blown down, I don't know. Our very worst alpine bivouacs were nothing compared with this unequal and exhausting struggle.

We were worn out and utterly weary, but the storm saw to it that we were kept wide awake.

Rébuffat and Terray, skeptical about the success of our attempt, went down toward camp two. When they arrived there, they found Couzy and Schatz, who gave them the latest news. Then they dropped with fatigue, and so, no doubt, did Pansy and Aila, for they disappeared into the Sherpa's tent and were seen no more that day. Couzy and Schatz, in excellent trim, were pleased to be on a rope together again. Early the following morning they left camp two, and, as arranged, they followed us up, one camp behind.

At camp two Terray gradually recovered. He felt that the final attack was imminent and set about his preparations with his usual meticulous care. Rébuffat was busy writing. Early in the afternoon, sleet began to fall.

"Hello, everybody!"

The white ghost who had just come in was Ichac!

"The others are coming up."

Oudot and Noyelle then appeared, shaking the snow off inside the tent with the cheerful carelessness of people coming from outside. It was 5:30.

"What! It's you!" exclaimed Ichac. "We were expecting to see Schatz and Couzy."

"No—it's only us."

And Terray went on to explain how they had had to retrace their steps the day before without having been able to establish camp five because of Rébuffat's feet showing signs of frostbite.

"We'll be off again tomorrow morning," said Terray.

Outside, the sleet had turned to snow. Oudot was impatient to find out to what extent oxygen would be of use. Displaying his usual authority, he insisted upon our liaison officer, Noyelle, going around with a mask on. His face became a snout connected by a tube to cylinders of Duralumin full of compressed oxygen. He might have been exploring the moon! Poor Noyelle, with his ridiculous hat pulled down over his nose and ears—he was the only one unable to appreciate the comic figure he cut.

After the tests, everyone collected in the tent, and Ichac took some flashlight photographs.

"Right now I'm going to establish a record for the highest flashlight shot."

As a matter of fact, this camp was not far off 20,000 feet high, and it was unlikely that many flashlights had been taken on Himalayan expeditions.

After dinner the sky cleared and the stars shone, and the Great Barrier was clothed in a mantle of white, lit up by the moon. The latest news on the radio was alarming: The monsoon had reached the north of Bengal, and, moreover, considerable disturbances were forecast from the west.

The following morning—June 2—the sky was brilliant; it was going to be a glorious day. As usual, Lionel Terray had timed his departure for an early hour. He left camp with Rébuffat and two Sherpa at six o'clock, before the sun was up. (At camp four we were still sleeping soundly.) Ichac took some telephotos of them as they went up the avalanche cone.

Now the whole mountain was inhabited, and as the hours

went by, activity increased. An onlooker would have seen an astonishing sight: At camp two, men were swarming round the settlement of tents. A little higher up, Terray and Rébuffat, with their two Sherpa, Pansy and Aila, were cutting fresh steps up the first slopes. Above, at camp three, Schatz and Couzy, accompanied by Angawa and Fourtharkey, were preparing to cross the great couloir. And, finally, Lachenal and I, with Ang-Tharkey and Sarki, were once again plowing through snow on the slope of the Sickle glacier.

During the afternoon, clouds appeared along the bed of the Miristi Khola and even on the plateau by camp two. Through a rent in them Ichac was able to see, at the foot of the spear-shaped rib, a new black speck that he guessed must be camp five. Would the final assault be made the following morning? That would be decided by the weather.

The mist grew thicker, and calls for help were heard. Noyelle and Ichac went out to see who it was and found Angawa and Fourtharkey wandering in the mist. Having only one tent at camp four—the other was at camp five—Couzy and Schatz had had to send their two Sherpa down.

The rest of the equipment for camp four was to be brought up the following day by the Rébuffat-Terray party, who would strike camp three and take it up with them. And the group at camp two would move up the day after and reestablish camp three.

At camp four morale was good, Rébuffat and Terray had just arrived, and everyone was in good form. Terray meditated upon the unpredictable nature of conditions in the Himalayas: Four days ago he and Rébuffat had climbed to camp three with the greatest difficulty, taking seven hours to crawl up. This time they had successfully carried out an ambitious program of which it would be hard to find the equivalent in the history of Himalayan climbing: Leaving camp two at dawn, they had succeeded in reaching camp three at about 11 o'clock in the morning; they had struck this camp and then carried everything on up to camp four, in this way gaining one precious day. Although there were only four of them, they carried two high-altitude units as well as 22 pounds of food. Rébuffat, like Lachenal, had made a magnificent comeback.

There were two people who were mighty pleased to see them, and these were Couzy and Schatz. Otherwise, the next day these two would have had to carry up a complete camp themselves, and they had not found this prospect particularly attractive. Thanks to aspirin and sleeping tablets and thanks, also, to a sense of tremendous well-being, caused partly by good physical condition and partly by the imminence of a happy outcome, everybody passed an excellent night.

On the third of June 1950, the first light of dawn found us still clinging to the tent poles at camp five. Gradually the wind abated and, with daylight, died away altogether. I made desperate attempts to push back the soft, icy stuff that stifled me, but every movement became an act of heroism. My mental powers were numbed; thinking was an effort, and we did not exchange a single word.

What a repellent place it was! To everyone who reached it, camp five became one of the worst memories of their lives. We had only one thought—to get away. We should have waited for the first rays of the sun, but at half past five we felt we couldn't stick it any longer.

"Let's go, Biscante," I muttered. "Can't stay here a minute longer."

"Yes, let's go," repeated Lachenal.

Which of us would have the energy to make tea? Although our minds worked slowly, we were quite able to envisage all the movements that would be necessary—and neither of us could face up to it. It couldn't be helped—we would just have to go without. It was quite hard enough work to get ourselves and our boots out of our sleeping bags—and the boots were frozen stiff, so that we got them on only with the greatest difficulty. Every movement made us terribly breathless. We felt as if we were being stifled. Our gaiters were stiff as a board, but I succeeded in lacing mine up; Lachenal couldn't manage his.

"No need for the rope, eh, Biscante?"

"No need," replied Lachenal laconically.

That was two pounds saved. I pushed a tube of condensed milk, some nougat and a pair of socks into my sack; one never knew, the socks might come in useful—they might even do as balaclavas. For the time being I stuffed them with first-aid equipment. The camera was loaded with black-and-white film; I had color film in reserve. I pulled the movie camera out from the bottom of my sleeping bag, wound it up and tried letting it run without film. There was a little click; then it stopped and jammed.

"Bad luck after bringing it so far," said Lachenal.

In spite of our photographer, Ichac's, precautions taken to lubricate it with special grease, the intense cold, even inside the sleeping bag, had frozen it. I left it at the camp rather sadly; I had looked forward to taking it to the top. I had used it up to 24,600 feet.

We went outside and put on our crampons, which we kept on all day. We wore as many clothes as possible; our sacks were very light. At six o'clock we started off. It was brilliantly fine but also very cold. Our superlightweight crampons bit deep into the steep slopes of ice and hard snow up which lay the first stage of our climb.

Later the slope became slightly less steep and more uniform. Sometimes the hard crust bore our weight, but at others we broke through and sank into soft powder snow, which made progress exhausting. We took turns in making the track and often stopped without any word having passed between us. Each of us lived in a closed and private world of his own. I was suspicious of my mental processes; my mind was working very slowly, and I was perfectly aware of the low state of my intelligence. It was easiest just to stick to one thought at a time—safest, too. The cold was penetrating; for all our special eiderdown clothing, we felt as if we'd nothing on. Whenever we halted, we stamped our feet hard. Lachenal went as far as to take off one boot, which was a bit tight; he was in terror of frostbite.

"I don't want to be like Lambert," he said. Raymond Lambert, a Geneva guide, had to have all his toes amputated after an eventful climb during which he got his feet frostbitten. While Lachenal rubbed himself hard, I looked at the summits all around us. Already we overtopped them all except the distant Dhaulagiri. The complicated structure of these mountains, with which our many laborious explorations had made us familiar, was now spread out plainly at our feet.

The going was incredibly exhausting, and every step was a struggle of mind over matter. We came out into the sunlight and, by way of marking the occasion, made yet another halt. Lachenal continued to complain of his feet. "I can't feel anything. I think I'm beginning to get frostbite." And once again he undid his boot.

I began to be seriously worried. I realized very well the risk we were running. I knew from experience how insidiously and quickly frostbite can set in if one is not extremely careful. Nor was Lachenal under any illusions. "We're in danger of having frozen feet. Do you think it's worth it?"

This was most disturbing. It was my responsibility as leader to think of the others. There was no doubt about frostbite being a very real danger. Did Annapurna justify such risks? That was the question I asked myself. It continued to worry me.

Lachenal had laced his boots up again, and once more we continued to force our way through the exhausting snow. The whole of the Sickle glacier was now in view, bathed in light. We still had a long way to go to cross it, and then there was that rock band—would we find a gap in it?

My feet, like Lachenal's, were very cold, and I continued to wriggle my toes, even when we were moving. I could not feel them, but that was nothing new in the mountains, and if I kept on moving them, it would keep the circulation going.

Lachenal appeared to me as a sort of specter—he was alone in his world, I in mine. But—and this was odd enough —any effort was slightly *less* exhausting than lower down. Perhaps it was hope lending us wings. Even through dark glasses the snow was blinding—the sun beating straight down on the ice. We looked down upon precipitous ridges that dropped away into space and upon tiny glaciers far, far below. Familiar peaks soared arrowlike into the sky. Suddenly Lachenal grabbed me.

"If I go back, what will you do?"

A whole sequence of pictures flashed through my head: the days of marching in sweltering heat, the hard pitches we had overcome, the tremendous efforts we had all made to lay siege to the mountain, the daily heroism of all my friends in establishing the camps. Now we were nearing our goal. In an hour or two, perhaps, victory would be ours. Must we give up? Impossible! My whole being revolted against the idea. I had made up my mind irrevocably. Today we were consecrating an ideal, and no sacrifice was too great. I heard my voice clearly:

"I should go on by myself."

I would go alone. If he wished to go down, it was not for

me to stop him. He must make his own choice freely.

"Then, I'll follow you."

The die was cast. I was no longer anxious. Nothing could stop us now from getting to the top. The psychological atmosphere changed with these few words, and we went forward now as brothers.

I felt as though I were plunging into something new and quite abnormal. I had the strangest and most vivid impressions, such as I had never before known in the mountains. There was something unnatural in the way I saw Lachenal and everything around us. I smiled to myself at the paltriness of our efforts, for I could stand apart and watch myself making these efforts. But all sense of exertion was gone, as though there were no longer any gravity. This diaphanous landscape, this quintessence of purity—these were not the mountains I knew; they were the mountains of my dreams.

The snow, sprinkled over every rock and gleaming in the sun, was of a radiant beauty that touched me to the heart. I had never seen such complete transparency, and I was living in a world of crystal. Sounds were indistinct, the atmosphere like cotton wool.

An astonishing happiness welled up in me, but I could not define it. Everything was so new, so utterly unprecedented. It was not in the least like anything I had known in the Alps, where one feels buoyed up by the presence of others—by people of whom one is vaguely aware or even by the dwellings one can see in the far distance.

This was quite different. An enormous gulf was between me and the world. This was a different universe—withered, desert, lifeless, a fantastic universe where the presence of man was not foreseen, perhaps not desired. We were braving an interdict, overstepping a boundary, and yet we had no fear as we continued upward. I thought of the famous ladder of St. Theresa of Avila. Something clutched at my heart.

Did Lachenal share these feelings? The summit ridge drew nearer, and we reached the foot of the ultimate rock band. The slope was very steep and the snow interspersed with rocks.

"Couloir!"

A finger pointed. The whispered word from one to another indicated the key to the rocks—the last line of defense.

"What luck!"

The couloir up the rocks, though steep, was feasible.

The sky was a deep sapphire blue. With a great effort we edged over to the right, avoiding the rocks; we preferred to keep to the snow on account of our crampons, and it was not long before we set foot in the couloir. It was fairly steep, and we had a minute's hesitation. Should we have enough strength left to overcome this final obstacle?

Fortunately, the snow was hard, and by kicking steps we were able to manage, thanks to our crampons. A false move would have been fatal. There was no need to make handholds—our axes, driven in as far as possible, served us for an anchor.

Lachenal went splendidly. What a wonderful contrast to the early days! It was a hard struggle here, but he kept going. Lifting our eyes occasionally from the slope, we saw the couloir opening out onto—well, we didn't quite know— probably a ridge. But where was the top—left or right? Stopping at every step, leaning on our axes, we tried to recover our breath and to calm down our racing hearts, which were thumping as though they would burst. We knew we were there now—that nothing could stop us. No need to exchange looks—each of us would have read the same determination in the other's eyes. A slight detour to the left, a few more steps —the summit ridge came gradually nearer—a few rocks to avoid. We dragged ourselves up. Could we possibly be there?

Yes!

A fierce and savage wind tore at us.

We were on top of Annapurna!—8075 meters, 26,493 feet.

Our hearts overflowed with an unspeakable happiness.

"If only the others could know. . . ."

If only everyone could know!

The summit was a corniced crest of ice, and the precipices on the far side, which plunged vertically down beneath us, were terrifying, unfathomable. There could be few other mountains in the world like this. Clouds floated halfway down, concealing the gentle, fertile valley of Pokhara, 23,000 feet below. Above us there was nothing!

Our mission was accomplished. But, at the same time, we had accomplished something infinitely greater. How wonderful life would now become! What an inconceivable experience it is to attain one's ideal and, at the very same moment, to fulfill oneself. I was stirred to the depths of my being. Never had I felt happiness like this—so intense and yet so pure. That brown rock, the highest of them all, that ridge of ice—were these the goals of a lifetime? Or were they, rather, the limits of man's pride?

"Well, what about going down?"

Lachenal shook me. What were his own feelings? Did he simply think he had finished another climb, as in the Alps? Did he think one could just go down again like that, with nothing more to it?

"One minute. I must take some photographs."

"Hurry up!"

I fumbled feverishly in my sack, pulled out the camera, took out the little French flag that was right at the bottom and the pennants. Useless gestures, no doubt, but something more than symbols—eloquent tokens of affection and goodwill. I tied the strips of material—stained by sweat and by the food in the sacks—to the shaft of my ice ax, the only flagstaff at hand. Then I focused my camera on Lachenal.

"Now will you take me?"

"Hand it over—hurry up!" said Lachenal.

He took several pictures and then handed me back the camera. I loaded the color film, and we repeated the process, to be certain of bringing back records to be cherished in the future.

"Are you mad?" asked Lachenal. "We haven't a minute to lose; we must go down at once."

And, in fact, a glance round showed that the weather was no longer gloriously fine, as it had been in the morning. Lachenal was becoming impatient.

"We must go down!"

He was right. His was the reaction of the mountaineer who knows his own domain. But I just could not accustom myself to the idea that we had won our victory. It seemed inconceivable that we should have trodden those summit snows.

It was impossible to build a cairn—there were no stones; everything was frozen. Lachenal stamped his feet; he felt them freezing. I felt mine freezing, too, but paid little attention. The highest mountain to be climbed by man lay under our feet! The names of our predecessors on these heights raced through my mind: Mummery, Mallory and Irvine,

Bauer, Welzenbach, Tilman, Shipton. How many of them were dead—how many had found on these mountains what, to them, was the finest end of all?

My joy was touched with humility. It was not just one party that had climbed Annapurna today but a whole expedition. I thought of all the others in the camps perched on the slopes at our feet, and I knew it was because of their efforts and their sacrifices that we had succeeded. There are times when the most complicated actions are suddenly summed up, distilled, and strike you with illuminating clarity. So it was with this irresistible upward surge that had landed us two here.

Pictures passed through my mind—the Chamonix valley, where I had spent the most marvelous moments of my childhood; Mont Blanc, which so tremendously impressed me! I was a child when I first saw "the Mont Blanc people" coming home, and to me there was a queer look about them. A strange light shone in their eyes.

"Come on, straight down," called Lachenal.

He had already done up his sack and started going down. I took out my pocket aneroid: 8500 meters. I smiled. I swallowed a little condensed milk and left the tube behind —the only trace of our passage. I did up my sack, put on my gloves and my glasses, seized my ice ax; one look around and I, too, hurried down the slope. Before disappearing into the couloir, I gave one last look at the summit that would henceforth be all our joy and all our consolation.

Lachenal was already far below; he had reached the foot of the couloir. I hurried down in his tracks. I went as fast as I could, but it was dangerous going. At every step one had to take care that the snow did not break away beneath one's weight. Lachenal, going faster than I thought he was capable of, was now on the long traverse. It was my turn to cross the area of mixed rock and snow. At last I reached the foot of the rock band. I had hurried, and I was out of breath. I undid my sack. What had I been going to do? I couldn't say.

"My gloves!"

Before I had time to bend over, I saw them slide and roll. They went farther and farther straight down the slope. I remained where I was, quite stunned. I watched them rolling down slowly, with no appearance of stopping. The move-

ment of those gloves was engraved in my sight as something
irredeemable against which I was powerless. The conse-
quences might be most serious. What was I to do?

"Quickly, down to camp five."

Rébuffat and Terray would be there. My concern dissolved like magic. I now had a fixed objective again: to reach
the camp. Never for a minute did it occur to me to use as
gloves the socks that I always carry in reserve for just such
a mishap as this.

On I went, trying to catch up with Lachenal. It had been
two o'clock when we reached the summit. We had started
out at six in the morning, but I had to admit that I had lost
all sense of time. I felt as if I were running, whereas in
actual fact I was walking normally, perhaps rather slowly,
and I had to keep stopping to get my breath. The sky was
now covered with clouds, everything had become gray and
dirty-looking. An icy wind sprang up, boding no good. We
must push on! But where was Lachenal? I spotted him a
couple hundred yards away, looking as if he was never going
to stop. And I had thought he was in indifferent form!

The clouds grew thicker and came right down over us; the
wind blew stronger, but I did not suffer from the cold. Perhaps the descent had restored my circulation. Should I be
able to find the tents in the mist? I watched the rib ending
in the beaklike point that overlooked the camp. It was gradually swallowed up by the clouds, but I was able to make out
the spearhead rib lower down. If the mist should thicken, I
would make straight for that rib and follow it down, and in
this way I should be bound to come upon the tent.

Lachenal disappeared from time to time, and then the mist
was so thick that I lost sight of him altogether. I kept going
at the same speed, as fast as my breathing would allow.

The slope was now steeper; a few patches of bare ice followed the smooth stretches of snow. A good sign—I was
nearing the camp. How difficult to find one's way in thick
mist! I kept the course that I had set by the steepest angle
of the slope. The ground was broken; with my crampons I
went straight down walls of bare ice. There were some
patches ahead—a few more steps. It was the camp, all right,
but there were *two tents!*

So Rébuffat and Terray had come up. What a mercy! I
should be able to tell them that we had been successful, that

we were returning from the top. How thrilled they would be.

I got there dropping down from above. The platform had been extended, and the two tents were facing each other. I tripped over one of the guy ropes of the first tent. There was movement inside; they had heard me. Rébuffat and Terray put their heads out.

"We've made it. We're back from Annapurna!"

WHEN THE WHOLE WORLD PRAYED

By Captain James A. Lovell

Suddenly and irrationally, in spite of all the tests and re-hearsals and reassuringly unflappable electronics, in spite of everything that had seemed to guarantee its certainty, the odds changed for Apollo 13. The word came crackling thinly, across an unreachableness of anguish, that something had gone wrong. Now these three men might not make it.

With the realization of that stark fact, overnight the names Jim Lovell, Jack Swigert and Fred Haise acquired the currency they should have had all along. The first critical hours of this third trip to the moon had gone smoothly, scarcely noticed by a world now accustomed to accepting the most incredible feats of coordination and precision as mere routine. Even the drama of blast-off had been scantily attended: no world figures on hand and only a fraction of the world press there at Cape Kennedy to witness this latest audacious attempt by man to prove that his wits and his guts could answer the taunt of space.

But now from spacecraft Earth, billions of people prayed, listened, watched and lived each tense moment as the men backed their desperate play with everything they had left. They monitored dials and flickering lights, talked with the men in Mission Control who were devising a way to save them and always kept their nerve. When the time came, they blew the bolts to ditch the service module, unlatched the LM and then waited with apprehension, hoping they'd make it home through the thickening layers of air.

Some people would call the mission of *Apollo 13* a failure. I look back on it as a triumph—a triumph of teamwork, initiative and ingenuity, on the ground and in the space-craft. The possibility of catastrophe in space has always been there. I recall John Glenn remarking that whenever you are dealing with high speeds, long distances, thousands of pounds of highly volatile fuel, vacuum pressure, thousands of pieces of machinery and electrical equipment—well, you are taking risks. We all know that, and we accept the risk. Of course, when you train to fly a mission, you never think that "it" will happen to you. Emotionally you feel that it won't happen to you, that it won't be your wristwatch that breaks down. But since I had already logged 572 hours in space before *Apollo 13* lifted off, I must have been as good a target for the law of averages as anyone. For whatever reason, "it" did happen on this mission. The turn of the dice came up, and we did have an accident. We then had problems, and they were serious. But we are going to have these things in the future. The triumph was in proving our ability to cope with these problems, solve them and get a crew back to earth under emergency conditions. Therefore, I like to think that *Apollo 13* contributed a great deal to "maturing" the space program and to realistic thinking about it. Continued success is a commodity too easily taken for granted. Things can go wrong, and it is well to be reminded of that. When "it" does happen, you simply do everything possible to keep going, to keep functioning, to stay alive.

Just before the accident, Fred Haise and I had done a routine telecast from inside the lunar module *Aquarius*. We had gone into *Aquarius* a little earlier than the flight plan called for because we were anxious to check the pressure on a helium tank. It was all right. Then we did our housekeeping chores, and while Fred worked in the LM, I did the camerawork and sent the pictures back to Houston. I crawled back into the command module *Odyssey*, followed by Fred, who was to close the hatch. We were 55 hours and 55 minutes into a mission that had been planned to last about 240 hours.

Then we heard the bang. You always get a bang when you close the hatch, but Fred had not finished doing that. Anyway, this bang was much too loud to have been caused by the hatch. Our first thought was that this was some kind of electrical problem that we could isolate. Then Jack Swigert saw the warning light. He was the first one to alert Houston that we had "a problem."

Fred immediately stopped work on closing the hatch, got into the right-hand couch to start checking out the systems and quickly spotted the state of the three fuel cells that generate the command module's power and keep its life-support systems going. One had already gone, and a second one was slowing down. I looked at the oxygen-pressure indicators. Tank number three read zero and tank number one was dropping fast. Without fuel cells *Odyssey* simply could not operate for a sustained period; there was reserve battery power, but those three batteries were part of the reentry system, and they just would not last long enough to take you to the moon—or even get home from where we were. Should we turn off the reactant valves? This was an irreversible decision, and I was reluctant to make it, because without those valves the fuel cells were gone for good and the moon mission would have to be aborted.

They were fast going anyway. When I moved over to the left-hand couch in *Odyssey* and looked out the window, what I saw was pretty alarming. The sun was shining on gaseous matter that was being vented from the service module at a tremendous rate. It was probably oxygen. At that time we were losing the number-one oxygen tank—the number-three tank had gone in about 50 seconds—so the oxygen must have been venting from number one. Now it was a question of survival without the fuel cells. It became apparent, and quickly, that the only way to do that was to get out of this powerless *Odyssey* and into the lunar module.

So Fred and I went back into *Aquarius* to power up the LM's systems, which operated independently of the service module. Simultaneously we had to maintain the integrity of our alignment on the inertial guidance platform; without that data, we might as well have been three schoolboys in a rain forest without a compass. Jack drew on battery power (the batteries could be recharged later, using the *Aquarius* systems, although we did not know that at the time) to keep the alignment in *Odyssey* "alive." We have a technique for aligning the lunar module's own guidance platform with the one in the command module, but in this case we had to move fast. We got the transfer, and that was the first big turning point. The *Aquarius* optics were less sophisticated, since they had never been intended for use in deep-space navigation and required movement of the entire spacecraft to get a sighting. Had we lost *Odyssey*'s alignment, the only way to get another alignment would have been to use the sun and the moon and the earth. Because of the gaseous cloud and the mechanical debris, we couldn't do star sightings.

So the first big question had now answered itself: The mission had to be aborted. We were not going to land on the moon, but getting home was not all that simple. We were, at the time "it" happened, 205,000 miles from earth, on a trajectory that would take us to within 60 miles of the lunar surface, but which was not designed to return us home if something went wrong. So Mission Control's first request was that we do a maneuver to get us back into the "free return" trajectory, which is sometimes called the "slingshot." This means going around the moon once, starting at the leading edge—roughly, the left-hand side of the moon as seen from earth—with the proper trajectory. The moon will then put you on a free-return coast when you come around the trailing edge after one pass on the back side. Free return is simply a free ticket home. That free-return trajectory was part of the flight plan for *Apollo 8, 10* and *Apollo 11*, but beginning with *Apollo 12* we went to a "hybrid" trajectory necessitated by the different landing sites but giving up one safety factor. Now we had to get that safety factor back.

The obvious thing to do was fire the descent-propulsion-system engine of *Aquarius*, which had been designed to power the lunar module on its final descent to the moon. Without that burn of the DPS engine, we would go around the moon, all right, but we would have wound up stranded a few days later in a weird, egg-shaped earth orbit. Our first order of business was to avoid this, because we never would have got closer than about 2950 miles from the earth, and there just wasn't anything we or Mission Control could have done then. It would have been a situation comparable to the one depicted in the motion picture *Marooned*, but for one difference: There would have been no possibility of rescue. I had seen the film, and I must admit that the parallel crossed my mind.

That was the worst time—those few hours after the accident. I was worried about the systems in *Aquarius*. Nothing in the lunar module had been designed for the work we were now asking it to do. And we had to have power. We might have been able to figure out a way to fire the big service-propulsion-system engine, which was built to get us into lunar gravity and out again, I still don't know. The best bet was to fire the DPS engine in *Aquarius;* if it failed, we might be able still to do something with the lunar module's less powerful reaction-control thrusters, but we couldn't be sure about that, either.

So there was the big feeling of relief when that engine fired for 30 seconds to boost us up and take us around the moon at an altitude of about 130 miles instead of 60 miles. Now we had our free ticket home—if our consumables held out: oxygen, electricity, especially water. That first burn of the DPS engine put us on a course that would land us in the Indian Ocean, but that was the least of my worries at this point—the very least of my worries. I didn't know until after I got back that so many nations had volunteered to help in a recovery operation, but any old ocean would do as long as it was on the earth. We could have survived for some time in the Indian Ocean, the South Atlantic or wherever waiting for a destroyer to pick us up. My primary concern was getting back before we ran out of the consumables. But since we wanted to get back fast without depending solely on free return, we wanted that DPS engine to fire again.

So, about 18 hours after the first burn, we fired the DPS engine again—a "big burn," this time, for more than four minutes. Now we were more or less on the right course, and the second burn had reduced the time of the trip home by about ten hours. Moreover, we were now targeted for the Pacific Ocean, where we had intended to come down in the first place. Our alignment was still not quite right, but it was good enough for the time being.

We powered down everything to keep essential things going—the glycol pumps, the fans, the communications. This was part of the water problem, because the more systems you had powered up, the more water you used for coolant. We never did use the high-gain antenna, which had been built for lunar communication; it required too much power. We continually switched the omnidirectional antenna manually from forward to aft to keep communications clear, but the ground thought the talk was still about as scratchy as it used to be in the old *Mercury* days.

With everything in the command module powered down, someone had to be awake at all times to keep an eye on things in *Aquarius.* At first we were all too keyed up to worry about rest; I slept hardly at all for the first 35 or 40 hours. Eventually it dawned on me that somehow we all had to get some sleep, and we tried to work out a watch system. We weren't very successful. Events kept upsetting it and making a sensible rotation impossible. Besides, the inside of *Odyssey* kept getting colder and colder. It eventually got down pretty close to freezing point, and it was just impossible to sleep in there. Fred and I even put on our heavy lunar boots. Jack didn't have any; so he put on extra long johns. When you were moving around, the cold wasn't so bad, but when you were sitting still, it was unbearable. So the three of us spent more and more of our time together in *Aquarius,* which was designed to be flown by two men— standing up, at that. There wasn't really sleeping space for two men there, let alone three; so we just huddled in there, trying to keep warm and doze off by turns. We didn't get any sleep in the true sense of the word. We considered putting on our heavy space suits, but the suits were so bulky that they would compromise our maneuverability in an emergency situation, and when you put on the suit, you were bound to perspire a lot. Soon you would be all wet and all cold, too, an invitation to pneumonia.

We knew after our first calculations, on board and on the ground, that we had enough electricity to get home if we conserved power and the *Aquarius* systems held out. We knew that we had more than enough oxygen but that water was going to be critical. A "surge" tank in *Odyssey* held reserve oxygen that could be used to force out drinking water left in the potable-water tank. We isolated the surge tank immediately after the accident to make sure we did not lose its oxygen, too, because it was required for reentry. On the trip back we turned it on only to get drinking water out of the water tank, and on the last day the tank went dry. We had access to the water in the environmental-control system of *Aquarius,* but we didn't want to use that, either. It was needed as coolant while we were coasting back to earth.

Then there was the carbon dioxide problem, which was serious enough but which was solved by a marvelous piece of improvisation suggested by the ground. This is one reason why I call *Apollo 13* a triumph of sorts—it challenged men to come up with solutions to problems they had never run into before. In this case the trouble was in using the available supply of lithium hydroxide to cleanse the air of the carbon dioxide we exhaled in breathing. If we continued to breathe unscrubbed air, we would get drowsy and eventually just go to sleep permanently. There were two big canisters and one secondary canister of lithium hydroxide in *Aquarius*, plus a small canister in each of the two PLSSs—the back-packs for the lunar walk we were not going to make on this trip. This did not add up to enough. We had all kinds of lithium hydroxide in the command module *Odyssey*, enough to run out of our ears, in fact, but how were we going to utilize it? The *Aquarius* canisters had round connections, and *Odyssey*'s two big canisters were square. But ground came up with an ingenious method of mating the two kinds of con-nections with tape, plastic bags, cardboard—anything we could find. It worked so well that we never did have to draw on that second big canister in the lunar module.

But we couldn't dump our urine. It sounds funny now, but it wasn't funny then. Normally we dump it through a little vent in the command module, but we were afraid to dump because that might cause a reaction that would change the trajectory of our spacecraft stack, and we had enough troubles there already. So we used all the bags in the lunar module, everything and anything we could find, and just stacked the stuff away.

Now we had less than 48 hours to go, and tracking was the primary concern. We were coming home fast—faster than the speed of escape velocity. We definitely wanted to get "captured" by the earth's gravity. Here we used a tech-nique that had been worked out during the around-the-moon flight of *Apollo 8,* in December 1968, but which I had never dreamed I would have to use in a situation like this. (If we had had this kind of accident on *Apollo 8*, Frank Borman, Bill Anders and I would now be long dead. We had no lunar module on that flight and, therefore, no reserve power.) The technique involved using the earth as a reference platform and using the earth's terminator (day-night line) and the position of the sun to align the spacecraft for a burn to make a necessary change of angle during reentry. At the time we made this alignment, we were coming home too "flat," and we would bounce off the atmosphere into space again, this time for good. We wanted to come in at an angle of minus

6.5 degrees. There isn't much margin for error in that figure, since you don't want to come in too "steep," either—and burn up. So, 37 hours before splashdown, we used the alignment data that we had got by sighting the earth's terminator and fired that DPS engine again. Now we were in the corridor leading to the Pacific Ocean recovery area, but about five hours before we were due to hit the atmosphere, we had to make still another midcourse correction, this time using the lunar module's smaller reaction-control thrusters. For some reason our reentry angle was always a little "shallow." We never did get it right, and I'm not sure why. There may have been an error on my part in flying the whole stack by translation controls; with *Odyssey* for the time being a dead bird, we did not have our normal attitude-control capability. And this constant venting from the tanks may have kept throwing us just a little bit off the path.

After we dropped the service module and our blessed little *Aquarius*, the rest was routine. We came home on the same systems—the same oxygen, the same battery power—that we would have used had the rest of the mission gone as planned. It would be foolish to speculate at this point on what happened to the service module. The meteoroid possibility has just about been ruled out, and if we assume an internal malfunction, there are many possibilities, including fire. But I would be shooting in the dark if I tried to make even an educated guess. It probably is just as well that we did not see the extent of the damage to the service module earlier; we were sufficiently worried without knowing that a whole side panel had been blown away (or had dropped away) and the service module's innards were just hanging out there.

During the flight, control of the docked *Odyssey* and *Aquarius* was very difficult. *Aquarius* was not designed to fly the docked spacecraft, and it took some time for the crew to learn a new mode of operations. And without *Odyssey*'s controls, the rocket stack was awkward to handle.

In any event, the accident could have been worse, much worse: If this had happened when Fred and I were on the moon, we would have lost a whole crew—like that.

ABOUT THE AUTHOR

William Parker, a magazine editor and writer in special-interest fields, previously edited an anthology of stories of Medal of Honor winners for Macfadden-Bartell Books. He has written articles on sports and general subjects for several national magazines, in addition to publishing and editing his own national golf magazine. He is an alumnus of Columbia Graduate School of Journalism and was a sports reporter for the *Baltimore Sun* and *New York World-Telegram and Sun.*